The Dynamics of Rules

The Dynamics of Rules

Change in Written Organizational Codes

JAMES G. MARCH

MARTIN SCHULZ

XUEGUANG ZHOU

STANFORD UNIVERSITY PRESS

STANFORD, CALIFORNIA

Stanford University Press
Stanford, California

© 2000 by the Board of Trustees of the
Leland Stanford Junior University

Printed in the United States of America
CIP data appear at the end of the book

Acknowledgments

In more than the usual sense, this book represents a collaborative effort. The project began with discussions among the three of us in the context of dissertations by Schulz and Zhou that evolved into several papers on rule development (Schulz 1992, 1993, 1998a, 1998b; Zhou 1991, 1993, 1997) and research by March on institutions and organizational learning that led to several publications during the same period (March and Olsen 1989, 1995; March 1991, 1994a). After a few years of pursuing our separate interests, we reestablished our collaboration in order to elaborate some general thoughts on rules and their dynamics and to reanalyze the Schulz and Zhou data on rules at Stanford in ways that illuminated more clearly the links to theories of organizational adaptation and that allowed a more systematic comparison of different kinds of rules.

Over the years, and more pointedly in the past two or three, the three authors have worked together in formulating the ideas contained here, have collaborated in working through the problems of gathering and coding the data, and have developed the analyses and interpretations. We have drawn from our individual works as well as our joint work and have tried to acknowledge a few specific instances in which one or the other of us has been especially responsible for the ideas (e.g., Zhou's work on historical period and agenda effects, Schulz's work on density effects, and March's work on organizational learning), but the book as a whole reflects no priority of authorship. To that end, the order of the authors' names is alphabetical. Each of us is equally culpable, and we could not, even if we wanted to do so, untangle the individual contributions.

Any project such as this relies on the help of others. The research has been supported by the Spencer Foundation, whose support has been not only generous but also remarkably uncluttered by the kind of impatience and bureaucratic impediments to research that typify many other granting agencies. In our relations, Spencer has been a model sponsor. We hope that the book may constitute a partial repayment for the sustained high quality of that sponsorship.

In less financial and more intellectual ways, we are grateful for the support of our colleagues in the organizational research community. In particular, we are indebted to Raymond Bacchetti, Frank R. Dobbin, Mooweon Rhee, Suzanne Stout, David Strang, Harrison White, and Moris Zelditch for thoughtful and helpful comments.

More generally, and in addition to our obvious debts to Max Weber and the tradition of scholarship that he spawned, we should like to acknowledge the insights in thinking about rules that we have gained from Robert Axelrod, David Braybrooke, Nils Brunsson, Michael D. Cohen, Jon Elster, Alfred Kieser, Kristian Kreiner, John W. Meyer, Douglas C. North, Johan P. Olsen, W. Richard Scott, Oliver E. Williamson, Sidney G. Winter, and Lynn G. Zucker.

We should like to acknowledge the decisive contributions to techniques for analyzing event history data that have come from Michael T. Hannan, Trond Petersen, Nancy Tuma, and Larry Wu.

For help in gaining access to, gathering, and coding the data, we are grateful for the contributions of Maurine Buma, Patricia Del Pozzo, Maureen Eppstein, Noel Kolak, and Robert Tanner.

Of course none of this would have been possible without the support of our families, especially three remarkable women: Jayne Dohr March, Katharina (Tinky) Schulz, and Zhaohui Xue.

Contents

Tables

Figures

The Dynamics of Rules

Introduction

This is a book about written rules in formal organizations. It uses observations drawn from the history of a specific organization, Stanford University, to develop speculations about the ways in which written rules change. Written rules are distinctive elements of organizational history; they shape organizational events and are shaped by them. They are created, revised, and eliminated in ways that leave historical traces. They have visibility and durability that elude nonwritten rules. Because of these properties, written rules provide natural data for an empirical probe into the dynamics of organizational history. They are by no means a complete record of that history, but they form an accessible archive of changes over time.

Although the research reported here includes some qualitative observations of specific instances of rule change, ours is primarily a quantitative investigation of the historical patterns and statistical properties of rule birth and change. The speculations drawn from those data are intended as modest contributions both to a theory of rules and to theories of organizational change and learning. They emphasize the patterns of rates of change in a population of rules, rather than the substantive content of the changes or the operation of a specific individual rule.

Organizational actions are rule based. Organizations respond to problems by focusing attention on existing and potential rules. Histories of written rules are produced by organizations solving problems, allocating attention, and learning as they pursue intelligence. When a rule is created, changed, or eliminated, it records a reaction to external or internal pressures on the organization. Changes in the external environment affect rules by creating problems and offering exemplars of possible rules. Direct experiences with rules and their consequences affect rules. Changes in internal structures and resources also affect rules. The flows of problems and responses to them create patterns of rule stability and change.

Written rules are repositories of organizational lessons, but the learning that deposits new lessons into rules and removes old ones is notorious for generating myopic, path-dependent, and inefficient histories. Thus we see the history of written rules as being produced by learning, but we do not see learning as inexorably leading to a unique set of rules predictable from the functional necessities of a particular situation or organization. Rather, we focus on the meandering, interactive paths that a history of interacting local adaptations reveals.

The adaptation of rules is local, but rules are not autonomous. Instead, they are bound together and separated from each other by barriers within an ecology of written rules and rule making. Local learning has systemic ecological consequences. Attention to rule making in one domain or at one time affects attention in other domains and at other times. The density of written rules affects both their mutual autonomy and the possibility of new rules. Changes in one rule can impinge on other rules, creating ripples of rule creation and revision through a system of written rules. The ripples are facilitated and constrained by the jurisdictional structure of an organization.

Most recent empirical studies of written rules are qualitative studies of the substantive content of individual rules. They examine the ways in which specific texts of particular rules are crafted or changed in response to the detailed texture of organizational history and the intentions of organizational stakeholders. Classic examples are found in the extensive literature on the birth and revision of the United States Constitution. These studies, and similar ones of organizational rules of lesser fame, elaborate the pressures, negotiations, and agreements that have produced rule texts.

Some of the explorations reported here are similar; however, our primary intentions are different. We focus on three critical events in a rule history—rule birth, rule revision, and rule suspension—and try to identify factors that influence their likelihoods. Rather than seeking to explain why a particular rule text exists, we seek to understand the propensities for changes in texts that underlie rule histories and the processes that affect those propensities. Our emphasis, then, is on the incidence of rule births and rule changes, rather than the content of such changes.

Underlying this emphasis is a conception of rule histories as richly detailed and complex in meaning and interaction but as possibly having comprehensible underlying causal structures of change that manifest themselves in observable regularities. For example, we consider the effect of a change in one rule on the likelihood of change in another. Such effects clearly depend on the contents of the rules involved, since they define the "distance" between the rules as well as the nature of their interactions; but our interest is less in the precise content of a change in a rule than in its occurrence.

Within this perspective, we elaborate a simple set of ideas about written rules and their dynamics. Those ideas emphasize the interplay among periodic major shocks to the system from outside, experiences with individual rules as they age and are revised, and the spread of effects through an interconnected set of rules. It is a story of a kind of learning in which changes introduced in one part of a rule system create adjustments in other parts, including the same rule later in time, as the consequences of the changes are experienced and as rule-making attention is mobilized, satiated, and redirected. These learning phenomena reflect, and are orchestrated through, a variety of organizational processes, involving the full panoply of political negotiation, symbolic competition, discussion, and problem solving that are typical of organizational decision making. We attribute rule histories to properties of the underlying dynamics of those processes.

As we shall see, rule births and rule changes result from relatively complicated combinations of external and internal signals and mechanisms that invite deeply contextual investigations of individual events. At the same time, however, they have general statistical properties that stem from their place in organizational life. Organizational rules develop in systematic ways. To elaborate the fundamental phenomena underlying the systematic properties of rule histories, we focus on three substantial issues familiar to the literature on rules.

The first issue deals with the relation between rules and learning. Rules in organizations can be seen both as products of learning and as carriers of knowledge. Indeed, it seems likely that any theory of organizational learning will want to treat rules as major factors in the accumulation of competence in an organization. We will show how rules evolve as organizations solve the political and technical problems they face and how they mediate interactions between the actions and lessons of the past and those of the present.

The second issue deals with the relation between rules and bureaucratization. Bureaucracy is associated with rules and more specifically with the tendency for rules to proliferate. Bureaucratic rules are also linked to ideas about bureaucratic stability and rigidity. We will show that rules tend to accumulate over time but that the accumulation occurs at a decreasing rate. And we will show that although the development of rules produces significant elements of stability in a bureaucracy, it also produces elements of instability and change. Rule systems become more stable over time, reducing both rule births and rule changes; at the same time, they become less stable through revision, as pressures from the environment force adjustment and as changes in one rule stimulate changes in other rules. The combination leads to a bureaucracy that is neither hyper-stable nor hyper-plastic.

The third issue deals with the efficiency of history. We ask whether individual rules develop autonomously out of individual functional necessity, reflecting current exogenous requirements for survival or effectiveness. Such a conception of historical efficiency underlies many speculations about rules. We show that the development of rules reflects an inefficient history. The learning that translates political and technical pressures into rules is a complex process in which attention, prior experience, and rule ecologies all operate to frustrate any simple hypothesis of a unique match between rules and environments. Rules develop through adaptations that are local in time and space and lead to rule sets that can be seen as collections of residues of past histories, that are themselves influential in shaping subsequent events and the interpretation of them. In that development, the ecological context of rules and the histories of rules make a difference.

ONE

Rules in Organizations

Although the topic suffers from a drab coloration, speculations about rules and their place in human societies have been common throughout recorded history. Indeed many elements of modern history, as well as of their early antecedents in oral traditions and myths, are organized around discussions of rules. This history of concerns about rules is reflected in the continuity of conceptions about them. For example, perceptions of written rules as being received from the gods echo in modern perceptions of rules as a prerogative of organizational leadership. This history of attention to rules extends into contemporary social organization.

Centrality of Rules

In a broad perspective, rules consist of explicit or implicit norms, regulations, and expectations that regulate the behavior of individuals and interactions among them. They are a basic reality of individual and social life; individual and collective actions are organized by rules, and social relations are regulated by rules. Indeed, rules are a general feature of human organization, both a basis of civilization and a bane of civilized existence. They provide bureaucracy with both capabilities and opprobrium. While they are often honored by avoidance or defiance, they permeate human existence.

RULES IN THEORIES OF INDIVIDUAL ACTION

Most individual behavior is rule based to a substantial degree. Rules impose cognitive and normative restrictions on appropriate behavior. Individuals act to fulfill identities, defining what is implied by a particular identity or what is expected, socially or morally, in a particular situation. From this perspective, action is driven less by anticipation of its uncertain consequences and preferences for them than by a logic of appropriateness reflected in a structure of rules and definitions of identities (March 1994a). Thoughtful individual actors are imagined to act by matching identities to situations. They ask: What kind of a person am I? What kind of a situation is this? How does a person such as I act in a situation such as this?

Rules, therefore, involve three constructions. The first is a construction of the self: Which of my identities is relevant? The second is the construction of reality: How do I code the situation in which I find myself? The third is the construction of a match between the two: What do my identities tell me to do in the situation as I have defined it?

The constructions of self, reality, and the match between the two involve interactions among individual struggles for identity, social interpretations of reality, and negotiations about appropriate ways to connect them. Part of those interactions are mediated by formal, written rules in an organization, rules that define identities, situations, and the matches between them. Rules are created and revised as old identities and situations become less relevant over time and as new ones emerge. Such a rule-based conception of human action has long been a hallmark of sociological visions of human behavior (Durkheim 1933; Merton et al. 1952; Douglas 1973; Edgerton 1985; Shils 1975), but in recent years its importance to psychological, political science, and economic conceptions has also become notable (Nelson and Winter 1982; Anderson 1983; North 1990; Zhou 1997).

Ideas of rule-based action have generally been contrasted with ideas of choice-based action. The latter vision ties action to anticipation of the consequences of alternatives, evaluated in terms of prior preferences, a logic of consequence, rather than a logic of appropriateness. Logics of consequence are the fundamentals of modern theories of rationality, including bounded rationality and multiperson strategic rationality (March 1994a). They presume that individuals anticipate the probable consequences of their actions and take those actions that best serve their interests. Those anticipations may be subject to various inadequacies, but the driving forces of action are expectations of consequences and evaluations of those consequences in terms of prior individual preferences. In this light, rules are instruments; they arise to serve the interests of the individual or of individuals, and they are revised or discarded when they no longer serve the purpose of relevant actors.

Debates over the two conceptions are sometimes made comical by the tendency of advocates of each persuasion to treat the alternative conception as a special case of their own. Rational instrumentalism is viewed as simply one set of rules by sociologists, and rules are viewed as simply rational solutions to some repeated game by economists. In recent efforts to describe human behavior, however, these postures of mutual subsumesmanship have generally been subordinated to a perspective that sees the two logics of action as intertwined, rather than as strictly competitive or mutually subsumable. Few enthusiasts for logics of appropriateness would deny the importance of rationality as a set of rules of appropriate behavior particularly likely to be evoked in some human situations, or as one of several methods used in resolving conflicts among identities (Goode 1973). And, as we shall see below, recent interpretations of consequential action have placed increased emphasis on the role of rules and institutions in specifying the constraints within which rational action takes place. The "rules of the game" have been conceived as vital aspects of consequence-based action.

RULES IN THEORIES OF HUMAN SOCIETIES

Rules and rule-based action are central features of all human societies of which we have knowledge. Human actions are organized around rules, and these rules fit together to create and maintain social systems. The position of rules as primary instruments of coordination and control is reflected in theories of law and governance (Dworkin 1967; Elster 1989; Fuller 1969; Brennan and Buchanan 1985; Walker 1988). Contemporary hierarchies, markets, and international relations are governed by institutions built around formal and informal rules. Rules of behavior have long been regarded as solutions to Hobbesian problems of anarchy (Parsons 1982). Reciprocity is recorded as a golden rule of social and economic exchange since ancient times. Solidarity and authority in both tribal and modern societies are seen as based on expectations of stable relationships stemming from explicit and implicit rules. Indeed, Durkheim (1933) argued that anomie is likely to result when mutually agreed rules regulating social interactions break down, as in the transition from a mechanical (feudal) society to an organic (market) society.

In part, the centrality of rules stems from their position as symbolic artifacts of collective life. They are symbols of order, even where their effects on behavior are limited. They are trophies of bargaining, recording the outcomes of conflicts. They are testaments to intentions and proclamations of virtue, serving in that way to juxtapose the morality of values with the compromises of situational action. They are the sacred texts of social order. Since the earliest recorded human history, systems of rules have been seen as fundamental to civilization.

Ideas of rules and rule following are manifest in studies of roles (Goffman 1967; Leblebici and Salancik 1989) and underlie substantial elements of contemporary work on individual problem solving (Anderson 1983) and social and political behavior (Searing 1991), as well as work on artificial intelligence (Zytkow and Simon 1988). They are a focus in recent policy research (Allison 1971; Levy 1986; Bromiley and Marcus 1987; Provan 1987). They also fill theories of governance and law (Hart 1961; Kratochwil 1989), political institutions (March and Olsen 1989, 1995), standardization (Brunsson and Jacobsson 1998), and philosophies of deontological justification (Braybrooke 1996). In particular, a conception of institutions as collections of rules and behavior as rule- and identity-based underlies virtually all "institutionalist" conceptions of action in political science (e.g., March and Olsen 1984), sociology (e.g., Meyer and Rowan 1977; Zucker 1997), economics (e.g., Hodgson 1994), and anthropology (e.g., Douglas 1986).

RULES IN THEORIES OF ORGANIZATIONS

Rules are ubiquitous in human behavior, but they are particularly conspicuous in formal organizations and are often seen as the prototypical instruments of organizing. Modern formal organizations are characterized by their structured and stable patterns of collective behavior, sustained by and reflected in routines, procedures, regulations, conventions, and other forms of organizational rules. Rules routinize organizational activities and define authority relations, connections among subunits, and decision-making structures.

The familiar organization chart is a visualization of the rules by which hierarchical levels are ordered and units coordinated. Entry into organizations is screened by rules of duty and responsibility specified in employment contracts; internal mobility is regulated by criteria embodied in policies of rewards and sanctions; the timing of arrivals and departures, as well as work activities, is regulated by rules. Rules define organizational identities and boundaries and stabilize linkages with other organizations. Accountants do what proper accountants do. Managers do what proper managers do. Each follows rules that define appropriate behavior for the role he or she plays.

Much of the effectiveness of modern organizations is credited to their ability to create and implement organizational codes in imaginative ways that reflect the lessons of experience, guide behavior, and symbolize organizational commitments. In many cases, written rules are followed in a highly calculated and conscious manner. In other cases, rule following in organizations occurs unnoticed because rules have been internalized, have become unconscious premises of action, or have been incorporated into firmly established and widely practiced routines and procedures. In still other cases, rules are glorified and supported as manifestations of organizational ideology, although they are hardly implemented at all.

As a result, theories of organizations—both traditionally and currently—are often theories of rules, rule making, and rule following. Rules have been portrayed as instruments of reliable organizations by Aristotle, Confucious, and Ibn Khaldoun, among others, but discussions of rules in the literature of organization studies invariably begin with Max Weber and the links he made between rules, bureaucratization, and modernity. At the turn of the century, Weber traced the rise of modern bureaucracy to a rationalization process accompanying the development of capitalist economies (Weber 1946).

Weber saw rules as a defining characteristic of bureaucracy (Weber 1946). The prevalence of rules distinguished formal organizations from traditional organizations and from informal groups glued together by intimate interactions. In fact, of the nine characteristics of bureaucracy listed by Weber, at least seven are explicitly related to rules and rule-following behavior (see Weber 1946, 196–98). He argued that rules together with other characteristics, such as hi-

erarchy, reliance on expertise, and delineation of jurisdictional areas produced
a form of social authority technically superior to simpler, less rational forms
(Weber 1946, 579).

Many subsequent authors shared the Weberian premise that rules are important components of modern organizations (although many of them did not
agree with Weber on the reasons for their empirical prevalence). Organizational rules were a recurrent theme in the classic studies of organizations that
appeared during the 1950s and 1960s. Gouldner (1954), Blau (1955), Merton (1957), and Crozier (1964) examined the place of bureaucratic rules in
regulating interpersonal relationships in the contexts of governmental agencies
and industrial organizations. Their studies adopted Weber's concept of bureaucracy as an analytical framework, although they deviated from Weber in
their emphasis on "dysfunctions" of bureaucratic rules.

March and Simon (1958) and Cyert and March (1963) started from the
observation that organizations were bounded in rationality, subject to shifting
political coalitions and constrained by routines, procedures, and decision rules.
Cyert and March (1963) elaborated the function of formal rules, such as decision rules and standard operating procedures, within the organization. They
noted, "These rules are the focus for control within the firm; they are the result of a long-run adaptive process by which the firm learns; they are the short-
run focus for decision making within the organization" (113).

These Weberian and post-Weberian conceptions of rules never disappeared
from theories of organizations, but during most of the 1970s and 1980s they
tended to be subordinated to conceptions of action that seemed initially to
place rules and institutions in a subordinate theoretical position. The rise of
theories of calculated rationality to positions of intellectual dominance within
the social and behavioral sciences seemed to relegate rule-based action to a minor role. Individual and collective actions were interpreted as stemming from
assessments of alternatives in terms of their consequences for prior preferences.
Theories of limited rationality came to emphasize cognitive constraints on a
consequential calculus rather than a rule-based logic of appropriateness (Nisbett and Ross 1980; Heiner 1983). And theories of organizations and institutions came to emphasize their dependence on their environments, thus to de-
emphasize the independent importance of rules.

The end of the twentieth century has witnessed a resurgence of attention to
rules and rule-based action (Brennan and Buchanan 1985; Burns and Flam

1987; Mills and Murgatroyd 1991; Pentland and Rueter 1994). Contemporary treatments of action in organizations, whether derived from theories that emphasize roles, identities, and appropriateness or from theories that emphasize preferences and expectations of consequences, are increasingly focused on rules. This focus on rules is shared by scholars who emphasize organizational rationality (Simon 1957; Hey 1981, 1982), bureaucratic power relations (Gouldner 1954; Crozier 1964; Rose 1984), evolutionary theories of economic change (Nelson and Winter 1982; Witt 1985), institutional theories of the development and diffusion of norms and rituals (Meyer and Rowan 1977; Meyer, Boli, and Thomas 1987; Zucker 1987, 1988; Mezias and Scarselletta 1994), and theories of organizational learning (Child and Kieser 1981; Levitt and March 1988).

Images of Rules

We can distinguish four different images of rules that are common in the literature. The first sees rules as conscious, rational efforts to organize intelligently. The second sees rules as proliferating organisms. The third sees rules as part of the construction of organizational reality. The fourth sees rules as encodings of history. The four images are not mutually exclusive, but they do lead to somewhat different views of how rules evolve.

RULES AS RATIONAL EFFORTS TO ORGANIZE

The longest tradition in interpreting organizations is one that sees organizing efforts as intentional attempts by rational actors to manage practices within a collectivity. Those attempts are sometimes seen as the leadership of teams, sometimes as the brokering of coalitions.

Rules in Teams

One of the oldest conceptions of rules in theories of organizations is a conception that sees rules as generated to improve the efficiency of a team, defined as a collection of individuals who share objectives. They face problems of communication and coordination in order to maximize the achievement of their shared objectives, but they do not face problems involving conflicts of interest (Marschak and Radner 1972; Mintzberg 1979).

In this conception, rules are conscious, intentional actions directed toward improving organizational performance. The problems of coordination and communication are approached by specifying rules that make actions reliable and consistent. Reliability and consistency of action are necessary to assure co-ordination among the various parts of the organization, particularly as participants leave and are replaced by new people (Pugh et al. 1969; Pugh 1993).

Rules have advantages due both to their impersonality and durability and to the fact that they allow considerable time and effort to be devoted to solving a coordination problem before it becomes critical. Furthermore, they presumably require less time in implementation. Such rules are particularly characteristic of organizational situations in which objectives are shared, decision time is short, in which predictability of the behavior of others is especially critical, and in which decentralized autonomy would result in serious coordination difficulties.

Rules in Systems Involving Conflicts of Interest

More commonly, however, organizations are seen as conflict systems involving multiple, conflicting interests. Managers are seen either as self-interested agents pursuing their own agendas, as representatives of particular interests (for example, the owner's interests in the case of a business firm, the regime's interests in the case of a public agency) confronting other actors (for example, workers) similarly pursuing their own interests, or as brokers seeking to arrange mutually beneficial exchanges among the contending interests. A large literature on congressional voting, public choice, and bureaucratic politics addresses these latter questions (Moe 1990; Goldburg 1994; Laver 1997), and a large literature on information asymmetries, principal-agent problems, and "shirking" addresses the former (Taylor 1947; Jensen and Meckling 1976; Schotter 1981).

When organizations are seen as combining multiple, conflicting interests, rules can be seen as negotiated (or evolved) contracts binding the participants (Nelson and Winter 1982). In such treatments, stories of organization are typically split into two parts: during the first part of the story the rules are negotiated through bargaining among self-interested participants. The results of such negotiations are seen by students of economic organizations as a set of implicit or explicit contracts (Williamson 1975, 1985; Hart and Holmström 1987). They are seen by students of political organizations as policies (Mayntz and Scharpf 1975; Egeberg 1998). Both usually either become or are supplemented by a set of written rules.

During the second part of the story, individual actors pursue their interests rationally within the rules. Since a clear problem in dealing with rational self-interested coalition partners is that of assuring rules are not opportunistically violated, the specification of rules that induce rational actors to be bound by them is an important part of the conception. For example, the recognition of moral hazard and principal-agent problems in recent economic literature has led to a framework of analysis focusing on "incomplete contracts." Because of the impossibility of specifying complete sets of rules to govern team members' behavior, other rules involving incentives, compensation, and monitoring must be used as organizational instruments (Holmström 1979; Grossman and Hart 1982, 1986). These rules have as their objective the alignment of objectives among participants with conflicting underlying interests. They elaborate an earlier vision couched in terms of an employment contract between employer and employee (Simon 1951). In this spirit, organizational economics focuses on rules of organizational design and human resource practices in hiring, training, compensation, and promotion, rules that elaborate and enforce the bargains made among conflicting rational actors.

RULES AS PROLIFERATING ORGANISMS

The second image treats rules as governed by self-evolving processes. Post-Weberian writers on bureaucracies (e.g., Crozier, Gouldner, Merton, Parkinson, M. W. Meyer, J. W. Meyer) rejected most notions of rationality and superior efficiency and instead emphasized less than rational reasons for bureaucratic proliferation, such as vicious circles (Crozier 1964), goal displacement (Merton 1957), problems of close supervision (Gouldner 1964), organizational complexity exceeding bounded rationality limits (Meyer 1985), and expansion and imposition of societal standards and institutions (Meyer et al. 1985), and so forth. Bureaucracy theorists (as well as much of the general public and many politicians) assume that bureaucracies breed rules. Frequently they imply that rule breeding intensifies as bureaucratization proceeds.

One can distinguish dramatic and moderate proliferation theories. The dramatic formulations of proliferation theories assume that rules breed rules. Several of Weber's arguments allude to mechanisms in which bureaucratization feeds on itself. This happens, for example, when bureaucratic expansion requires the establishment of control agencies that supervise the adherence to rules and create rules limiting the authority of officials (Weber 1978, 271). A second feedback mechanism results when new rules are created to unify and systematize existing rules and laws, sometimes in response to the interests of the bureaucratic officialdom generally interested in "clarity" and "orderliness" of the law (Weber 1978, 848). A third feedback is produced by the tendency of rules, introduced to solve problems, to create new problems requiring new rules. All of these positive feedback mechanisms are likely to result in exponential growth of the number of rules.

More moderate theories assume that organizations breed rules at a continuous, but relentless pace (more precisely, at a rate greater than the rate of rule suspension). For example, Max Weber, in *The Protestant Ethic* (Weber 1988, 181), argues that rationalization, the driving force behind the erection of great bureaucracies, is really the result of an ascetic mind-set carried out of monastic cells into everyday life. This would suggest the presence of a simple diffusion (e.g., proselytizing) process over the population of organizations (or their employees), and a subsequent, steady rule generation process in the "infected" organizations. The result would be a continuous, linear expansion of the number of rules.

Even more moderate theories assume that organizations breed rules at a decreasing rate, that bureaucratization continues but at a decreasing rate. One version of such theories is a variation on standard learning theories. As the technical superiority of bureaucratic administration (Weber 1978) produces rules, there is decreasing marginal return to additional rules. The early rules produce major gains; later rules produce lesser gains. As long as the return is positive, rules may continue to accumulate, but at a slower and slower rate as they compete with alternatives. A second variation postulates a rule-breeding exhaustion process. It imagines that rules, by virtue of their success in solving problems, eliminate problem opportunities. Especially in situations of relative environmental stability, this endogenous reduction in the supply of organizational problems amenable to regulation leads to a reduction in the rate of organizational rule production. Proliferation proceeds at a rate that declines with the density of rules already existing in a domain.

RULES AS CONSTRUCTIONS OF MEANING

Organizational rules are not only templates for action; they are also representations about an organization, its members, and its processes (Douglas 1973).

Formal rules permit an organization to be classified and evaluated. They are to be understood in terms of the way they communicate meaning to the observer. They are the "talk" of organizations, and organizations are understood, in part, by their "talk."

As the written code of an organization, rules represent claims about the ways things happen, or ought to happen. This organizational creed tells something about the organization that proclaims it. Organizations are judged by their rules. They secure formal and informal certifications by virtue of having rules that meet expectations about the kinds of rules that proper organizations have (Brunsson and Jacobsson 1998). For example, modern quality-control certifications of manufacturing organizations are almost entirely certifications of rule systems. Agencies enforcing regulations with respect to safety, fair treatment of ethnic minorities or women, and humane treatment of prisoners do so in large measure on the basis of an audit of rules.

Because organizations secure certifications in terms of the rules they have, there is a tendency for rules and action to become loosely coupled. Organizations are involved with two somewhat different environments (Brunsson 1989). The first environment is an environment for rules. Significant elements of the environment care about the rules the organization has. Those elements demand proper rules, and organizations wishing to secure a favorable position in their environments learn to be responsive to such demands. The second environment is an environment for actions. Significant elements of the environment care about the actions taken by the organization. Those elements demand proper and effective action, and organizations wishing to secure a favorable position in their environments learn to be responsive to such demands.

Although the two environments are connected, they normally involve somewhat different groups and are subject to different internal variations in attention. As a result, an organization tends to respond with written rules that satisfy one group and with actions that satisfy another group, recognizing that some groups care more about the latter than the former, while other groups care more about the former than the latter. The same feature of the construction of rules has been noted in the crafting and implementation of legislation (Baier, March, and Sætren 1986).

Finally, rules are trophies. Political struggles in an organization are partly about specific substantive concerns, but they are also usually about standing. When groups contend, they care about who wins and who loses as symbols of their own importance. This orientation extends to observers, and much of modern media analysis of organizational life is couched in terms of victories and losses for contending participants. As implicit records of the outcomes of past judgments and disagreements, rules are scorecards of disagreements and their resolution. They record who won and who lost, and by that recording alone they remove the necessity of renewing the dispute or implementing its outcome. A rule can be a declaration of victory even if it is never implemented or even evoked. The trophy character of rules contributes to the tendency for rules and action to become uncoupled.

RULES AS CODINGS OF HISTORY

It is also possible to imagine that rules carry the lessons learned from history. As memories of the lessons of experience, rules are depositories of knowledge. They store inferences from prior experience in an easily retrievable form. Such a vision of rules as carriers of knowledge gives rules some claim to wisdom since they may summarize a broader range of considerations than any current actor can recognize and evaluate. A feature of this conception, however, is that the inferences from history come to be significantly disconnected from the experiences on which they are based. The lessons of history—but not history itself—are relatively easily retrieved.

In one version of history-dependent rules, the experiences of history systematically eliminate rules that fail to serve the community of individuals. In the most extreme form, this idea presumes an efficient history. An efficient rule history is one that shapes a population of rules rapidly to form a set of rules that optimizes the joint interests of the participants. Thus rules evolve to a form uniquely predicted from knowledge about the current environment. A version of this perspective is found in the many efforts to show how a particular institution is a solution (in some sense) to a repeated game among rational actors. The presence of information asymmetry, incompleteness and ambiguity induces the use of rules as a device of organizational memory to ensure cooperation among self-interested players (Axelrod 1984; Kreps et al. 1982).

It is improbable that history can be represented as invariably efficient in selecting a uniquely optimal set of rules. The adaptive mechanisms are often quite slow relative to the rate of change in conditions. There are often multiple local equilibria, and it is quite possible for a rule system to be quite stable at something less than a global optimum. And rules and environmental conditions coevolve; the rules affect the environment even as they are affected by it. Furthermore, conventions may be formed through an endogenous process of "spontaneous order" with little regard to efficiency (Sugden 1989; Langlois 1986). As a result, current rules cannot be seen as responses simply to current conditions. Rules evolve over time through a sequence of experiences, and understanding the population of rules that exists at any particular time requires close attention to the history of their development, particularly to inertial forces in that history.

Written Rules and Unwritten Rules

Our focus in this book is on rules that are recorded in written form. We readily concede the limitations of looking only at written rules. Many important rules in an organization are not written, and many of the rules that are written are only loosely connected to actual behavior. Social norms, tacit understandings, standard practice, and rules of thumb are all powerful components of a rule-based world. They guide the behavior of individuals and thereby become core mechanisms of social order (Parsons 1968; Coleman 1990). Nevertheless, the focus on written rules is not simply a manifestation of academic perversity. There are pragmatic and theoretical reasons for it.

REASONS FOR STUDYING WRITTEN RULES

An obvious pragmatic reason for a focus on written rules is that, for all practical purposes, formal written rules are the only rules that leave clear enough historical traces to allow their histories to be studied in any detail. Written rules are likely to require documentation and updating when things change. Unwritten rules can deal with changes in conditions by relatively casual failures of memory or reinterpretation. Written rules also are subject to reinterpretation, but they are more likely to require some formal change to some sacred text, thus requiring more elaborate procedures and approvals.

As a result, more accurate information is likely to be available about the time and extent of rule changes when the rules are written. Changes in written rules tend to leave records that can be collected, analyzed, and used as data. Such traces are left behind when rule makers keep old rule versions or old rule books in archives (sometimes for legal or financial reasons), if they keep records documenting rule change events, or if invocations of rules involve production or modification of records, which are then kept (for example if a travel rule requires that reimbursement forms have to be filled out). When informal rules change, they leave fewer traces.

Written rules also are of theoretical interest. On the one hand, they share enough similarities with unwritten rules to serve as a possible lens through which to understand all rules. On the other hand, they represent a major modern phenomenon. Much of contemporary life is organized around written rules. One of the primary concerns of decision makers in contemporary organizations is the making and changing of formal rules. By virtue of their explicit, recorded nature, they are more frequently overtly contested. People care about them, partly because of their coercive nature, partly because of their symbolic standing. And they represent significant parts of modern organizing technology.

SIMILARITIES BETWEEN WRITTEN AND UNWRITTEN RULES

Formal, written rules have many of the characteristics of informal or unwritten rules and rule systems. First, both written and unwritten rules are maintained and communicated through socialization. Individuals learn what is appropriate to an identity in a situation through observation, mentoring, practice, and training. Just as young children learn the rules of proper eating, talking, and toilet behavior, new participants in organizations learn the rules of proper work behavior (Van Maanen and Schein 1979). Learning to be a proper citizen involves a combination of learning attitudes toward the laws and practices of the community and of learning what those laws and practices are.

Second, both written and unwritten rules create standards of appropriateness that balance the tendency of the consequential calculations made by an individual to be myopic with respect to the distant future, to the interests of distant others, and to the interests of collectivities. Both written and unwritten rules are used to civilize relationships. Many social norms, as well as legal and organizational rules, impose limits on individually rational "opportunism" (Williamson 1975, 1996). Rules sometimes mitigate informational disadvantages and enfranchise constituents (McCubbins, Noll, and Weingast 1987). They define behaviors appropriate to such identities as friend, lover, employer, and coworker,

RULES IN ORGANIZATIONS   19

behaviors that are expected even in the face of adverse personal consequences. They regulate action in the face of overlapping loyalties, install informal and formal checks and balances on self-serving action, specify procedures of employment and termination, responsibilities and duties, record keeping and reports, all of which frequently frustrate immediate individual self-interest.

Third, both written and unwritten rules—if widely known and accepted as legitimate—are often virtually self-enforcing. Compliance is internalized as a part of personal identity. Even where internalization is incomplete, rule following is enforced by other actors who are present (Coleman 1990). Identities are interlocked so that the fulfillment of one requires the fulfillment of others. And rules create interests that lead self-interested others to demand compliance. The public status of encounters is sufficient to assure the monitoring of conformity to rules and encourage spontaneous enforcement.

Fourth, both written and unwritten rules serve to reproduce social structure. There are numerous threats to social stability. Actors, clients, and audiences move in and out of institutions and decision situations (Cohen, March, and Olsen 1972). Their involvement in different particular domains fluctuates over time. This creates problems of consistency and coordination across structures and time. Solutions to rare problems found in the past are easily forgotten as their inventors leave. Perpetual renegotiations of coalition agreements and coordination procedures threaten to absorb attention and time. Rules are an important part of the social solution to these problems. They provide guidelines for action and inventories of competencies that endure through turnover in individuals. They accumulate experiences over several generations of rule followers (Levitt and Nass 1989).

SPECIAL PROPERTIES OF UNWRITTEN RULES

Previous studies of rules focus primarily on unwritten rules—the norms that regulate behaviors among members of tribal societies, or the "invisible hand" of market institutions in coordinating individual decision making (Hayek 1967; Sugden 1989). Unwritten rules are usually seen as evolving over time in response to experiences, including experiences that relate informal norms to their symbolic roles and often produce rules with considerable ambiguity. For the most part, however, studies of unwritten rules explain their existence and form as stemming from their organizational or social function.

Two properties of norms are particularly important: first, norms are shared understandings among members of a group. Anthropologists use the existence of shared norms to explain stable cooperative behavior within a culture without explicit social organization (Douglas 1973, 1986; Geertz 1973). Insiders are distinguished from outsiders on the basis of the norms they share, and cooperation extends to the former but not the latter. Consider the well-known case of the prisoner's dilemma (Axelrod 1984). If two or more rational individuals interact only on a "spot market," cooperation is unlikely to emerge, since defection is the dominant strategy. A critical escape from this dilemma involves developing some expectations of future interactions. A norm of cooperation is likely to emerge when rational individuals engage in repeated games. Shared interpretations of each other's past moves, often represented in "reputation," become effective mechanisms for regulating behavior (Dasgupta 1988).

Second, norms are seen as responsive to the survival needs of social groups. In recent game-theoretic variations on a functionalist approach, the emergence of norms is often credited to rational anticipation of future transactions (Kreps 1990). Efforts to overcome the tragedy of the commons, either based on collective or individual interests, may give rise to some kind of normative rules among members of the community. Organizational rules arise to manage uncertainties as well as unforeseen contingencies. These rules can be seen as derived from the functional needs of carrying out transactions potentially beneficial to all parties involved.

Because norms are based on shared understandings that are created and sustained through interactions among group members, their effectiveness in regulating behavior decreases with increases in the size of the group. The denser the relationships, the more powerful the norms. The larger the group, the less likely that norms can be learned and enforced effectively and the more likely that norms or informal rules will deteriorate and disappear.

SPECIAL PROPERTIES OF WRITTEN RULES

Codes of written rules are conspicuous features of formal organizations. They are frames for action within an organization, and they are artifacts of the history of an organization. They specify procedures to be followed and penalties associated with failing to do so. They are found in policies, operating manuals, handbooks, regulations, job and product descriptions, and contracts. In that sense at least, they are different from the habits, customs, and practices that comprise informal, unwritten rules, and they have some special features that stem precisely from their formal and written status.

Written rules are impersonal, explicit, and can be anticipated. As organizational size and complexity increase, written rules tend to substitute for unwritten rules because the effectiveness of informal rules is limited by the size of the group and the complexity of the task. In the organizational context, it is often argued that written rules are used as substitutes for direct managerial supervision. The substitution, it is argued, has advantages of saving managerial effort, minimizing the dysfunctional consequences of making differences in status overt, and avoiding direct confrontations involving conflicts of interest (Gouldner 1954; Crozier 1964).

By virtue of their public and explicit nature, written rules also seem to have some advantages as signals or symbols of organizational virtue. Rules may be coupled with behavior or based on shared understandings, but they need not be. They are symbols that appeal to the outside world, and may have little to do with beliefs or internal operations. Organizations that appear to be stable, accountable, and legitimate gain a competitive edge in business transactions with other organizations and regulatory agencies. Written rules convey the image of orderliness, authority structure, appropriate policies and practice. These functions cannot be performed as well by informal rules, which are difficult for an outsider to discern and fathom.

Written rules have some advantages as carriers of history. In a stable society with stable members, experience can be retained in the unwritten rules of individuals and groups and maintained and reinforced through everyday interactions. In a formal organization, however, such stability is not assured. Individuals come and go; positions are created and eliminated. As a result, it is difficult to retain organizational experience on the basis of personal memory and interpersonal communication alone. Written rules augment unwritten ones. They provide a depersonalized organizational memory, a storehouse of organizational knowledge.

Finally, written rules serve as foci for organizational discourse. They are accessible to many individuals and their interpretation can become a focus for debate. Within a university organization, for example, rules related to affirmative action, the use of grievance procedures, and tenure criteria are all subject to multiple interpretations and, at times, serious contention. By the same token, insofar as written rules retain an organization's history, they retain a history that can be explicitly contested.

Theoretical Issues

Much of the recent literature on rules and rule following has been directed at establishing the importance of rules, identities, and the logic of appropriateness as factors in human action (March and Olsen 1989; March 1994a; Zhou 1997). Students of rules and rule-based action have emphasized their fundamental skepticism about theories of action that depend exclusively on calculations of consequences and evaluations in terms of prior preferences. Although we share the skepticism, the present book is not directed toward that argument. It proceeds from the assumption that understanding rules is important to understanding organizations. Once the importance of rules is acknowledged, however, as it has been in large parts of the literature, a rule-based perspective confronts the problem of developing a theory of rule development.

THREE PROBLEMS FOR THEORIES
OF RULE EVOLUTION

The elementary conception of rules implicit in most contemporary discussions is one that assumes actions are translated into histories, history is translated into rules, and rules are translated into actions. Thus:

Rules → Actions → History

Understanding the consequences of the three translation processes as a system of interacting parts requires attention to three vital ambiguities: the first is the ambiguity of implementation, the complications involved in translating rules into action. The second is the ambiguity of history, the complications involved in understanding the relations between actions and histories. The third is the ambiguity of adaptation, the complications involved in translating history into rules.

Problem of Rule Implementation

The first problem is *rule implementation*. The rules found in any collection of rules are numerous, ambiguous, and conflicting. As a result, action depends on what rules are evoked, what meaning is given to them, and how conflicts among them are noticed, interpreted, and acted upon. Any idea of rule-based action has to clarify the ways in which a complicated mosaic of rules and identities is converted into action in particular situations (Bendor and Hammond 1992).

It is clear that actions are rarely uniquely specified by rules. Rules are generic; situations are specific. Any particular situation has a number of different interpretations and may evoke a number of different identities with different rules. Relevant rules may be overlooked, particularly if the collection of rules is large. Any particular situation may evoke several rules with quite different implications.

The processes by which individuals come to embrace and recall particular identities and by which situations are framed in one way rather than another form a large part of modern research on human decision making. That research reveals substantial ambiguity in moving from a collection of rules to action in a particular situation, an ambiguity well known to the traditions of jurisprudential thought.

Problem of Historical Interpretation

The second problem is that of *historical interpretation*. The complete cycle of learning requires that the actions produced by rules be translated coherently into the histories from which rules learn. Individuals in organizations develop stories of history to interpret their experiences, particularly the relation between their actions and the outcomes they realize. These stories exhibit some familiar biases (March 1994a). The outcomes of history are seen as more likely than they actually were *ex ante*. The likelihood of events that actually occur is systematically overestimated. Similarly, the role of human agency in history is exaggerated. As has frequently been noted, the contribution of individual action to history is often obscure. It is certainly difficult to establish the impact of particular actions on events in many organizational situations, particularly by any kind of direct observation. Nevertheless, history is seen as produced by the intentional actions of identifiable human beings. This inclination is particularly noteworthy in interpreting the cause of outcomes that are clearly favorable to the actor/interpreter. And the ordinary interpretation of history tends to assume that big changes must be produced by big causes, underestimating the role of feedback loops that multiply small differences into large differences and make history remarkably path dependent.

Problem of Rule Adaptation

The third problem is *rule adaptation.* How are rules created and changed? How does the population of rules evolve? Much of the recent social science consciousness of and theoretical interest in rules has been categorized as being "institutional" in character. That label has become particularly well known in recent years to refer to two conspicuous sets of "institutional" ideas. The first comes from the interest of economists in the limits of markets and other forms of rational exchange. Under some conditions, rules are seen as necessary to regulate self-interested negotiation and exchange. Observed rules are explained as calculated or evolved solutions to hypothetical metagames among the actors by which they agree to be bound by certain regulations. The idea is to imagine that historical processes more or less inexorably drive economic institutions to adopt rules that have some properties of evolutionary dominance. The precise process by which this solution is reached is ordinarily not specified. This functionalist imperative has been a major feature of the history of speculation about rules, but it has been given new vigor and imagination in work, both in economics and in political science, that has come to be called the "new institutional economics" (Hodgson 1994).

The second "institutional" development is also functionalist in form, but it is centered in sociological research and emphasizes the ways in which institutional survival involves satisfying the "taken for granted" presumptions of a population of institutions. Enduring institutions are pictured as securing legitimacy by adopting rules that are normatively accepted, coercively imposed by formal authority, or imitatively copied from rules observed in successful institutions. Legitimacy provides competitive advantage. Thus, by a process not ordinarily specified very precisely but involving competition, institutions that adopt socially defined appropriate rules come to dominate those that do not. Within the sociological view, the legitimacy provided by exhibiting allegiance to normatively approved rules plays a major role in institutional survival (Scott 1995).

Although these two sets of ideas are properly pictured as stemming from quite different perspectives, they share a common tendency to avoid questions concerning the details of the mechanisms by which rules develop. The new institutional economics, for the most part, assumes that rules are solutions to some metagame among self-interested actors and assumes such rules are discovered and become dominant as a result of the pursuit of efficiency. The new institutional sociology, for the most part, assumes that rules are given and focuses primarily on the ways in which rules spread to create pockets of homogeneous institutions, independent of any technical imperative.

RULE CREATION AND REVISION

Except incidentally, the present book does not examine the problems associated with problems of rule implementation or historical interpretation. Our primary concern is with the adaptation of rules. Rules are created, changed, and suspended, and any idea of rule-based action has to clarify the mechanisms by which rules become what they are. It is not adequate to see hypothetical rules as "evolving" or "arising" in some mysterious way and being implemented without complication. The processes of evolution of real rules and their implementation—including their main mechanisms and surprises—need to be explicated and placed in a social and historical context.

The literature on organizations suggests that rules are created and change as a result of several familiar processes (March 1981; Tushman and Romanelli 1986). Rules adapt to history through *selection* (Nelson and Winter 1982). By a selection process, in this context, we mean a process of birth and death among stable rules. Invariant rules survive or fail to survive depending on their continued use within an organization and depending on the survival of organizations using them. Their use in a population of organizations expands as organizations using them survive and grow; their use contracts as organizations using them die or shrink. Thus it is entirely possible to imagine a population of rules that adapts to its environment through differential diffusion and survival even though individual rules are entirely stable.

For example, Langton (1984) proposed that bureaucracies evolve through a process of Darwinian evolution in which bureaucratic elements are selected and retained. He assumed (Langton 1984, 337) that organizations retain bureaucratic elements that provide efficiency advantages. Less rationalistic, but equally inspired by Darwinian models, has been the work of researchers in the organizational learning tradition (Zhou 1993; Warglien 1995; Barnett and

Hansen 1996; Schulz 1998b). Finally, economists (Nelson and Winter 1982) have taken a selection perspective on organizational rules and routines and have developed models that treat organizational routines essentially as genes of organizations.

Rules adapt to history through *problem solving* (Radner and Rothschild 1975; Posner 1989). If organizational performance targets are not met, an organization increases search, looking for ways to restore performance to an acceptable level. The search involves a quest for new alternatives, for ways to reduce slack, and for ways to modify targets (Cyert and March 1963). The search is subject to a variety of cognitive errors and organizational biases that affect the solutions discovered. The resulting solutions are coded into new or changed organizational practices. These approaches tend to see organizations as being distinctively cognitive in character. They see them as thoughtful (Weick 1979) and ideational (Sandelands and Stablein 1987).

Rules adapt to history through *political processes* (Cyert and March 1963). Organizations respond to the changing pressures of their internal and external environments through bargaining and negotiation with power holders. For instance, it has been widely noted that organizational rules often reflect accommodation to organization members' interests (Crozier 1964; Perrow 1986). And it has been widely noted that organizational rules respond to authoritative normative specifications of what rules are appropriate for a legitimate organization (Meyer and Scott 1983). In this light, formal organizational structures and their rule systems are the outcome of explicit negotiation and conflict through which organizations acknowledge the power of sources inside and outside organizational boundaries.

Rules adapt to history through *experiential learning* (Levitt and March 1988; Beck and Kieser 1997). Organizational rules, such as routines, standard operating procedures, policy statements and regulations, change as a consequence of inferences drawn from experience with them. Rules that lead to outcomes defined as successful are reinforced; rules that lead to outcomes defined as failures are extinguished (Lave and March 1975; Herriott, Levinthal, and March 1985; Covington 1985; Comfort 1985). Organizations substitute new rules for old ones on the basis of learning from experience. Such changes involve processes of observing and interpreting history, processes of converting interpretations of history into organizational rules, and processes of retrieving rules from previous experiences and reconciling them with more recent experience.

A key assumption is that there is a more or less continuous updating of rules, although that process may be quite slow relative to changes in the environment and subject to various forms of myopia (Levinthal and March 1993; Barnett and Hansen 1996).

Rules adapt to history through *diffusion* of rules from one organization to another or among parts of a single organization. Understanding the diffusion of rules involves understanding the networks through which contacts are made and understanding the factors affecting the likelihood that a rule will be transferred if contact is made (Axelrod and Cohen 2000). The impact of networks of contacts on diffusion has been explored both in markets and in populations of organizations (see Strang and Soule 1998, for a review), as have some factors in the ease with which rules transfer (Cohen and Levinthal 1989) and the ways in which rules are transformed at the same time as they are transferred (Czarniawska and Joerges 1995).

As we will suggest in the following chapters, rule change can reasonably be described in any of these terms, or in combinations of them. The descriptions are not mutually exclusive and, indeed, tend to blend together in some treatments. Rules are constructed consciously to solve recognized problems; however, that construction involves conflicts of interest and the full panoply of political maneuvers. Rules spread from one organization to another, but that diffusion involves elements of past learning and anticipatory rationality. Rules are changed through incremental adjustments to experience, but populations of rules change through differential survival and reproduction. The processes are all mechanisms of a history-dependent development of rules.

TWO

Rules at Stanford

The locale of the empirical studies we report is Stanford University, a private American university. We were fortunate in being able to find an organization with good records of the history of rules. As always, good fortune comes with some risks. It is possible that organizations that keep good records of rules have rule histories that are not representative of organizations without such records. Archival histories are cursed by the fact that they are dependent on archives, and archives are not entirely products of chance. On the one hand, it is imaginable that rule histories are created and retained in anticipation of their being used in a particular way. Since the records of history often reflect efforts to influence the writing of it, one must question whether rule history records are strategic moves by self-conscious actors interested in corrupting the vision of future scholars or those of the legal system or other authorities. The risk that willful efforts to influence scholarship have produced a sample bias is, we believe, small, and we have attempted to treat efforts to influence authorities through rules as part of the story.

A greater risk, however, is the possibility that nonstrategic factors in the maintenance of archives may be related to features of an organization that are also related to the way they deal with rules. In particular, it seems plausible to picture both rules and archives as instruments of order. It is a reasonable speculation that organizations that maintain distinctively good order in their records of rules and rule changes are likely also to have an orientation to the creation and revision of rules that differs from that of organizations indifferent to historical records.

Is Stanford different? Yes, certainly it must be. Like any large, modern university, Stanford is simultaneously a bureaucratic organization, an institution of learning and research, a community infused with values, norms, and standards, and a corporate organization engaging in competition for resources. An American private university is a special kind of organization, sharing many features with business firms and public bureaucracies, yet it is different from either in important ways. In addition, Stanford University has numerous features that distinguish it from many other private American universities and colleges—its relative youth, its comprehensiveness, its distinction, its location, and its constituencies.

Is Stanford different in a way that makes a study of rules at Stanford irrelevant to understanding rules in other universities, military organizations, business firms, or church organizations? We doubt it. In a sense, ours is a case study. We focus on a single organization and the evolution of its rule systems. We examine the quantitative structure of changes in those formal rules, focusing on the likelihoods of changes, rather than their specific substantive content. Obviously, the findings might be sensitive to the idiosyncratic features of the organization and the organizational context for the population of rules. The particular structure we observe is quite possibly unique, and the specific quantitative estimates are likely to be unique too; but we think the robustness of the major results reported below across domains at Stanford gives some hope that they may be more generally robust. Stanford is a specific organization, but it shares many common features with other organizations, including organizations that function in quite different environments.

The Historical Background

Our studies cover the period from 1891 to 1987. During that period, Stanford University grew from an institution with fewer than 500 students and 37 faculty (*Stanford University Register 1891–1892*) to a large, complex, bureaucratic organization. By 1987, after 96 years of life, Stanford had 1,335 faculty members and 12,524 matriculated students. The organization was complex. By 1987, it was organized into seven schools, more than ninety departments and academic programs. In addition, there were seven standing university committees, nineteen administrative, advisory groups, and special administrative panels. There were an additional seven standing committees in the Academic Council, four standing committees in the Faculty Senate, and four student legislative, judicial, and advisory bodies (*Stanford University Bulletin, Stanford Directory*).

When Stanford University opened in 1891, higher education in the United States was at the beginning of an "academic boom" (Veysey 1965). Toward the end of the nineteenth century, student enrollment in major institutions began climbing upward, and new institutions of higher learning mushroomed. This was a turning point for American higher education. College education increasingly became part of normal career training. One hundred years later, the boom seemed to be over; but American higher education and Stanford University had both been transformed.

During the first twenty-five years of the university's history (1891–1915), Stanford was very much a local university, with few ties to other universities. Unlike the pattern fifty years later, the minutes of the Academic Council, which recorded main academic decisions during this period, seldom made reference to other universities or to the federal government. Despite the fact that this was a period of growth and prosperity for American higher education, Stanford struggled to survive. The founder, Leland Stanford, died in 1893, and only eleven months later the United States government filed a claim for $15,000,000 against the still unsettled Stanford estate. In 1906, a major earthquake struck Stanford and inflicted $3,000,000 worth of damage. These were huge sums in the currency of the time and in comparison with university assets.

In ensuing years, Stanford developed from a local university to one of the leading universities in the United States. It shifted from an institution in which scholarship was primarily an adjunct to teaching, to an institution in which scholarly research was a major function. It grew from a small group organized by informal authority relations to a formal bureaucracy. Over the same period, American higher education shifted from a relatively remote social sphere to become an important institutional center. By 1987, education was almost indispensable for social mobility. Professional work had become a standard career.

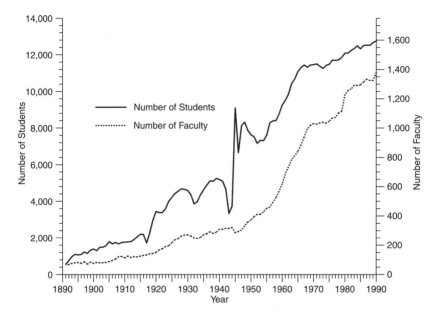

Figure 2.1   Number of students and number of faculty at Stanford University, 1891–1990

Both the state and society were firmly linked to higher education, shaping and being shaped by it.

In its history up to 1987, Stanford grew steadily except for the interruptions of the two World Wars. Figure 2.1 shows the numbers of undergraduate and graduate students and faculty during this period. The faculty grew steadily in numbers during the period, with the most dramatic increase coming during the 1950s and 1960s. The increases in the student body were similar but less steady. Student enrollment growth was disrupted in the late 1910s, early 1930s and early 1940s. Two of those periods coincided with the two world wars of the twentieth century.

The diversity of units within the organization is a common measure of complexity in organization literature (Scott 1975). In the university setting, the number of academic programs indicates the extent to which loyalties and disciplines are diversified and require coordination. In these terms, Stanford University became more complex over its first one hundred years. Figure 2.2 displays the historical trends for the number of academic programs. The figure

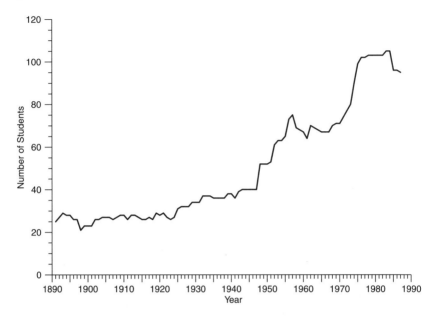

Figure 2.2 Number of degree programs at Stanford University, 1891–1987

suggests that the number of academic programs grew in spurts. Until the end of World War II, the number of academic programs showed a relatively small growth increment over the years. Complexity increased rapidly in the 1950s, changed little during the 1960s, and then accelerated again in the 1970s.

After World War II, Stanford University grew rapidly, became more complex, and augmented its reputation until by 1965 it had become one of the leading research universities in the nation. This trend paralleled the rapid growth of American higher education at the same time. Universities expanded and student enrollment increased drastically. Resources were also relatively abundant. Overall, this was the most trouble-free era for both Stanford University and American higher education.

Beginning about 1965, American higher education entered a period of turbulence and reconstruction. Two major features of the period deeply affected the higher education sector, and their effects were still visible in 1987. The first was the student protest movements associated with the Vietnam War. Student demonstrations of the late 1960s and early 1970s were the most serious social uprisings in the history of American higher education. Demonstrations in op-

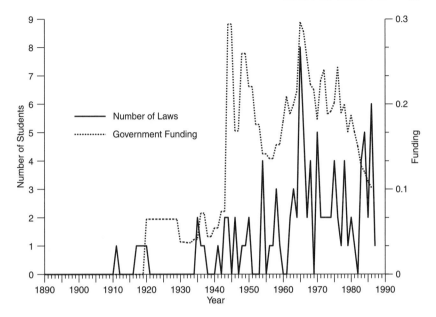

Figure 2.3   Proportion of total revenue of all U.S. institutions of higher education coming from federal funding and number of laws regarding higher education enacted by the U.S. Congress, 1891–1987

position both to university governance and to federal governmental intervention in South Asia diffused to university campuses across the nation. These
demonstrations posed a serious challenge to universities and left long-lived
marks on their institutional structures (Wallerstein and Starr 1971; Mayhew
1979). Stanford University was no exception. Student demonstrations and the
issues linked to them led to important changes in university rules and in the
rule-making system.

The second noticeable feature of the period after 1965 was the increasing
role of the federal government in higher education. Figure 2.3 shows the time
trends in the number of legislative acts dealing with higher education and governmental financial support for higher education. State governments had long
been major sources of support for higher education, although not significantly
at Stanford because of its status as a private university; but prior to 1946, the
federal government was a minor participant. This new role in higher education
occurred mainly through increasing federal support of research in universities.

In the four decades after World War II, governmental funding became the major single source of revenue for institutions of higher education (Andersen 1981). Concurrently, governmental regulations penetrated campus life not only as an adjunct of financial accountability but also through legislation. For instance, the Civil Rights Act of 1964 led to a series of affirmative action programs in universities.

During the university's history, rules had become a prominent feature of life at Stanford. To some degree, this development reflected the evolution of a decentralized organizational structure. In important respects, Stanford was more like a cluster of separate professional organizations (schools, departments), each organizing its own semiautonomous operation, than it was like a traditional bureaucracy. University-wide administration orchestrated a social life and culture for students, provided services and coordination, made policies, and organized ceremonies. But, to a large extent, professional activities in both teaching and research were organized around a system of discipline-based units. Throughout this structure, activities were regulated by routines, written and unwritten rules.

Rules and Rule Making

The university originally drew its governance model explicitly from Cornell University and Johns Hopkins University (*Stanford Faculty Handbook* 1997). The structure was quite conventional for American universities. Throughout most of the first one hundred years of its history, the university was organized into two intertwined systems of authority: one was a system that assigned staff members, faculty, and students to academic units connected through an authority hierarchy to the president of the university; the other was a system of faculty governance that played a substantial role in matters of academic personnel and policy. Both systems were formally subordinate to a self-perpetuating board of trustees, although in practice they operated with considerable autonomy.

Each of the units within the university had its own rules, many of them informal and unwritten but some of them written. The university as a whole had a variety of written rules regulating the activities of employees, faculty members, and students. Eventually, these rules were organized into written handbooks provided routinely to members of the university community. The rules dealt with the entire range of activities that occurred in the university, specifying such things as procedures for spending money, keeping records, supervising students, taking disciplinary action, and reporting results.

In this study, two specific sets of rules are considered. The first deals with the administrative policies of the university; the second deals with academic policies and student and faculty conduct. We refer to them as "administrative rules" and "academic rules," respectively.

ADMINISTRATIVE RULES

Administrative rules refer to those (mainly procedural) rules used by the administrative branch of the university in areas such as expense reimbursement, sick leave, surplus property sales, control of sponsor-owned property, campus facility planning, and the like.

We can distinguish two historical periods in the development of administrative rules. The first period extends from the founding of the university until 1961. The second period covers the period from 1961 to 1987. The early period was one of gradual, uncoordinated development. In the early days, Jane Stanford (the wife of the founder) was the main administrator of the university. Most of the bookkeeping was done by her (by hand) and her accounting system was simple, using only a small number of accounts. She made the rules and implemented them.

As Stanford grew larger in terms of the numbers of students, faculty, and employees, new methods for making rules were developed. In particular, much of the impetus for administrative rule making at Stanford originated with the controller's office. Early efforts to establish formal rules focused on accounting and budgeting. For example, budget procedures usually included written instructions (from the provost or the vice president for finance and business) on rules for spending money. Accounting rules were established to assure compliance and uniform application of accounting standards across departments. Later, personnel administration became a main source of rule production. The focus began with payroll processing, but later was extended to include rules regulating benefits, terminations, and layoffs.

The importance of accounting and personnel rules is reflected in the archives. Only two pre-1961 collections of administrative rules are retained in Stanford's archives (no information about rule changes are retained for either of these). One is the "Controller's Office Instructions." These instructions consist of a set of sheets containing rules (each about one paragraph in length) about payroll processing. The version retained in the archives is dated 1954. Some of this material was later (probably after some revision) integrated into two compilations: the *Administrative Guide* established in 1961, and the "Payroll Manual" established in the early 1980s. A second pre-1961 collection retained in the archives is the set of sheets called "Personnel Policies for Non-Academic Employees," which carries a revision date of May 15, 1951. This collection appears to have been issued by Stanford's personnel department. It appears that most of the materials in this set was later (after some revision) integrated into the *Administrative Guide*.

Before 1961, administrative rule making was fairly localized and relatively informal. Individual offices would develop small collections of local rules, mostly in the form of memos, dedicated to the tasks of that particular office. The individual offices would keep and maintain their own rules, sharing them with other offices that might be involved in a given process. Formal approval of local rules by higher administrative officials was not uniformly required and was uncommon.

Although this local rule-making process afforded a great deal of flexibility and responsiveness to shifts in conditions, it also had drawbacks. Some of these were discussed in archived correspondence between officers in accounting and personnel. The process did not ensure wide dissemination of administrative rules, nor did it provide continuity in the face of turnover. And it did not produce a consistent set of general, organization-wide policies.

On February 15, 1961, the controller's office issued the first edition of the *Administrative Guide*, initially called the "Administration Manual" with the subtitle "Guide to Administrative Organization Policies and Procedures." The *Guide* collected together earlier less formally defined and more scattered policies in a single place. This publication marked the beginning of the second period and was a tool to overcome the shortcomings noted above. Compared to the earlier, memo-based process, rule making during this period was made more formal. Policies were issued by a centralized unit, in this case the *Administrative Guide* office, managed by a person in charge of maintaining policies (the editor of the *Guide*) who was normally an administrator in the controller's office. The policies were disseminated to all university offices, and they were subject to formal approval by the vice presidents of Stanford.

The *Administrative Guide* rule-making process did not completely replace the memo-based rule-making process, but it significantly reduced the number of memos issued by individual departments. According to Maureen Eppstein, the editor of the *Administrative Guide* from September 1981 onward, special care was taken to assure that new policies were quickly integrated into the *Guide*, reducing the need for memo-based rule making. Changes of policies were handled by the editor of the *Administrative Guide*. There were five editors between 1961 and 1987.

By 1987, the *Administrative Guide* was a loose-leaf binder, which allowed individual administrators to record changes by substituting new pages for old ones. Several times each year (approximately four to five times but with varying dates) the *Administrative Guide* was updated. On these occasions revision notices were sent to the departments of the university. The revision notices instructed the users of the *Guide* (i.e., administrators in the various departments) which pages were to be inserted and which were to be removed from the loose-leaf collection.

In contrast to the procedures prior to 1961, the process of change of individual policies became relatively formalized. Policy changes were usually initiated because someone suggested that a policy should be created or revised. In most cases this person was either a "policy owner" (the person who was responsible for the area pertaining to a given rule) or the editor herself. The editor occasionally inspected the policies to determine if particular policies were outdated. She also picked up opportunities to create new policies from informal contacts and from administrative memoranda. In these cases the editor contacted the policy owners and initiated a policy change process. Policy owners communicated their suggestions to the editor, and she initiated a policy change process. Then the editor and the owners of a policy created a "list of experts," that is, a group of people who were expected to be experts on the subject of the policy to be changed, or whose interests were particularly affected. The experts produced a proposal for a new or revised policy.

The editor communicated the proposed policy text to a group of administrators the editor quite affectionately called "guinea pigs." These were administrators of various departments who supposedly would have to work with the policy. They provided feedback on the wisdom of the proposed policy, any ambiguities they saw in it, and any problems they foresaw in its implementation. Feedback from the "guinea pigs" was blended into the policy text, and the final draft was sent to the vice presidents for approval. Usually a vice president designated a person on his or her staff as *"Guide* liaison person." The *Guide* liaison persons (or the vice presidents themselves) gave feedback on the proposed policy. After agreement was reached on the policy, the vice presidents (or their liaison officers) recorded their formal approval. After that, the policy was reproduced and added to a revision package of other policies that was sent out to the departments.

ACADEMIC RULES

Academic rules are rules regulating academic affairs, such as graduate and undergraduate programs, requirements for degrees, as well as rules on faculty appointments, promotions, responsibilities, and protections, including tenure policy. Academic rule making evolved with changes in the academic authority in the university, and the historical evolution of the university academic authority structure is crucial for understanding changes in its rule system. Procedures for making academic rules was initially not remarkably different from procedures for making administrative rules, but they diverged very early and by 1987 were radically different from administrative rule procedures.

In its early years, the university, in its academic as well as administrative activities, was run mainly by its president. This was not unique to Stanford. At that time, "presidents wielded pre-eminent power at most of the major universities . . ." (Veysey 1965, 303). At Stanford, the first group of faculty was chosen by President David Starr Jordan himself. At the first faculty meeting, only two days after the opening day, Leland Stanford announced that the president "was invested with veto power over any action taken by the assembled faculty" (Mirrielees 1959, 58). This veto, however, was never actually exercised, because during this period the university faculty never took collective action that deviated enough from the president's wishes to elicit his opposition. The president of the university appointed all the committees and department heads and removed them at will (Mirrielees 1959, 121). The president chaired the executive committee of the Academic Council, which handled most of the academic affairs. In the early years, Jane Stanford and the board of trustees were also very active in campus affairs. Basically, "a system of University government grew up without reference to the Faculty" (Academic Council Minutes [ACM] January 12, 1912).

Rather quickly, however, Stanford University witnessed the transference of academic power from the administration to the faculty. The first major change of the authority structure came after Jane Stanford's death in 1904. At that time, the board of trustees assumed full responsibility for university governance and began a relatively rapid delegation of authority to the faculty. The board established Articles of Organization by which the Academic Council (a body consisting of all regular faculty members) was created with "the power and authority of the whole University faculty resting in it" (Mirrielees 1959, 123). Since then, authority for academic decision making and rule making has resided formally, and to a large extent informally, with the faculty.

The faculty organization to exercise faculty authority over academic rules has evolved over time. In 1912, the board of trustees initiated an interpretation of the Articles of the Academic Council. All standing committees specified in the Articles of Organization were made committees of the Academic Council, chosen by the council and responsible to it. Responsibility for initiating proposals for the council was given to the council itself, and such proposals were to be accepted or rejected on the basis of a vote by the council. An advisory committee, elected by the council, was established to advise the president.

During the period between 1904 and 1968, the making of academic rules was mainly governed by the Academic Council, that is, by the faculty as a whole. The Academic Council met once a quarter during the academic year. Between meetings, an executive committee handled routine rule-making issues. Major decisions were reported to and approved by the Academic Council. After 1912, all committees on academic affairs were responsible to the Academic Council. Standing committees were established to handle routine issues in specific areas, such as graduate and undergraduate studies. Unexpected, emergent issues were assigned to ad hoc committees.

This system collapsed in the late 1960s. The growth in the size and contentiousness of the faculty had made the Academic Council an ineffective legislative body, and large-scale social protests at the university challenged the governance structure, exerting strong pressures for intensive legislative work in many areas of the university, especially in academic affairs. As a memo proposing a change noted: "The strains on our present institutions have been demonstrated by the events of the past few academic years. . . . The Executive Committee is being progressively handicapped by its inability to give adequate simultaneous attention to the diverse issues which confront it. Further, it is not empowered to make final decisions on important issues, but must instead always refer them to the Academic Council" (Subcommittee of the Executive Committee of the Academic Council June 13, 1967).

In 1968, an elected Faculty Senate was established as the legislative body of the Academic Council. The senate consisted of fifty-five members elected from constituent areas and met monthly or biweekly to discuss and make decisions on academic matters. Furthermore, the university administration and other offices routinely, either by requirement or convention, reported to the senate on issues and decisions made in their areas. Rule-making processes in the Faculty Senate were highly structured with well-established procedures. Most proposals for change were referred to standing committees and subcommittees in the senate. Standing committees dealt with regular issues, such as undergraduate studies and tenure recommendations. When unexpected issues or external shocks emerged that could not be handled within the existing committee structure, ad hoc committees formed. In some cases, such committees were created by administrative officers, but any rule changes in academic areas had to be approved by the senate.

Despite this clear authority, some rules in academic areas were occasionally made by other offices. Administrative offices, such as the provost's office and the Office of Sponsored Projects, sometimes announced rules of their own that impinged on academic policies and procedures. One such case was described in an interview with assistant provost Noel Kolak:

> A few years ago, there were cases where questions involved whether the faculty gave proper credit to co-authors on papers. A couple of times, faculty felt accused. The Faculty Discipline Policy didn't give them the due process. We saw these people who felt the case had already been decided against them before they had an opportunity to state their views. That led the Provost's Office to think that we had to do something about it. So what happened was that the Provost's Office simply wrote a memorandum and then it became a policy. Then we incorporated that into the Faculty Handbook. This policy provides a period of time before any charge is made so that the faculty member is fully informed what is being said. (Kolak 1988)

In our study, we included both those rules that were made in the Academic Council or Faculty Senate and those made by other offices. The overwhelming majority of those rules were made in the Academic Council or the Faculty Senate.

Stories of Rule Change

Most of our focus in the remainder of the book is on describing the quantitative structure of rule change at Stanford, trying to identify some empirical regularities in the incidence of changes in rules. Such efforts need, however, to be placed within a more textured context of stories of rule change histories, to the ways in which participants in rule change processes describe the episodes surrounding specific changes. We use short sketches of such stories both to make the context clearer and to suggest a possible structure to the quantitative analyses.

EPISODES IN THE REGULATION OF ADMINISTRATIVE CONDUCT

As the university grew, it became more decentralized. Specialization and division of labor introduced problems of coordination and control that led to an expanded administrative apparatus and an accumulation of rules. For example, in 1929 an effort was undertaken to improve the gathering of budget statistics. This led to the adoption of a five-digit general ledger code and initiated a history of increasing complexity in administrative procedures. In 1948, the university established several quasi-independent divisions, and its balance sheet was divided accordingly. This change required general and widely disseminated rules (especially accounting rules), which would be practiced uniformly across divisions and thereby would ensure consistent accounting.

Technological change added to the expansion of the administrative apparatus. The increasing use of computer technology for accounting and other administrative tasks increased the level of skill required to perform these tasks. For example, in 1948 Stanford acquired a new IBM-407, a computer which used keypunch cards. It was used to process accounts payable and, subsequently, payroll accounts. As a result of such developments, new rules were established that would specify how the new accounting and payroll procedures were to be performed. By 1987, Stanford used administrative computer systems, an alphanumeric-coded ledger, and employed more than 3,000 employees who performed accounting and administrative tasks. The changing technology and the growth of the university provided additional impetus to the establishment of rules to help guide and train administrators in using the administrative systems.

The evolution of Stanford's administrative apparatus was also related to external changes. Increasing legislation in the area of higher education contributed to many administrative rules (e.g., equal opportunity legislation). As Stanford grew larger, its involvement in research expanded, making it more dependent on funding agencies, particularly the federal government. Requirements of these funding agencies had to be disseminated to departmental decision makers, and their implementation had to be monitored. This resulted in an expansion of rules related to research funding and government property. Additional impetus came from experience with management and auditing. As Stanford became more sophisticated in its accounting methods and more embedded in a national system of accounting rules, internal rules were added and changed. Requests by outside audit and consulting firms resulted in more extensive and sophisticated rules. As a result of these pressures, the rules of the *Administrative Guide* experienced considerable change from 1961 to 1987. Not only did the number of rules grow over time (from 34 to 127) but also many were revised several times while others were suspended.

Finally, it should be noted that throughout this period, causal effects were not uniformly directed from the environment to the university. Some external institutions were very much influenced by Stanford's administration. For example, the Association of College and University Business Administrators developed an administrative manual (called the *CUBA Manual*) in 1948 which became widely adopted by many universities in the United States. Some Stanford administrators who were members of the association became key contributors to the drafting of this manual.

EPISODES IN THE REGULATION
OF STUDENT CONDUCT

In the early days of Stanford University, President Jordan delegated his authority on student conduct to the Student Affairs Committee (SAC), which consisted entirely of faculty members appointed by him. This committee was charged with the responsibility for promulgating and implementing rules on student conduct. During this period, there were extensive regulations. An emphasis on Victorian decency and morals led to restrictive rules on student behavior and severe penalties for those who violated them (Mitchell 1958, 10–104). These restrictions came to be seen as too severe even before the emergence of student power in the 1960s. Student revolts, most of them outside the formal student governance system, against SAC decisions were not uncommon during this period. Friction between the SAC and students resulted in frequent turnover in committee membership and various crises over the regulations. Tension between the faculty and the student body led to additional pressures for reform. As a result, in 1911, the SAC delegated its authority over student conduct to organs of student government, subject to continuing oversight by the SAC. Finally, in a series of dramatic events in the late 1960s, authority on student discipline was formally transferred to a legislative council consisting of representatives of three parties: university officials, the faculty, and the students.

Organizational rules have evolved in response to these changes. Ever since the collapse of the SAC as an instrument for the enforcement of detailed faculty conceptions of appropriate student conduct in 1911, Stanford has organized its regulation of student conduct around a few general rules, rather than a detailed code. We consider three such general rules. The first is the Fundamental Standard, a general rule about behavior. Soon after the university opened, the first president of the university, David Starr Jordan, stated his expectation of student conduct, which a few years later was formalized as the Fundamental Standard: "Students at Stanford are expected to show both within and without the University such respect for order, morality, personal honor and the rights of others as is demanded of good citizens. Failure to do this will be sufficient cause for removal from the University."

A striking characteristic of the Fundamental Standard is its remarkable stability. In 1989, an article appearing in *Stanford Daily* observed: "In just 44 words, the Fundamental Standard has defined the code of student conduct at Stanford for 83 years." The Fundamental Standard proved to be quite durable and flexible in dealing with a variety of student misconduct. It even survived the political turmoil of the 1960s, 1970s, and 1980s without serious questions being raised in this area. However, by the end of 1980s, a formal Interpretation to the Fundamental Standard was promulgated. This interpretation was triggered by a series of racial slur incidents on campus. After a long and contentious debate, this interpretation formally extended the Fundamental Standard to a new area for the first and only time in its entire history.

The second general rule regulating student conduct is the Honor Code, a general rule about the ethics of academic competition. At the core of the

Honor System, established in 1921, is the statement: "The primary responsibility for the Honor System rests upon each individual student who is pledged not to receive or give aid in examinations." Although there were many initial doubts about the effectiveness of the Honor Code, it gained wide support among the students and the faculty over time. In 1954, on the initiative of the Association of Students at Stanford University (ASSU), the expectation of faculty cooperation was incorporated in the ASSU bylaw on the Honor Code.

The understandings, trust, and sense of community among students, faculty, and the administration that were essential to the Honor Code were, however, seriously compromised by the turmoil of the late 1960s. Subsequently, beginning in 1977, the Honor Code was "clarified" by a set of interpretations that were made a part of it. Gradually, the clarifications were elaborated into a relatively detailed list of "interpretations" of the basic Honor Code, which maintained a small distinction between the code and its interpretation, although the two were usually printed together and the distinction between the two might well have been more obvious to a historian than to a participant.

The third general rule governing student conduct is the Policy on Campus Disturbance, a not-quite-so-general rule stimulated by the phenomena and sophistication of campus demonstrations. In contrast to the Fundamental Standard and the Honor Code, the Policy on Campus Disruption has a short history. It was initiated in response to the student protests of the 1960s as part of the administration's effort to restore and maintain order on campus. In 1964, faculty representatives and university officials adopted a formal "Policy on Campus Demonstrations," which stated that "the rights of free speech and peaceable assembly are fundamental to the democratic process" but added that the university must "maintain on the campus an atmosphere conducive to academic work" and "preserve the dignity and seriousness of University ceremonies" (*Stanford Daily* October 11, 1965).

When subsequently the student government declared that it would not enforce the policy, the university president, on his own authority, declared the Policy on Campus Disruption in 1967, which was similar to the policy on campus demonstration. The Policy on Campus Disruption has never been changed, but it was supplemented during 1970–1971 by several detailed pronouncements made by the president and by student government in response to specific crises. These supplements seem to have disappeared after the turbulence of the 1960s and 1970s, but the Policy on Campus Disruption was used in the 1980s to deal with a few instances involving students in the occupation of university offices and blocking building entrances.

The rule-based regulation of faculty conduct at Stanford can be similarly illustrated by considering briefly three key components of academic tenure. The first component includes rules establishing the protections of tenure. In the early years after Stanford's opening in 1891, the president of Stanford, like his colleagues at other universities, opposed the idea of permanent tenure for professors (Veysey 1965, 398). Both at Stanford and elsewhere, such sentiments gradually gave way to an ethos of academe in which academic freedom, tenure, and academic excellence were bound together (Miller 1987, 96), but the change did not occur over night.

In 1900, Edward A. Ross, an economist, sociologist, and political activist, was fired by the president. Among other things, his campaigns for free silver, a ban on immigration from the orient, municipal ownership of utilities, and public scrutiny of the Southern Pacific Railroad had offended Jane Stanford. She demanded that he be fired, and he was. The case became an immediate and dramatically public cause célèbre both at Stanford and throughout the country. Significant members of the faculty organized a protest, and just two weeks after dismissing Professor Ross, President Jordan issued a statement concerning professorial tenure, which stated: "The appointments of professors, associate professors, and assistant professors are now for life, unless connection with the University is severed by resignation, retirement, or removal" (ACM January 20, 1907). In 1905, the board of trustees reconfirmed this policy and extended it to include all appointments in those ranks made prior to the year 1905.

Tenure protections did not become secure immediately. Despite considerable furor, a tenured associate professor was dismissed in 1910 when his position was abolished. This action led to a revision of tenure policy to grant tenure to any assistant or associate professor who had served at least six years. Tenure protection rules at Stanford remained essentially unchanged from 1910 to the 1960s, undergoing only minor additions and modifications in those five decades.

The 1962 President's Statement on Tenure Policy contained words virtually identical to those in the 1910 Academic Council resolutions (President's Office memorandum 1962). Those words were refined but essentially maintained in a 1967 Statement of Policy on Appointment and Tenure at Stanford University. In 1971, a tenured faculty member was fired from Stanford (only the second such case in the university's history) for actions during a demonstration on the campus. The firing came after a lengthy hearing and on recommendation of an elected faculty review board.

By 1987 there were substantial criticisms of tenure policies from two major sources. On the one hand, tenure was criticized as protecting the incompetent and unmotivated, denying to the university control over the quality of its faculty. These criticisms did not secure much faculty support at Stanford. On the other hand, there was some support for those who viewed the criteria for tenure as inappropriate. These criteria for tenure comprise the second component of the tenure-based regulation of faculty conduct.

Before the 1970s, policies on tenure criteria were contained in the Procedures for Appointment, Reappointment, and Promotion issued by the Provost's Office. They stated that "each new member of the Faculty shall be the best available in his age group or at his proposed rank, and the most accomplished in his field" (*Faculty Handbook 1972–1973*, 27). During the 1970s, considerable debate focused on the precise meaning to be given to "the best available" and "his field," and various individuals and schools attempted to make the criteria more precise. For example, the dean of the School of Humanities and Sciences clarified the school's tenure criteria as follows: "It is the position of this school that any individual who is to be recommended for appointment or promotion to tenure must be truly superior as either a teacher or scholar and at least very good at the other. He or she should be demonstrably the best person available" (Dean's Office memorandum 1972).

Beginning in the 1970s the criteria were also challenged in terms of the weights to be given to scholarly research, teaching, and public service. Official university policy attempted to gloss over the dispute by presenting teaching and research as substantially equal partners in promotion decisions. The policy was contested through several specific cases involving the denial of tenure for popular teachers. These struggles ultimately resulted in a 1985 statement on criteria for tenure issued by the dean of the School of Humanities and Sciences: "The first criterion for tenure is that the individual has achieved, or gives every promise of achieving, true distinction in scholarship. The published materials must clearly reveal that the person being proposed for tenure is among the very best in the field." As for the weights given to research, teaching, and university service, this statement made it clear: "Both scholarship and teaching are important prerequisites for tenure at Stanford because the University is dedicated to outstanding achievement in both." On the other hand, "The basic policy is that service, however exemplary, cannot substitute for deficiencies in scholarship or teaching." The statement hardly quelled either the conflict over specific cases or discussion of the principles involved.

The third component of tenure involves the obligations of tenure. Until the late 1960s, Stanford had no formal rules concerning faculty discipline except a vague sentence in the Statement on Appointment and Tenure, which stated that faculty would be subject to discipline for "reasons of substantial and manifest incompetence, substantial and manifest neglect of duty, or personal conduct." The terms of penalty and the content of such "misconduct" were left unspecified. The era of social protest in the late 1960s and early 1970s changed that. In 1968, the Faculty Senate adopted a resolution extending the Policy on Campus Disruption, originally seen as regulating student conduct, to include faculty members as well. And in 1973, a Statement of Faculty Discipline dealing with many of the same issues was finally adopted after a long and heated debate. In the 1980s, issues of campus disruption and faculty involvement in them became much less salient, but problems of faculty obligations and discipline surfaced strongly in two other areas. The first was the area of sexual harassment. Changes in laws and social mores combined to make concerns about the sexual misuse of faculty power a major concern. The second area was the area of research malpractice. Partly as a result of pressures toward research productivity, faculty members in significant numbers at Stanford and elsewhere were being accused of such kinds of research malpractice as mistreating subjects (particularly human subjects), exploiting assistants, and falsifying data.

In Search of Understanding

These brief stories of the history of administrative and academic rules at Stanford are reflections of the ways in which rule changes have been experienced at Stanford by the people involved in them. They are familiar stories, fitting standard ideas of proper narratives about such things. They emphasize the dramatic details of major historical developments. It is in the nature of such stories that they tend to describe memorable events in a history and thus introduce a bias in understanding something as mundane as organizational rules. The bias is manifest in the brief stories we have told in the sections above. They emphasize specific historical contexts and particular events that produce specific substantive changes in rules. They come from the drama of rules, rather than from their routine. Since our interest is in a more general look at the rates of rule birth, revision, and suspension and the factors that affect them, there is a mismatch between the way stories are told about rules and their changes and our concerns.

We do not attempt to say much about the factors that produce specific substantive changes in rules. We wish, however, to use the story lines of history to develop some general ideas about properties of rule histories. Our examination of these sketchy stories of rule development suggest three general things that might be further explored quantitatively: first, an organization searches for solutions to unexpected problems with which current routines fail to deal. These problems often occur in the context of crises, and their resolution often involves conflict. Second, rule changes are sensitive to and regulated by the ways in which organizational attention is organized and allocated. Not everything can be attended at one time, and problems and solutions diffuse through the organization. Third, rules become embedded in an organization, developing links to other rules and to the competencies of individuals using them.

PROBLEMS, CONFLICTS, AND
THE MAKING OF RULES

Today's rules are often the solution to yesterday's problems. Rule changes are often preceded by incidents, crises, or controversies. For example, our examination of the general pattern of rule making about tenure at Stanford University from 1891 to 1987 shows that changes in tenure rules were made infrequently and were clustered into a few periods, notably in the 1900, 1909, 1966, and 1973 academic years. Each of these flurries of rule-making activities was associated with some sort of incident, crisis, or controversy. In other words, these were the periods in which the continuity and regularity of previous institutional patterns were disrupted.

This kind of pattern has long been recognized in organization studies (Cyert and March 1963). Rule change requires events with magnitudes large enough to draw attention above a threshold, so as to put the issues related to the rule system on the organizational agenda and activate the search process. This means that the rules concerned must be recognized as being a problem area at several levels of the organization (Hilgartner and Bosk 1988). When existing solutions fail to deal with emerging problems successfully, a search is activated and new solutions become new materials for the making of new rules.

That search often either stems from or leads to conflict. As we have noted before, changes in tenure rules in Stanford's early history were triggered by a controversial administrative decision. At a later time, administrative attempts to deal with the financial crisis of the 1970s by tightening tenure rules generated pressures for the making of new rules or the elaboration of existing rules (especially the rules regarding the tenure criteria). At the same time, it is equally true that the effort to change rules leads to controversies and conflicts. For instance, an attempt to restrict student expressions of racial prejudice led to intensified confrontation between those who supported such regulations and those who were against them. An attempt to develop a rule dealing with faculty discipline created heated debate and tensions between the faculty and the administration.

Several factors are likely to be related to the supply of problems in any given area. It is likely that large, heterogeneous problem areas (such as the population of all academic rules) generate more problems than narrow, homogeneous problem areas (e.g., rules regarding specific stakeholders such as government or donors). Populations in close contact with the environment (e.g., procurement, marketing) produce more problems than areas shielded from the environment (e.g., accounting). Finally, conflicts of interest are likely to play a large role. Areas plagued by such conflicts between top policymakers and those who implement them are likely to provide many impulses for rule making (e.g., personnel rules or rules about reimbursement of expenses), whereas areas less subject to those conflicts are likely to have a smaller arrival rate of new problems.

The rules that emerged in the Stanford rule histories involved elements of problem solving with shared goals, but they also were political treaties and commentaries on them. For example, the struggles over student conduct and tenure rules have involved compromises and casualties. The close association between rules and organizational conflicts has been noted in the organization literature (Cyert and March 1963; Crozier 1964). The present stories about rule making are quite consistent with this association and suggest that there are several facets to it.

First, decisions on rules were choice opportunity garbage cans (Cohen, March, and Olsen 1972). They provided arenas into which groups could throw demands. These inputs entered the decision-making process, colored by rhetoric, symbols, and strategic information and punctuated by limited attention, temporary coalitions, and variations in patience. As a result, although rules seemed to result from a problem-solving process, the solution often did not address the original problems that triggered search. Among other things, there was a tendency for an immediate case to be decided in one way and for a rule to be rewritten another way (more or less in a way that made the resolution of the instant case counter to the rule). For instance, a formal interpretation of the Fundamental Standard was triggered by racial incidents on campus. According to the university official responsible for its implementation, however, the new interpretation's applicability to the original problem was quite unclear. This decoupling appeared to reflect elements of a garbage can process, suggesting that the link between problems and rule changes may be more complicated than the language of problem solving might imply.

Second, rules are often part of efforts to manage conflicts. Often rules are created to manage tensions, reduce arbitrariness, and provide protection for administrative officers, especially in times of crises and uncertainty. The promulgation of the Policy on Campus Disruption is such a case. It was made in response to campus protests that involved sit-ins and violence that disrupted the normal university operation. The same mechanism, although accompanied with less bombast, is part of the creation of administrative rules regulating the treatment of budgets.

Third, rules are used to punctuate conflicts. They declare an end (possibly temporary) to hostilities. The interpretation of the Fundamental Standard was such a case. It was a compromise that satisfied almost no one. Some charged that it was so narrow and vague that it was useless. Others saw it as threatening the free exchange of ideas in the academic setting. The decision on the rule was, in effect, a proposal to direct attention elsewhere. Such punctuations may, of course, be ignored. Indeed, there is a sense in which they often are. Rule changes seem to open up discussion of other related rule changes. The activation of the rule-making process signals organizational attention to this area, which serves the role of diffusing political pressures that are mobilized around particular issues and channel them into a well-structured process.

A general inference drawn from these observations is that organizational rules are closely related to problems and crises in an organization. They are often a "natural" organizational response to these circumstances. At the same time, however, these observations also raise questions about the way sporadic episodes of conflict and crisis management in an organization interact with a more continuous and less dramatic evolution of the rule system.

ATTENTION ALLOCATION AND THE MAKING OF RULES

Given the openness of the rule-making process and the variations in the supply of problems, attention allocation, and its manipulation are crucial to rule dynamics. For example, during the 1970s and early 1980s, officials periodically released information concerning violations of the Honor Code. These releases had the effect of stimulating attention to possible problems with the Honor Code, although a survey in 1981 found that student honesty remained essentially unchanged (and at a high level) during the two decades (*Stanford Observer* February 1981).

Two crises during the 1970s probably altered the balance between the administration and the faculty in the tenure rules decision-making process. Awareness of these crises was fostered by the administration through attention management. The first crisis was that of faculty maturation. The demographics of faculty recruitment and tenure was such that when faculty growth slowed substantially, the age distribution of faculty tilted toward a concentration of older faculty, and opportunities for appointing new young faculty declined. This aging of the faculty became suddenly alarming in late 1971, when President Richard W. Lyman pointed out the problem. In retrospect, the problem of faculty maturation may well have been identified at a time when the problem was lessening; but attention was both instrumental in solving the problem and persistent after the peak had passed.

The second crisis was that of the budget deficit. In the 1974–1975 academic year, at the end of a five-year budget balancing effort, a further deficit appeared in the university operating budget. Although fiscal difficulties were indeed present at the time, it provided an occasion for the organization to manage attention and induce organizational change. Vice-Provost Raymond Bacchetti, who was in charge of budget planning during this period, remembered the experience:

> In 1974, we [the administration] realized that we had serious financial problems due to the decrease in governmental funds, the OPEC oil crisis, a declining stock market, and increasing inflation. We needed to get the seriousness of this situation across to the faculty quickly. We decided to use the budget deficit to send a signal, since everyone understands what the deficit means. So, in that year, we loudly and clearly projected an operating budget with deficit. That led quite smoothly to a new budget balancing program, despite our just ending the previous program. (Bacchetti 1988)

Obviously, faculty maturation and financial difficulties were real problems during this period, but their salience for rule making depended on their being defined as crises. Under the shadow of financial crisis, the administration came to play a larger role in tenure decisions and led the faculty to refining and tightening tenure processes and requirements.

Attention to problems and solutions was contagious. Often times, solution to one problem led to the search for problems in other areas. Problems were noticed in one place because they were noticed in another. Solutions were adopted in one place because they had been adopted in another. The development of the Honor Code can be understood in this light. The self-government of student conduct in nonacademic areas provided the momentum for similar changes in the academic area. This made the proctoring system problematic and led to the adoption of the Honor Code in the academic area.

The contagion of rules and rule making was not exclusively internal to Stanford. Problems are defined in terms borrowed from outside; solutions are borrowed to solve the problems. Since the 1960s, the making and revising of rules often involved references to other campuses and legal institutions. For example, the risks of legal intervention in tenure cases were recognized outside of Stanford and communicated to rule-making bodies in the university, as were solutions involving the elaboration and formalization of procedures and policies in the tenure area. Thus, during one debate in the Faculty Senate, James Sienna, legal advisor to the university president, said: "It is no longer acceptable to say that a decision is so personal and subjective that its rationale can't be articulated. That is just no longer acceptable in court" (*Campus Report* June 19, 1974). Discussion of the Fundamental Standard occurred in a larger social context where many other universities were grappling with similar issues, including Emory, Yale, UCLA, and the University of Michigan. Similarly, the discussion of the Honor Code at Stanford in the early 1970s was triggered by reports of student academic cheating at other universities.

At the population level, then, we observe the convergence of the definitions of problems and of institutional forms and practice among organizations. Universities come to perceive similar problems and to deal with them by adopting similar rules. The problems and rules of Stanford were copied from or imposed by outside institutions. Several features of stories of the evolution of rule change are consistent with this pattern. For example, the evolution of authority in the area of student conduct parallels changes in the larger social context. The delegation of presidential power to student self-government, and especially the ultimate transfer of authority to the student legislative body are not isolated phenomena. Rather, they reflected, even as they influenced, changes in governance structures throughout higher education (Veysey 1965).

THE STABILITY OF RULES THROUGH COMPETENCE WITH THEM

The episodes of rule making in the areas of administrative rules, student conduct, and faculty tenure policies suggest a discontinuous problem-solving process: rules are stable and unproblematic as long as the institutional patterns based on these rules are unproblematic. When conditions change substantially, problems are created, attention is directed at problems, and a search for solutions stimulates change. In such a world, the stability of rules is as impressive as is their change.

That stability, however, is not just a product of inattention and the absence of external pressure to change. It is also a consequence of considerable and accumulating competence in using rules. In all of these areas, Stanford has individuals who have learned how to operate within rules, extending the meaning of rules to new situations, molding them to encompass new problems. Rule changes involve long processes and several levels of decision making. Occasional problems are often dealt with by allowing exceptions to rules or changes in interpretations, rather than the revision of formal rules. Much of this development is implicit, rather than explicit, in the stories of history that are told, for the stories emphasize the occasions of change; but it appears to be a

pervasive feature of rules at Stanford. For example, the changing interpretations to both the Fundamental Standard and the Honor Code are impressive
symptoms of the development of skills in coping with problems within a fixed
rule structure.

Stories and Statistics

One of the better-documented features of human understanding is a tendency
to prefer stories to statistics. Most of the time, human beings of virtually all
walks of life and all forms of education accept, store, and retrieve information
that is organized in the form of stories more readily than information that is
less concrete and more elaborately quantitative. This predilection lies at the
heart of many strategies for writing, teaching, and advertising. Nevertheless,
in the rest of the book, we move away from episodic snapshots of organizational rules, such as those summarized in the brief stories above, to a systematic examination of basic statistical regularities in the patterns of rule dynamics and to the underlying processes that generate these changes and stability.

The change is not predicated on any presumption of the inherent superiority of statistics over stories. A great deal can be learned from examining detailed stories that are told of rule development in a particular organization at a
particular time. Such stories deal well with the rich intermingling of contexts
and events that produces critical episodes in organizational history. They illuminate ideas of a complicated, path-dependent history by specifying the contingencies of history, the ways in which minor factors at critical times produce
permanent effects and the ways in which processes of history are orchestrated
in an organization.

Observations gleaned from key historical episodes in rule change are vital
to understanding rule dynamics, but they have clear limitations. They focus
on the dramatics of rules, on events that are recorded in memories and archives with enough detail to be recovered. They are histories of vivid crises,
articulate monarchs, and glorious conquest without consciousness of the overwhelming significance of mundane problems, ordinary people, and prosaic
events. We think that important features of the latter can be learned by study-
ing the former, but we wish to examine the underlying dynamics of the evolution of rules. And for that we need to supplement the texture of historical con-

creteness with a look at some broad theoretical ideas about the quantitative statistics of rule development.

Our intent is to contribute to a scholarship on rules that draws from both stories and statistics. To accomplish this, we consider the histories of rules—their births, revisions, and suspensions—but we attempt to tie those histories both to explicit measures of the contexts that surround them and to ideas that have been derived from more qualitative methods. Some elements of those ideas have been sketched above. We now turn to a more detailed elaboration of the ideas we will explore, ideas drawn from the traditions of organization studies and stories about rules but cast in a way amenable to a more quantitative analysis.

THREE

Speculating about Rule Dynamics

Rules are born, develop, and, sometimes, die. There is no shortage of ideas about the underlying processes by which rules are created and changed. Some of those conceptions see rules as responses to pressures external to organizations; some see rules as responses to features of organizational structure; some see rules as having an internal dynamic in which changes in rules at one time and place affect subsequent changes. In this chapter, we try to identify a few central speculations about the development of rules that might provide a basis for sorting among and integrating those conceptions.

Basic Ideas

We focus particularly on three general notions: first, rules evolve over time in response to problems. Their histories are constructed as part of an organization's dealing with the internal and external problems that it confronts. When problems arise, organizations attend to them, drawing resources from the organizational vicinity of the problems. They attend to problems by using existing procedures if they can, otherwise changing procedures or creating new ones.

The problems, like the rules, are organized into areas of concern with their own associated problem spaces and rule makers. As problems are addressed, rules are created and the problem space contracts. Problems frequently originate from outside the organization; and when they do, they frequently come in surges of concerns that mark a particular historical period. As a result, clusters of rules share a common beginning. Subsequently, each rule follows a path of stability and change that is particularly responsive to features of the internal organizational experience with it.

Second, rules are interrelated within an organization. They compete for attention, channel attention allocation, and introduce sources of rule dynamics that cannot be inferred from studies of individual rules. Those ecological connections matter, and we need to treat the development of organizational rules as a coevolutionary process within a population of interconnected rules. Attention to rule change opportunities is initiated by some signal of a problem, then moves through a rule system as new problems are created or discovered and as attention capabilities and problems are matched. Change in one rule at one time affects the stability of that rule, as well as other rules, at subsequent times. The result is that each problem initiates a ripple of attention that is dampened by competition from the attention claims of other ripples and by the barriers to contagion created by the organizational structure.

Third, rules both record history and reflect learning within the organization. Organizations and their environments gain competence with rules, and those changes in competence affect the development of the rule system. In particular, the generation and contagion of problems are affected by the gains in competence that experience brings. As organizations accumulate experience with particular sets of procedures and problems, they develop competencies that reduce the need for new procedures. As rule makers accumulate experience with making rules, they develop competencies that increase their propensities to make them.

Within such a perspective, organizational propensities for rule change in individual rules depend on three fundamental sets of processes. The first two are: (1) processes for the *generation of problems* associated with rules; and (2) processes for the *allocation of attention* to problems. Both of these sets of processes occur within an *ecology of rules*. The context of problems and rule change for one rule is the pattern of problems and change in other rules. This context is structured by the ways in which individual rules are connected to each other and by the ways in which rule regimes are constructed to regulate the flow of attention to problems. The third set of processes involves *competence accumulation* with rules, learning how to implement and adapt written rules without changing them, and learning how to change them. As these three processes unfold over time, they create histories of rules that are path dependent. The events of one time period create the premises of the next, and the stability and substance of rules depend not only on their current environments but also on their histories.

Generation and Recognition of Problems

A pattern of relative stability and continuity of organizational rules characterize, we suspect, most of organizational history. However, there are times when organizations recognize problems with existing rules and move to change them. We assume a familiar bounded rationality/satisficing organization that monitors its environment for internal and external signals of failures or impending failures (March 1994a, Chapter 2). Organizations respond to rules and rule domains that have come to be defined as problems. An initial response involves the application of existing organizational skills at operating within and around existing rules. If problems persist, then an organization turns to creating new rules or modifying old ones to deal with them. Thus, rule production can be seen as "feeding" on problems, and problems are a (possibly scarce) resource for rule creation.

EXTERNAL SOURCES OF PROBLEMS

A major (initial) source of problems comes from the organization's environment. The embeddedness of organizations in their social, political, and cultural context is a familiar theme of the literature on organizations (Scott 1981; Granovetter 1985). Students of institutional diffusion (Meyer and Rowan 1977; DiMaggio and Powell 1983; Zucker 1987; see also Strang and Soule 1998, for a review) have argued that organizations adopt rules that have become legitimate in the external environment, such as rules that have been created through state and federal legislation, rules that are espoused by actors in the environment that provide necessary resources, such as governmental agencies or corporate donors (Pfeffer and Salancik 1978; Oliver 1991), or rules that have managed to find wide acceptance or are just taken for granted by large numbers of actors in the environment.

It seems virtually axiomatic that organizational rules adjust to changes in surrounding conditions, to the changing mix of participants and their interests and experiences, to new currents of organizational conduct, to emerging problems and solutions. Some events in rule histories are the result of highly focused, relatively dramatic crises that mobilize many forces outside and inside the organization. During the late 1960s, for example, rules governing student and faculty conduct in universities in the United States were swamped by pressures for change stemming from widespread student and faculty political and social action. In many universities, the rules of 1975 were significantly different from the rules of 1960. Although the changes came about through internal confrontation, political bargaining, and tests of power, the primary stimulus was global more than local.

Other events in rule histories are less dramatic but reflect continuing forms of exogenous attention generation. During the period from 1945 to 1960, for example, many American universities developed and modified accounting rules dealing with federal research grants and contracts. The rules of 1960 differed significantly from the rules of 1945, but the changes were more incremental and the political and administrative negotiations more muted.

Several lines of arguments recognize the importance of external environments for organizational survival. They portray an organization as dependent on resources controlled by external institutions and thus as responsive to them. The arguments are not always mutually consistent, however. One view emphasizes the role of the institutional environment in shaping the internal operations of organizations (Meyer and Rowan 1977; DiMaggio and Powell 1983; Tolbert and Zucker 1983; Edelman 1990; Mezias 1990; Abzug and Mezias 1993; Sutton et al. 1994). As the institutional environment becomes more intrusive, it will solicit a closer linkage between organizational practice and external requirements. In this view, the rate of rule birth and rule change should increase with increased importance of external actors.

A second view emphasizes the ways in which organizations substitute external regulations for organizational rules, adopting the regulations imposed on them and thus reducing their own inclinations to create or change rules (March and Olsen 1995, 35). The rule-making proclivities of subordinate colonial offices are dampened by being tightly integrated into a rule-imposing empire. In this view, the rate of organizational rule birth and change should decline when the importance of external actors and regulations increases.

A third view describes organizations as building buffers between themselves and their environments, in particular by trying to decouple rule acceptance and rule implementation (Meyer and Rowan 1977; Brunsson 1989; Elsbach and Sutton 1992). In this view, rule adoption as symbolic compliance to external environments should increase, but, at the same time, rule following should decrease. This would also suggest that rates of rule birth and rule change would differ depending on the centrality of the rule area. Areas located on the boundaries of an organization might be expected to have higher rates than those close to the technical core.

These various arguments make it quite unclear what kind of relation we should expect between external pressures and organizational response. Organizations attend to their external environments, but they do so in many ways. Some rules may be used for the purpose of symbolic compliance. Others may be used for managing internal processes.

The impact of the state and political authorities through legislative attention and financial support stand out as especially important for both dramatic changes and their more incremental cousins (Tolbert and Zucker 1983; Edelman 1990). The most common proposition is that the greater the external legislative and financial dependency of an organization, the more elaborate are its linkages to the political and legal system. The argument is that the necessary cost of financial support is the elaboration of rules demanded by the source of the funds. Universities adopt rules mandated by external regulations and do so particularly where the financial consequences are large. This suggests that the number of external rules and the level of external financial support will have a positive effect on university rule production.

However, converse predictions can also be derived from the same ideas. First, increased involvement with outside groups sometimes translates into increased slack resources. These translate into a decrease in the need for controls and thus a decrease in the production of rules. Second, the process of attention may be more complicated. The existence of multiple external institutions with conflicting demands leads to predictions that organizations will seek to "decouple" various activities through sequential attention or organizational differentiation. Moreover, the delays in response and variations in the impact of pressure on different rule guardians may translate into hard-to-understand "waves" of diffusion of practices. Third, organizational rules and external laws and regulations can be seen as mutual substitutes. If a law exists, then a rule is not required. This suggests a negative relation between legislation and university rule production. Similarly, an increasing proportion of professionals in the labor force may also facilitate the use of implicit professional norms and expectations—as substitutes for formal rules.

INTERNAL SOURCES OF PROBLEMS

Early pioneers on the subject of organizational rules saw rules as outcomes of the expansion of rational-legal authority forms (Weber 1978), as a result of organizational differentiation (Blau 1970), or as the result of organizations seeking to match their structures to environmental contingencies (Pugh et al. 1969; Pugh 1993). Within this tradition, attention has been given particularly to the effects of two central features of bureaucracy that create problems for organizations—increases in scale and increases in complexity.

Speculations about the relation between size and complexity abound. A positive correlation between organizational size and formalization (or complexity) has frequently been reported in empirical studies (e.g., Blau 1970). Although some recent work (Abdel-Khalik 1988) has suggested that the correlation might be a result of underlying mathematical features of hierarchical structures, most explanations of this empirical regularity have emphasized the matching of complexity to size by virtue of the competitive advantage it provides. As organizations grow and undertake more elaborate tasks, it is argued, they confront difficulties of organization. Complex organizational structures provide the advantages of subdivision of work (creating simple tasks that can be executed by unskilled labor or machines), of responsibility (concentrating focus and allocating duties), and of organization into specialized subunits.

Any correlation between organizational size and complexity makes it difficult to establish the independent effects of either on the elaboration of rules, as does the fact that both may be consequences of environmental change that may also directly affect rule generation and change. If organizational size and complexity are responses to environmental conditions, then it is likely that many other things are also determined directly by the same environmental conditions and cannot be attributed to the independent effect of size and complexity. In the absence of experimental controls, the problems are hard to avoid.

It is commonly hypothesized that increases in either organizational size or complexity or both will lead to increased use of written rules, which are alternatives to informal relationships and understandings. A small, homogeneous, simple world can, it is argued, be coordinated and controlled through shared values and beliefs that make explicit rules unnecessary and even wasteful. As organizations grow in scale, diversity, and complexity, these informal and value-based mechanisms become less feasible. Relevant people are not connected to one another, or if connected, they do not share understandings, experiences, or meanings.

By this analysis, rules are substitutes for informal understandings. They will be more frequently created (and perhaps more often subject to revision) as organizations become more heterogeneous. For example, some sociologists of organizations have noted the role of conflict in stimulating the creation of formal rules to protect the interests of employees (Perrow 1986), to reduce the arbitrariness of management (Crozier 1964), and to substitute for close supervision (Gouldner 1954). Since interests might be expected to multiply with the scale and complexity of an organization, differences in scale or complexity should, on average, be associated with differences in the rates of generation and change of rules.

The arguments presume some kind of mechanism, most commonly some process of rational choice, learning, or competitive selection, by which organizations move toward rules when they "need" them. Such a presumption discounts any possibility that the very features of organizations that make rules functionally attractive may also serve to make them more difficult to enact and refine. The processes by which rules are created, suspended, and revised are likely to become more cumbersome as organizational size and complexity increase, thereby producing some indeterminacy in the prediction. Although in the long run it might be imagined that larger, more differentiated organizations will tend to have more rules than more homogeneous organizations, it is not clear that the rates of rule birth and change will be directly related to the contemporaneous size or complexity of an organization. Indeed, changes in the number of rules (or the rates of rule birth and change) seem likely to be more closely connected to *changes* in size and complexity than to the *levels* of those variables.

SOCIAL CONSTRUCTION OF PROBLEMS

Organizations attend to problems, but the presence of a problem is not entirely dictated by either external environments or internal complexities. Whether a problem exists is socially constructed: that is, problems exist if they are recognized as existing. As a result, any theory of rule change includes a theory of problem recognition. Such a theory begins with the observation that, as in most cases of social construction, the recognition of a problem is not arbitrary. A claim of a problem must be granted credence, and the negotiation of credence often requires some manifest plausibility. Organizational complexity, institutional environments, and external shocks are potential bases for such plausibility, but they do not determine it.

We note, in particular, two key components of problem recognition. First, organizations are thermostatic in their attention. As long as performance is satisfactory in a particular area, problems tend not to be noticed. When performance falls below a critical point, attention is directed to the area associated with the failure. Problems that were previously not noticed receive attention. Attention continues until performance is raised to a "cut-off" point that is higher than the "turn-on" point. Thus, problem solving tends to generate a discontinuous wave of rule changes. There are (relatively long) periods of low rates of change when problems are attended by routines or exceptions to routines. But there are also episodes of problem solving when the rate of change is high. These patterns are influenced critically by the "turn-on" and "cut-off" points (commonly called aspiration levels or targets). Since these thermostat settings are themselves subject to modifications with experience, the translation of exogenous flows of problems into their recognition as organizational problems tends to dampen the fluctuations in problem incidence. When there are many problems, the criterion for problem recognition is raised. When problems are scarce, the criterion is reduced.

Second, parts of the patterns of problem recognition are produced by the "demand" for problems, rather than the "supply." Rule makers without a supply of problems tend to promote minor annoyances into serious difficulties. New administrators see the problems they have inherited more vividly than their predecessors did. Individuals with experience and competence using old rules are less likely to see problems with those rules than will new individuals, and experienced individuals are more likely to see problems with new changes.

The existence of an attention agent, such as safety inspector, ombudsman's office, or committees on academic misconduct, may affect the threshold of problem recognition, increasing problem recognition when the supply is low, decreasing it when the supply is high. Individuals and groups that seek attention for problems will direct those problems to areas where the competition for attention from other problems is relatively weak and where the collection of rules is relatively undeveloped.

Ecological Structure of Rules

Rules are linked to other rules in functional and procedural ecologies that place any particular rule in close proximity to some other rules and more distant from others. Rules occupy domains, sometimes crowding the domains, sometimes not. As a result of these linkages, specific rule births and changes are likely to be inadequately understood unless they are located in the ecological context of rules.

PROBLEM ABSORPTION AND RULE DENSITY

Rule density is analogous in a general way to the density of organizations in population ecology studies (Hannan and Freeman 1989; Carroll and Hannan 1989). Just as organizational density refers to the number of organizations within a given niche, rule density refers to the number of rules in a given organizational rule domain at a given time. Rule density changes over time, generally increasing as an organization grows older and larger (Pugh et al. 1969; Blau 1970).

We wish to explore the extent to which the number of new rules born per year (the birthrate) depends on the number of rules already in the organizational rule population (Schulz 1998b). A positive density dependence of the birthrate would mean that the rule population grows more rapidly when there are many rules already in a domain than it does when there are fewer. Conversely, a negative density dependence of the birthrate would mean that the rule population grows more rapidly when there are only a few rules already in a domain than it does when there are many. A negative density dependence of the rule birthrate means that the growth of the rule population slows down as the number of rules increases. It does not mean that the rule population declines in number.

A basic hypothesis suggested by bureaucratic theory is that the rate of rule birth increases with rule density, as existing rules spawn new rules. That is, rules create problems which create the need for new rules, and the number of rules increases exponentially. This is a possible interpretation of much of bureaucratic theory. Within that interpretation, the internal dynamics of rules lead to explosive growth. Limits to bureaucratic rule proliferation, if any, must come from the outside, perhaps from technological or cultural changes (e.g., Crozier 1964, 294), perhaps from public disaffection with bureaucratic forms (Meyer 1985, 195).

An alternative idea is that the relation between rules and problems is one in which rules solve problems. When issues can be handled successfully within a rule system, they are dealt with in a routine way. Rules become stable and unproblematic. They "absorb" problems. Once they have been addressed by a rule, problems are less available for further rule production (within the jurisdiction of the same rule-making body). Moreover, old rules are extended to deal with new problems. Even when rules provide only cosmetic solutions, they absorb problems. They reduce or eliminate the pressure for change by appeasing external stakeholders. Finally, the flow of problems into an area is not entirely exogenous, but rather depends on the attractiveness of a domain to problem instigators, people who generate problems in order to stimulate discussion and rule making. As the density of rules in a domain increases, the attractiveness of that domain as a target for problem instigators declines, and problems are discovered or created in other domains.

One possible consequence is that the elaboration of rules is self-regulating. In particular, potential new rules face competition from existing rules in being linked to problems. As the number of rules in a particular domain increases, new problems are likely to encounter numerous existing rules. New rule opportunities are reduced. By such a competition mechanism, the rate of rule production should decline with the number of rules in the population. We should observe negative density dependence.

Different problems have different rates of recurrence: some kinds of problems occur more frequently than others. The rate at which particular problems are absorbed depends on their frequency of occurrence. Recurring problems receive more attention and are absorbed by rules at a more rapid rate than are rare problems. This sorting by frequency of recurrence removes recurring problems from the problem space more reliably and faster than it does less frequently recurring problems. The set of remaining problems not yet absorbed by rules consists increasingly of rarely occurring problems.

A reduction in the number of rules in a domain can be imagined to open new possibilities for new rules. In the absence of an influx of new problems into the domain, the supply of problems available for organizational rule attention and production is a negative function of the density of rules already in existence. Conversely, rule suspensions reduce competitive pressures on new rules. When a rule is suspended, problems previously regulated by that rule are once again available for attention and to being re-regulated by new rules. Delacroix, Swaminathan, and Solt (1989) refer to such a process as "recycling." At the same time, as the number of suspensions increases and thereby decreases rule density, the attractiveness of the domain to problem instigators rises. Thus, the birthrate of organizational rules should be expected to increase as the number of suspended rules in a population increases.

So far, our discussion has focused on endogenous sources of problems—absorption restricting the supply, and suspensions replenishing it. Much of the variation in the flow of problems is, however, exogenous. The world changes. Environmental turbulence introduces new problems and makes old rules and competencies with them partially or entirely obsolete. Because of new rule opportunities provided by turbulence, the negative effect of density on the birthrate of rules should be weaker in more turbulent areas than in less turbulent ones. Such turbulence is more likely in boundary-spanning areas, areas involving conflict, and areas that cover a large, heterogeneous domain.

The effects of rule density might be expected to depend on the distances among rules and problems. Two rule populations are close if they are interconnected functionally or procedurally, and it seems reasonable to predict that some rule subpopulations will find problems in other nearby subpopulations. When clusters of domains form close ecological communities (Astley 1985; Fombrun 1986; Astley and Fombrun 1987), one might expect that rule density within each community would affect rule production throughout the domains within it. On the other hand, if rule populations are relatively autonomous functionally and procedurally, density effects might be expected to be confined within the local populations.

ECOLOGICAL CONTEXT OF PROBLEM
RECOGNITION AND ATTENTION

Rules do not change automatically. They are changed by relatively conscious processes of learning, problem solving, discussion, conflict, bargaining, and decision making. Those processes require that individuals and procedures be activated and energy be addressed to the issues. When the attention of decision makers is focused on rules or a particular domain of rules, the probability of rule change is increased. Therefore, we expect to find that the rate of rule change in a specific domain will be positively related to attention allocated to that domain.

Contagion and Competition Effects

Within the constraints of an attention structure, attention allocation is shaped by two major (and potentially countervailing) ecological phenomena. The first is the contagion of problem recognition and attention, the way attention in one part of the system spreads to other parts. This contagion, or multiplier, effect leads to change in one rule increasing the likelihood of change in another. Political and organizational attention are likely to precipitate rule changes. Such attention is likely to diffuse through a whole domain of rules. Thus, attention to problems of grade inflation spreads through a family of academic rules. When decision makers see problems in a particular rule or a particular domain of rules, the probability of rule change in nearby rules is increased.

A classic example of the contagion of problem generation is tinkering with a technology. Changes in a technology designed to accomplish intended improvements by correcting known problems or introducing expected embellishments characteristically introduce unintended and unanticipated difficulties and improvement opportunities, which invite further attention. These problems occur in the rule that has changed and in rules that are near to it. For example, a change in rules about the creation of a particular report is likely to lead to changes in rules about its review and dissemination. Thus, problem recognition spreads from a specific rule at a specific time to the same rule subsequently and to neighboring rules at the same time. Also it is noticeable that organizational attention is seldom strictly rule specific; rather it is often organized by some area-specific apparatus (e.g., the committee on undergraduate studies in the Faculty Senate). As a result, once organizational attention is activated, it is likely to produce changes in nearby rule areas but not in more distant areas. Boundaries between different arenas in an organization restrict the flow of attention. The permeability of the boundaries depends on the magnitude of external shocks and the persistence of problems, as well as upon the overlapping nature of the links that constitute an organizational structure.

The second phenomenon is competition for attention, the way attention in one part of the system detracts from (or substitutes for) attention in other parts. For the most part, theories of organizational decision making that start from a bounded rationality/satisficing base are theories of attention allocation (March and Simon 1958; Cyert and March 1963; March 1988, 1994a; Kingdon 1984; Shapira 1997). They assume that a prime factor in decision making is the way in which a scarce attention resource is allocated among alternative problems. If attention were an unlimited resource within an organization, then the processes of attention generation and contagion would saturate rules with attention. That is not what is observed. Rather, attention is constrained by the availability of decision makers to concern themselves with rules.

Rule changes often require mobilization, negotiation, and elements of consensus. Even when rule change is not particularly contentious, rules require scarce attention and energy. Given scarcity, attention to rule making will reduce attention available for other activities. Rule-related items on the agenda of a rule-making body direct organizational attention to the rule system, hence increase the probability that the rule system will undergo changes. Rule-unrelated items, on the other hand, direct organizational attention away from the rule system, decreasing the rate of rule revision. Because attention is limited, competition for attention is also a major factor in determining the attention given to any particular rule change opportunity. The organizational machinery for dealing with rules can accommodate only a limited number of rule issues at any one time (Kingdon 1984). As a result, conscious attention allocation and manipulation are factors in rule dynamics, as are stable organizational processes that structure attention without deliberate intention.

In the early stages of a specific rule regime, attention is mobilized to attend to rules. Rules are created and revised. However, the same level of attention cannot be maintained indefinitely; as other problems attract the attention of the organization, and as the apparent organizational and political return from attention to a specific set of rules declines, the energy devoted to modifying that set of rules is reduced. As a result, organizational learning with respect to a particular rule is not a continuous process. Learning occurs when attention is focused on a problem area. When attention shifts or becomes scarce, the learning rate declines (Winter 1971; Radner and Rothschild 1975).

This suggests that organizational rule making is often activated in response to crisis, uncertainty, and the disruption of routine processes—"putting out fires," as Radner and Rothschild (1975) call it. On these occasions, previous rules seem inadequate, and organizations search to find solutions to the new problems. Those solutions often take the form of formal rules. The financial crisis that Stanford experienced in the late 1980s and early 1990s attracted attention from many administrative offices, schools, departments, and individual faculties and almost certainly diverted their attention from other possible problems. Similarly, when an academic rule-making body directs its attention to issues or crises in the student area, it tends to neglect issues in the faculty area. For example, when rule-making institutions are focusing on problems of grade inflation, they are less likely to focus on problems of faculty retention.

The effects of competition for attention are felt within a particular attention domain. That is, competition for attention occurs among rules that share a common pool of decision makers and a common universe of problems. Thus, change in one rule seems likely to decrease the likelihood of change in another. In particular, when the political and procedural pressures leading to rule change are primarily symbolic, action on one rule tends to substitute for action on another.

Somewhat similar arguments apply to the effects of the distribution of attention across time. There is, however, a difference between the two situations. Although contagion of attention can be imagined to occur across time, so that attention in a prior time period may stimulate attention in a subsequent one, the effects of competition for scarce attention resources across time are more problematic. As a result, we would expect that the effects of contagion (relative to competition) would be greater with respect to attention across time than with respect to attention across domains. If there are effects of the distribution of attention in previous times on rule changes in current times, then we would expect them to be positive.

These considerations also illuminate the effects of centralization of decision making in organizations. In a highly centralized organizational structure, the authority of rule making is concentrated. As a result, we may expect the effects

TABLE 3.1

Competing hypotheses about the effects of change in
one rule domain on changes in another

	Positive effects of change	*Negative effects of change*
Functional interdependency	MULTIPLIER Changes in one rule necessitate changes in others, thus increase changes elsewhere	SUBSTITUTE Changes in one rule substitute for changes in others, thus decrease changes elsewhere
Attention interdependency	CONTAGION Changes in one rule generate attention to other rules, thus increase changes elsewhere	COMPETITION Changes in one rule distract attention from other rules, thus decrease changes elsewhere

of attention competition to be accentuated. On the other hand, in highly de-centralized structures where rule-making responsibilities are dispersed, we may expect greater decoupling of rule-making activities across areas and weaker effects of attention competition.

The ecological effects on problem generation and the allocation of attention can be summarized in a simple two-by-two table, Table 3.1. As the discussion and the table suggest, there are ample theoretical grounds to expect that change in one rule will increase the likelihood of change in another, as well as ample grounds for expecting that change in one rule will decrease the likelihood of change in another.

The joint effect of the contagion of problem generation among close domains and the competition for attention within a structure of attention boundaries produces ecological patterns of change that resemble the patterns of iron filings responding to multiple magnets on a surface with barriers. Although the details depend on the timing of the arrival of problems and the structural restrictions on attention, we would expect the attention competition effect to be dominant in cases in which the rules belong to the same "region" of rules but not the same "locality." In such cases, we expect to find that the rate of rule change in a particular domain is inversely related to the rate of change outside that domain. Where two rules belong to the same "locality," however, we would expect the contagion of problem recognition effect to be dominant. In such cases, we expect to find that the rate of rule change in one rule will be positively related to the rate of change in another.

Ecological Structure and Distance

The spread of problem recognition through a population of rules is not random. Ideas about the diffusion of problem recognition presume an ecological structure that defines distances and boundaries among rules. By determining the patterns of diffusion, the structure of that ecology has pervasive effects on the contagion of problem generation and recognition. This structure is, of course, not fixed in most organizations. Rather, it can change over time. Boundaries around problem areas and distances among them can shift, for example, when the organization expands into new activity domains. Rule-making bodies can change. In longitudinal studies of rule populations, such changes have to be considered.

We think of an organization as being partitioned by semipermeable membranes that restrict, but do not totally prevent, the flow of information from one broad domain ("region") to another. The network of perceptual and procedural interdependencies among possible rule changes has a structure that makes it possible to speak of "distances" among rules. Contagion of problem recognition is likely to occur more readily among "neighboring" rule change opportunities.

The most obvious dimension of distance among rules is a functional interdependence one. Rules are connected by the way the execution of one rule affects the execution of another. Functional interdependence arises routinely in the operation of rules. For example, rules about faculty conduct in a classroom are linked to rules about student conduct. Rules about legitimate travel expenditures are linked to rules about making travel arrangements. On average, two academic rules are closer to each other than either is to most administrative rules, and two administrative rules are closer to each other than either is to most academic rules.

A second dimension of distance among rule changes is a procedural interdependence one. Rule agents, problem areas, and organizational responses are organized around clusters of rules. When rules are partitioned into clusters or domains, and each domain is delegated to a specialized attention agent, it creates procedural interdependence in that attention is given not to a single rule but to the domain in which the particular rule resides. The process of creating or changing one rule affects the process of creating or changing another connected rule. Rules are connected by sharing common procedures for changing them, or by sharing the same rule agent. For example, one of the rule-making bodies of the rules analyzed in the context of this study was administered by only one person (the "editor" of the administrative rule book) who would occasionally assemble small groups of "rule owners" (i.e., relevant administrators from a given area) to discuss rule changes in their area.

A third dimension of distance among rules is a temporal one: rule changes are connected by time. Recognition of problems in a rule domain at one time may spread to a subsequent time. By this mechanism, we would expect a positive link between attention at one time and attention at a subsequent time. Alternatively, problem solving in a domain at one time may decrease the likelihood of problem recognition in the same domain in the immediate next periods. This might occur either because the problem space is reduced or because there is a limited attention span on the part of rule-making bodies.

Competence Accumulation within Rules

A prominent notion in theories of organizations is that age has a positive effect on the persistence of organizational structures (thus in this case a negative effect on revisions and suspensions). The main argument of persistence theories is that organizational rules become more resistant to change the longer they survive—it is a familiar argument. The concept of liability of newness was first introduced to studies of organizations by Stinchcombe (1965). He argued that organizations face a liability of newness which makes them more prone to fail immediately after the time of founding. This argument that age produces stability is echoed in institutional theory (e.g., Zucker 1987; Selznick 1957), ecological theory (e.g., Freeman, Carroll, and Hannan 1983), and theories of organizational learning (e.g., Levitt and March 1988).

Two major mechanisms are involved in increasing persistence with age. The first is the infusion of rules with values. Organizational participants infuse value into rules and these values subsequently impede change (Selznick 1957). The longer a rule has existed, the more it becomes linked to the values of organizational stakeholders. It comes to be viewed as "natural" and "taken for granted." Endurance transforms a rule from being subject to human choice to being an unexamined object of the environment (Zucker 1977, 729).

The second mechanism is the adaptation of rule users and rules to experience with rules, the development of competence. The longer a rule exists in an organization, the more experience is accumulated with it, giving rise to rule improvements and improved skills in using the rule. Improvements in rules and enhanced abilities to use them (rule-specific knowledge) reduce incentives for revision. Rules are the technologies of organizational life and become stabilized through competency traps (Levinthal and March 1993) much as other technologies do (Arthur 1989). Most activities within an organization are based on routines. Most of the time, problems are contained by using existing rules, refining existing rules, or making exceptions to rules. As a result, experience with a particular population of rules accumulates. In the interplay between rules and rule users, confidence and competence grow.

We examine the implications of these routine-based learning processes for rule dynamics. In particular, we distinguish three important types of competence gained by an organization as a result of experience with rules: the first is increased skill at operating within existing rules; the second is increased skill at making or changing rules; and the third is increased capability of rules to absorb problems.

LEARNING TO OPERATE WITHIN RULES

Competence enhancement can be described in terms of two time-dependent processes of learning. The first process is one of learning within the organization. Organizations become better at doing the things they do. Over time, an organization collects more experiences with existing rules and becomes more competent in operating within (or around) them. This expanded experience and the resulting lessons can be encoded in two places—in rules and in people. When organizational rules are revised, experiences and lessons learned up to that point are encoded in the new rule version. Because each new revision adds new experiences made since the last revision, the knowledge encoded in the new rule version is based on a larger pool of experiences and thus is likely to be more comprehensive and more accurate, resulting in a reduced need to change the rule again. The encoding of experiences has a similar effect. The longer a rule exists in an organization, the more likely it is that rule followers will have confidence in it and the more likely that skills will be gained in using it. As they gain experience with particular rules, members in an organization not only transform rules from being subject to human choice to being unexamined objects of their worldview but also they increase their skills in dealing with the rules they have, learning from experience (Perrow 1986; Levitt and March 1988; March and Olsen 1989). They accumulate competence in interpreting rules, developing exceptions to rules, and understanding the boundaries and flexibilities of rules. As a result, rule age can affect the rate at which an individual rule will be suspended or revised.

The second process is one of learning within the organizational environment. Organizational rules and practices are intertwined with each other and with the rules and practices of others; and they become more so over time. The process of entanglement is an obvious feature of the development of higher education in the United States (Meyer, Boli, and Thomas 1987; Thomas and Meyer 1984). The rules found in universities have coevolved and their interconnections reduce the independent plasticity of each. At the same time, both the state and society are firmly linked to higher education, shaping and being shaped by it. As an organization and those with whom it deals gain competence in fitting the organization's rules into a larger structure of rules and expectations, the ability of all concerned to function within the existing system improves relative to the ability to function within an alternative system. This gain in competence with the existing system reduces the capability of any organization to change autonomously. A change would incur heavy costs in loss of competence for those who are connected to the rule system (e.g., suppliers, customers, patrons, governmental agencies); thus it is resisted by them.

These two processes in combination produce gradual change in the factors affecting rule creation and revision as a rule ages. Learning enhances competence, and competence results in fewer new rules and fewer revisions of old rules.

LEARNING TO MAKE OR CHANGE RULES

Organizations also gain competence at changing rules through experience in doing it. As a result, they become more inclined to change rules. If rule making and rule changes are solutions to problems, then the cumulative competence in making and changing rules turns rule making into an attractive solution to emerging problems. These gains in competence at rule making and in the proclivity to engage in them stem from several sources. On the one hand, skills at working within a rule-making agency accumulate with experience. Individuals involved at rule making become better at it over time. They learn how to recognize problems in rules, how to mobilize attention to those problems, how to organize coalitions of support for changes. The more experience, the greater the competence. The greater the competence, the greater the willingness to see rule change as desirable.

Part of this competence gained from experience is competence at recognizing the side benefits of engaging in rule change. Experienced rule makers recognize that the act of making a rule or changing a rule, or even talking about a rule, may by itself resolve problems. Once problems are channeled into a rule-making process, the demands of attention and the time delays that such a process requires are likely to overload some key participants, particularly those with short time horizons or tenure, thereby reducing the pressures for substantive change. For example, it is commonly observed that whenever there are large-scale controversies on campus, they are likely to lead to some sort of rule-making and rule change activities. Typically, these rule-making processes take two to three years before any specific changes are adopted. Often, the adopted solutions are not directed to the original problem. But once the problems are channeled into the rule-making process, attention is diverted and uninstitutionalized pressure evaporates. In this sense, the rule-making process itself, not the substance of the rules, is the solution to the problems. The organization learns that initiating rule change discussions solves problems in the sense that it makes sustained attention to the problems by outside advocates difficult. Rule makers learn some variation of the "short shelf life of problems" hypothesis.

It may be well to note that organizational competence at operating within rules and organizational competence at making rules may develop in different parts of the organization. Rule makers tend to become skilled at making rules; rule followers tend to become skilled at using rules. As a result, we might speculate that the longer a rule endures in an unchanging environment, the fewer problems will be found with it by users (because of their competence at operating within the rule) and the greater the likelihood that those problems that are found will result in rule changes (because of the competence of rule makers at making rules).

LEARNING TO ABSORB PROBLEMS

An important aspect of organizational learning is the refinement of rules. Organizations learn not only by establishing new rules but also by revising existing rules. This occurs typically when an old rule code does not fit new experiences. The main impetus of rule refinement is an enhancement of a rule's capability to absorb problems arising in its (intra- and extraorganizational) environment. Refinement can involve many forms. It can involve adding provisions that specify appropriate and efficient solutions to problems, but it also can involve broadening the scope of a rule by allowing more flexible interpretations, hence making it more ambiguous.

Refinement can be seen as a case of learning by rules. Organizational rules learn organizational responses that absorb the problems emerging from their current environment (see also March and Olsen 1989, 18). Although there is no assurance that the process leads to any optimal absorption rate or pattern, rules come to exhibit features that provide a satisfactory level of problem absorption and thereby promote their own survival.

From a slightly different angle, refinement could be seen as a form of sampling that pools organizational experiences. Each time an organizational rule is revised, the organizational rule makers in charge sample current conditions relevant to the rule, derive a model about surrounding conditions (e.g., assess if it is appropriate to consider certain expenses as reimbursable, or which forms of rule evasion are likely to occur), and adjust the rule accordingly. In refinement, new experiences are consolidated with previous experiences stored in the rule. The samples drawn at consecutive rule change times are pooled with previous samples (although, possibly with greater weights attached to more recent samples). Such pooling of experiences over recurrent adjustments and extended time periods increases the sample size and thereby the reliability of rules. Refinement makes rules more "fit" to a stable environment, but potentially less able to cope with change. For example, after a series of rule adjustments a reimbursement rule might become less ambiguous, appear to be more just, easier to follow, better at preventing efforts to circumvent it, more in tune with other rules, and so forth. By the same token, this increased specificity and interconnectedness probably makes a rule less pliable in the face of change.

In practice, the accumulation of experiences in rules is probably more complex. One complication arises from difficulties of retrieving old experiences.

Rules store the lessons of past experiences, but typically not the experiences leading to those lessons (March and Olsen 1989, 38). Especially in times of high personnel turnover, prior experiences are likely to be irretrievable, potentially resulting in a bias of rule refinement toward current experiences. Another complication arises from fluctuations of attention within an organization, fluctuations that are likely to make both memories of the past and its relevance unstable.

MANIFESTATIONS OF COMPETENCE ACCUMULATION

If they survive an early period of vulnerability, organizations tend to endure for relatively long periods. This is particularly true of American universities, which historically have had a comparatively low risk of failure (Marshall 1995). Long-enduring organizations seem often to have histories characterized by extended periods of moderate, orderly change punctuated by occasional dramatic shocks, shocks that overturn the basic regime of the system (March and Olsen 1989). Competence accumulates in a number of ways throughout organizational histories and rule histories. We focus on four of them.

Rule Regime Age

Long-enduring organizations occasionally reconstitute themselves in ways analogous to the reconstitution of nation-states through the establishment of new rule-making regimes. They restructure relationships and overturn systems of rules. Thus, the processes of aging in rule systems are subject to a "resetting" of their clocks (Amburgey, Kelly, and Barnett 1993). When rule regimes change, rule making changes, and the effects are often immediate. New rule regimes are likely to be associated with a flurry of problem recognition and rule making.

As a rule regime ages, an organization becomes more competent in rule making and more competent in operating within (or around) the rules. As a result of the first competence, an organization is likely to generate more rules and more revisions of rules. As a result of the second competence, it is likely to generate fewer rules and fewer revisions. The development of these competencies may not be even; one tendency may come to dominate and having done so become even more reinforced by the resulting differential strengthening of competence. In general, we expect rule regimes to become more comfortable with existing procedures as they age, losing the will to change rules and elaborating skills at operating within the existing system. Thus, we expect the rates of rule birth and of rule change to decrease as a rule regime ages. When environments change dramatically, as happened in the 1960s in American higher education, however, the change triggers dramatic changes in the system for making rules, what we call *rule regime changes*. Such external shocks to the rule regime give rise to doubts about the collection of rules as a whole, inviting new scrutiny and new interpretations. Thus, when the rule regime itself changes, the age clock is reset and liability of newness is reintroduced.

Rule Age

Regimes are not the only things that grow older. Individual rules also age. At any particular moment in the history of a rule regime, some individual rules will be older than others. Rule age can affect the rate at which individual rules are suspended or revised, independent of the effects of rule regime age. As a rule ages, it also is likely to change through revisions. The effects of rule change need, however, to be distinguished from the effects of rule age. Rule age affects the fit of a rule to its environment primarily by affecting the adaptation of the organization and its environment to the rule. Thus, the mechanisms are mechanisms of learning by the users of the rule. Rule change, on the other hand, affects the fit of a rule primarily by affecting the adaptation of the rule to the organization and its environment.

Although the idea of increasing persistence with age is quite prevalent in theories of organizations (e.g., Singh, Tucker, and House 1986; Hannan and Freeman 1984), it is not a self-evident idea. Organizational rules, like other structures, are embedded in a myriad of social, economic, and technological conditions. Rules are created and updated in a specific context at a specific historical time. A rule text created at a given historical time is based upon conditions and experiences valid at that time (Boeker 1989; Tucker, Singh, and Meinhard 1990). These conditions change over time, sometimes very rapidly. To assume that rules become increasingly persistent in the face of continual change is a strong claim. If the new conditions differ from those experienced when the rule was created, then it is likely that a rule will become obsolete. Thus, a speculation counter to that of persistence theories is that rules become more vulnerable to change the longer they are in existence. More formally, rule age has a positive effect on rule change.

A possible reconciliation of these two speculations can be obtained by observing that the age of a rule at any point consists in two components. The first component is the time from the birth of the rule to the time of its most recent revision. The second component is the time from the most recent revision to the current time. The first component could be seen as a measure of the rule-related knowledge summarized by the current rule version, since it counts only the time that has elapsed between the birth of the rule and the revision of it. According to the first speculation, age at the time of last revision might be negatively related to rule change, since the older the age at last revision, the greater the knowledge represented by the current rule version. The second component, on the other hand, could be seen as a measure of the obsolescence of the current rule version, since it counts only the time since revision. According to the second speculation, the time since the last revision might be positively related to rule change. By these interpretations, any observed relation between overall rule age and rule change would be a confounded consequence of these two effects.

Rule Plasticity

As rules age, they may change. The longer they endure, the more changes they are likely to experience. Rule age and rule changeability or plasticity are not the same, however. We ask whether, controlling for the age of a rule at the time of last revision, prior changes in the rule affect its subsequent stability. What might affect the relation between previous changes and subsequent changes? The most obvious answer is that rules might become "refined" through recurrent adjustment processes, changing less in the future the more they were adjusted before. From this perspective, rule changes are part of the improvement in rules that makes them better equipped to deal with problems. Each change extends the capabilities of the rules.

Alternatively, rules might be destabilized by change, changing more in the future the more they have changed in the past. The classic example is tinkering with a technology. Changes in a technology designed to accomplish intended improvements by correcting known problems or introducing expected embellishments characteristically introduce unintended and unanticipated difficulties, which invite further changes. New rules or changes in rules might very well, on average, introduce more problems than they solve. A second example is "repetitive momentum." Amburgey, Kelly, and Barnett (1993) proposed a model of organizational change in which change becomes routinized and organizations develop increasing competencies with change. Increasing competencies at change leads to increases in the likelihood of further change. A similar process might occur in change histories of rules. If rule makers develop competencies at changing a particular rule, their competencies might well increase with the number of changes introduced. The result would be a positive effect of prior changes on subsequent changes of the rule.

Thus, the process of rule change can result either in a path of gradual refinement by which the technology improves, or in a path of gradual disintegration in which each change encourages further changes or even introduces more problems than it solves until the technology collapses.

A more complicated possibility is that the improvement made by a single change declines with the number of previous changes made to any particular rule, but the contribution of a single change to the creation of new problems is a constant. Then, rules would be stabilized by change early in their history, when the improvement effect is greater than the new problem effect, and destabilized by change late in their history, when the new problem effect is greater.

Density Revisited

There is a direct analogue between the ideas about competence gains and the earlier discussion of density effects. Density at a particular time is defined as the number of rules existing at that time. Thus, it is the number of births from the beginning of the rule regime up to that time minus the number of suspensions during the same period. The previous arguments examined density effects in terms of occupancy of a problem space, arguing that the creation of rules absorbed problems and the suspension of rules released problems for subsequent absorption. If the number of problems were fixed (or controlled for), therefore, we expect the number of previous births to reduce the birthrate of rules, and the number of previous suspensions (as well as the number of contemporaneous suspensions) to increase the birthrate. This means that we expect density (previous births minus previous suspensions) effects on the birthrate to be negative and current suspension effects to be positive. Those ideas are contrasted with ideas that assume simply that rules breed rules.

Similarly, the ideas about competence gains contrast two visions of competence gains. One vision is that experience in rule making increases the skills at rule making and therefore the utilization of rule-making capabilities. Previous

TABLE 3.2

Competing hypotheses about the effects of previous births and
previous and current suspensions on current birthrate

	Problem space and density	*Bureaucratic proliferation*
	Learning of competence in rules	*Learning of competence in rule making*
Effect of previous births	NEGATIVE	POSITIVE
Effect of previous suspensions	POSITIVE	POSITIVE
Effect of current suspensions	POSITIVE	NO PREDICTION

rule births and previous suspensions both provide experience at rule making;
thus they would affect the birthrate of rules positively. The alternative vision is
that experience with rules increases skills at using the rules that exist and therefore decreases the pressure for new rules. Capabilities for using the existing rule
set is gained by the endurance of rules, lost by the suspension of rules. Competence in using the rule set should be associated positively with the total number of years of existence represented by existing rules but is approximated by
the number of existing rules or density if rule regime age is controlled.

The link between the ideas of problem absorption and competence gaining
(or knowledge accumulation) is a general one. The conceptions of problem
solving that we have proposed presume that there is a problem space that is
given, that the amount of problem-solving opportunities are proportional not
to the problems already solved but to those remaining to be solved, and that
the problem space can be augmented either by exogenous additions or by recycling previously solved problems as currently unsolved. Conceptions of learning and unlearning ordinarily presume that there is something to be learned,
that the amount of learning per experience is proportional not to what has al-

ready been learned but to what remains to be learned, and that the amount to be learned can be augmented either by exogenous additions to the knowledge space or by unlearning of previously gained knowledge.

From both a problem-solving and a learning perspective, the critical comparison is between the two sets of predictions portrayed in Table 3.2. One set of predictions associates previous rule-making (births) or rule-unmaking (suspensions) experience with an increase in rule births and suspensions, but makes no prediction with respect to current suspensions. The other set of predictions associates previous rule suspensions and current suspensions with an increase in the birthrate, and associates previous rule births with a decrease in the birthrate.

FOUR

An Event History Approach

We examine the development of a rule system by means of a quantitative analysis of rule histories. Such analyses are conspicuously absent from the literature on rules in bureaucracies. For the most part, previous quantitative explorations of bureaucratization have been limited to considering the expansion of organizational size or scale (e.g., Blau 1955, 1970; Meyer 1985; Strang and Chang 1991). The expansion of rules has been treated as derivative of the expansion of size. Our interest is different. We look at the fine detail of the history of rule birth and rule change within the context of a single organization. We assess what such data can tell us about the factors involved in the development of an organizational rule system.

The Strategy

Our research strategy is in the traditions of event history analysis (Tuma and Hannan 1984) and event count analysis (Cameron and Trivedi 1986; Brannas and Rosenqvist 1994). We consider rule histories composed of three kinds of vital events: rule births, rule revisions, and rule suspensions (deaths). A rule is

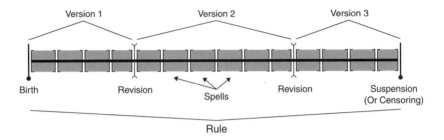

Figure 4.1   The structure of a rule history

born when a new rule document is put into force in an organization. A rule is suspended when it is removed from the organization's records and no successor version of the rule is put in place. Suspensions are empirically much less frequent than the other events. The third kind of vital event in rule histories is a rule revision, which involves adding or removing provisions from existing rule documents. Rule revisions are distinguished from rule births by the existence of an identifiable predecessor rule document (i.e., an earlier version of the rule). For rule births, no predecessor can be identified.

A rule history is a sequential record of the dates of such events. A rule is born at the time it is put in force. Subsequent revisions of the rule create new rule versions. The last version of the rule ends in a rule suspension. Figure 4.1 displays the structure of the rule history of an individual rule and the way in which the data for a particular rule history were treated. Each rule has a birth date. It may have any number of revision dates and may ultimately have a suspension date. The figure shows the way in which each period is divided into spells. For administrative rules, the length of a spell is two months (unless a rule change event occurred). For academic rules, the length is one year.

In the following chapters we present event history and event count analyses of administrative and academic rules at Stanford as they are born, revised, and suspended. We use Poisson regression models to examine processes of rule birth, and hazard rate models to analyze processes of rule revision and suspension. We use maximum likelihood estimation techniques to estimate parameters for covariates of theoretical interest (Tuma and Hannan 1984; Cox and Oakes 1984; Cameron and Trivedi 1986). Our analytical focus is on the rates of rule birth and rule change, where a rule change is either a revision or a suspension of a rule. We ask whether there are regularities in the rule histories that cast light on the rule dynamics. By looking at changes recorded during almost a century of history, we hope to be able to identify some systemic properties that might otherwise be overlooked and to test alternative ideas about the processes that generate the observed patterns. In particular, we test hypotheses about rule dynamics derived from the basic ideas highlighted previously in Chapter 3. The ideas sketched in Chapter 3 are ideas about some characteristics of rule birth and change within a population of rules. We examine quantitative features of rule birth and change suggested by those ideas.

The Data

The data for the studies are drawn from the rule archives of Stanford University. Written rules leave marks of their histories in ways that unwritten rules typically do not, so we were able to obtain relatively complete records of rules and rule changes in two major areas of university rules. The first is the domain of administrative rules; the second is the domain of academic rules. The records are somewhat different, but they are fairly complete.

ADMINISTRATIVE RULES

Data on the evolution of Stanford's rules of administrative practice between 1961 and 1987 were taken from Stanford's collection of administrative policies, called the *Administrative Guide*. In 1961 a collection of 34 formal administrative polices was issued and distributed to all departments of Stanford. Over time, new policies were created and added to the collection, existing policies were revised, and others were suspended. In 1987 the collection consisted of 127 policies. Stanford has a well-maintained archive on its administrative policies, and we used the information in that archive to construct rule history data.

Administrative rule changes are recorded in revision notices. Revision notices are sheets of paper accompanying a new set of rules. They provide instructions regarding rule changes. The format of the revision notices has changed during the lifetime of the *Administrative Guide*. However, revision notices are dated and thus recorded when the policy changes occurred. Usually, a revision notice lists the policies that are changed, their "memo number" (i.e., a number which indicates the location of a rule in the *Administrative Guide*), the name of each policy, and sometimes also the previous date of change of that policy. Often there is also a short summary of the policy changes or the contents of the new policies. Sometimes pointers to related changes in other policies are provided.

To explore the rule dynamics of administrative rules, we recorded each change in the rule population and categorized it as either a rule birth, a rule revision, or a rule suspension. Distinctions among rule births, revisions, and suspensions are sometimes ambiguous. We defined revisions as changes in which an identifiable successor policy was issued on the date the predecessor version was removed. If a revision notice used the term "suspension," or asked to "remove" a policy from the *Guide* and did not mention that a new version was issued, then the change was classified as a suspension. Similarly, if a revision notice did not speak of modifying or replacing an existing policy, the change was defined as a birth. The date of the birth, revision, or suspension was defined as the date of the revision notice.

ACADEMIC RULES

Information on academic rules is less readily available than is information on administrative rules. First, there are multiple rule-making agents, including the Academic Council, the Faculty Senate, and several administrative offices. Second, there is no single depository for information on academic rules. Information on academic rules was collected from the minutes of the Academic Council and the Faculty Senate. Additional data on rule changes were collected from various editions of the *Stanford Faculty Handbook*, the *Stanford University Register*, the *Stanford University Bulletin*, and the Stanford catalogue, entitled *Courses and Degrees*.

The academic rules we recorded included both policy statements that provided explicit regulations, requirements, or procedures and also resolutions specifying the purpose or intention of the legislative body without explicit procedures for their implementation. Examples of the former include procedures for granting degrees to students and tenure to faculty. Examples of the latter include resolutions expressing the position of the Faculty Senate on such matters as "campus disruption."

We recorded each change in the population of academic rules and categorized it as either a rule birth, a rule suspension, or a rule revision. A rule birth was recorded when a new rule was incorporated into the rule system as an independent identity. In cases in which the content of a rule may have already existed before the rule was formally established, our procedure was to record the event and the time when the content was formally established as an independent rule.

A rule suspension was recorded when an existing rule was terminated through a formal process, such as action by a rule-making body or a formal announcement. Where rules were dissolved into other rules, dissolution was recorded as a suspension. Where rules appeared to disappear quietly from rule books, the case was treated as "censored" since we did not have information on the final outcome.

A rule revision was recorded when the content of the rule was altered. However, if the name of the rule was changed substantially or the content of the rule was totally rewritten, the change was recorded as a suspension of the old rule and the birth of a new one.

For rule events noted in the minutes of the Academic Council or Faculty Senate (a majority of the events), we recorded the year, month, and date when the resolution passed in which the specific rule was established, suspended, or revised. For rule events recorded in university annual publications, such as *Courses and Degrees* or the *Faculty Handbook*, we recorded only the year in which the rule event occurred.

DESCRIPTIVE PATTERNS OF RULE BIRTHS AND
REVISIONS OVER TIME

The events in our data include the births, suspensions, and revisions of recorded administrative and academic rules at Stanford. We believe we have identified all such change events in the evolution of academic rules between 1891 and 1987, and in administrative rules between 1961 and 1987. We recorded 217 births, 567 revisions, and 92 suspensions of administrative rules during the twenty-eight years from 1961 through 1987. And we recorded 343 births, 672 revisions, and 88 suspensions of academic rules during the ninety-seven years from 1891 through 1987.

Figure 4.2 shows the annual number of administrative rule births and rule changes (revisions plus suspensions) from 1961 to 1987. The pattern is er-

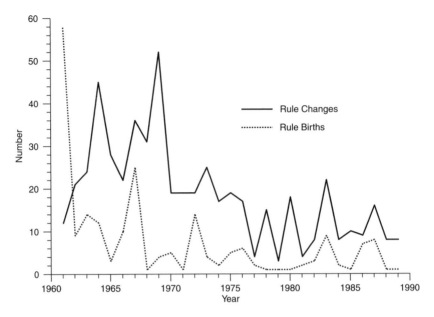

Figure 4.2   Number of rule births and rule changes, administrative rules, 1961–87

ratic, but after the initial flurry of rule making in 1961, the number of births declines fairly steadily with occasional small peaks. After a low initial level, the number of changes rises sharply, then after 1970 it declines fairly steadily. Since the total number of rules in the system increased from 58 in 1961 to 127 in 1987, this pattern means that the change *rate* declined quite significantly during the period.

Similarly, Figure 4.3 shows the annual number of academic rule births and academic rule changes (revisions plus suspensions) from 1891 to 1987. The number of births shows bursts of activity associated with the founding of the university (1891), World War I, the late 1920s, and the mid-1950s. A major explosion in births occurred in the late 1960s, associated with the period of student protests and the founding of the Faculty Senate at Stanford. Subsequently, the number of rule births declined, although not to the levels experienced before the explosion.

The annual number of changes of academic rules shows a somewhat similar pattern. After an initial very small rate of change, the number of changes

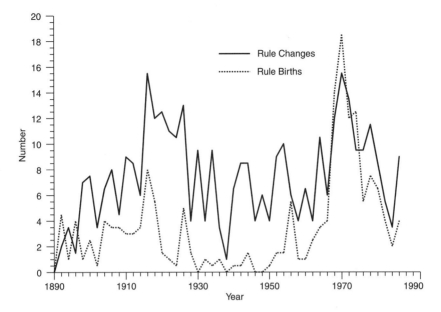

Figure 4.3   Number of rule births and rule changes, academic rules, 1891–1987

fluctuates significantly with peaks averaging about eleven changes per year. The changes associated with the creation of the Faculty Senate in 1968 pushed the number of changes up to a temporary level of about twenty per year. Thereafter, the number declined, but not to the pre-1968 level. During this period, the number of academic rules in the system increased, so that except for the late 1960s the predominant pattern is one of a declining rate of change.

The Covariates

A conspicuous feature of the ideas we have discussed above is that alternative theoretical formulations yield conflicting predictions about rule births and rule changes. Plausible, well-grounded arguments can be made that lead to quite contradictory predictions. At the same time, the arguments are sometimes couched in broad enough terms as to defy operationalization. The intent of the analysis in this book is to specify simple measures for the variables, to define a class of models, and to choose among the competing arguments by estimating the coefficients associated with measured covariates. Thus the analysis is couched almost entirely in terms of the signs of coefficients within standard statistical models. We ask whether a particular variable will be significantly associated with rates of birth and rates of change, and if so, whether its effects will be positive or negative. To capture the speculations outlined above, we have defined a number of covariates, which are treated essentially as independent variables that measure the underlying processes affecting the rates of rule birth and revision. Most of the covariates are dynamic; that is, they are updated at certain time intervals. The method of updating varies between the analysis of births and rule changes and depends on the sources of the data we obtained. The analysis of rule births is entirely based on time series, and updating occurs annually. The analysis of rule changes is based on event history data, and updating occurs at the beginning of each spell, although some covariates are by definition or due to data source constraints constant over several spells.

The analysis is conventional and useful, but it has clear limitations. We note some specific limitations in discussing specific results. However, it may be well to record two general limitations at the outset. First, the procedures are vulnerable to the effects of unmeasured variables or unnoticed explanations that may be correlated with those that are measured, thereby seriously overestimating the explanatory power of some variables considered. Second, the procedure is limited to estimating the net effect of a variable that may be associated with multiple mechanisms having quite different consequences, thus seriously underestimating the effects of some mechanisms. The limitations are hardly unique to this particular instance of research, but they need to be kept in mind.

MEASURING THE VARIABLES

In order to explore the factors involved in rule births and changes over time, the theoretical ideas about rules sketched earlier have to be translated into observable variables that make them empirically concrete. In some cases, the translation is not transparent. For example, such variables as "age of a rule regime," "political and legal involvement," or "organizational structure" do not automatically convert into standard measures. In other cases (e.g., "rule age") statistical considerations affect a choice among alternative specifications. In this section, we describe the specific operational definitions of the covariates we use.

Age of a Rule Regime

The twentieth century has seen two distinct periods in the history of rule-making regimes at Stanford University. The watershed divide between these two periods is the decade of the 1960s. Early in this century, at Stanford as elsewhere at American universities, university presidents tended to make rules relatively unilaterally (Veysey 1965, 303). There was little consultation with the faculty (Mirrieless 1959). As the university grew, there was a gradual increase in consultation with the faculty about academic rules, but formal rule-making procedures were largely unaffected. Most decisions in academic areas were delegated to committees and subcommittees of the Academic Council. Constitutional changes in rule making continued to be slow after the Second World War, being subordinated to a spirit of entrepreneurial opportunism that permeated the American system of higher education. Resources were abundant and demands for higher education were high (Altbach and Berdahl 1981). Rules changed, but there was substantial continuity in the rule-making apparatus. Because of the long intervals that usually separated Academic Council meetings, attention to rules in academic areas was limited. The pace of rule making and of rule changes was slow.

In the late 1960s, however, two conspicuous pressures transformed the rule-making systems of Stanford, as well as those of American higher education in general. The first pressure came from the increased attention of external institutions. Universities were growing rapidly, and the costs of higher education were rising at a substantially faster rate than the general economy. This growth resulted in new requirements for resources that could be assured only through renegotiated relations with public institutions, foundations, private donors, and students. The second pressure came from the challenge of student protests in late 1960s. Issues of university governance became salient and rules as well as procedures for making them became a focus of attention.

One of the consequences of these crises at Stanford was a significant change in the mechanisms of rule production. The two most obvious dates that marked this change were 1961, when the *Administrative Guide* was created as a codification of administrative procedures, and 1968, when the Faculty Senate was created as an institution with primary responsibility for establishing academic rules. The introduction of systematic procedures for maintaining and changing administrative rules heralded the beginning of a fully rationalized administrative rule structure. Similarly, the introduction of the Faculty Senate focused responsibility for academic rule making. After the establishment of the Faculty Senate, the role of the Academic Council diminished gradually. It changed to an annual meeting only, a meeting that was normally entirely per-functory. Rule-making procedures became more formalized, and rule-making meetings became more frequent.

To reflect this situation, we construct rule regime "clocks." In the case of ad-ministrative rules, the rule regime clock starts at zero in 1961 and increases until the end of the observation period (1987). The increments are equal to one year for the time-series-based birth models and equal to two months for the event history analysis of rule changes. In the case of academic rules we construct two partially overlapping clocks. The first rule regime clock, called the "Academic Council regime age" clock, starts in 1891 and increases until 1987. The second rule regime clock, called the "Faculty Senate regime age" clock, starts (at zero) in 1968 and increases until 1987. Increments for both clocks are equal to one year for both the birth and change models. Using two partially overlapping clocks for the academic rules allows us to test if the age dependencies of the two regimes are different (i.e., if the effects of the second regime clock differ significantly from zero). Additionally, we can observe in the case of academic rules whether the basic level of rule production or change shifts with the shift of regime.

Involvement of the Political and Legal System

To measure changes in the external environment, in particular the role of the federal government intervention in the higher education sector, we collected information on two variables: federal legislation regarding education, and fed-eral funding of higher education. More precisely, the first is the number of leg-islative acts enacted by the federal government that were related to higher ed-ucation. This variable was measured on an annual basis. The second is the proportion of the total revenue of higher education institutions in the United States that came from the federal government. This variable was also measured on an annual basis.[1] For a plot of those two variables over time, see Figure 2.3 in Chapter 2. Three-year moving averages of these two variables were used to smooth the year-to-year variability.

Organizational Structure

We measured two dimensions of organizational structure: organizational size, and organizational complexity. Organizational size is measured by the logarithms of the number of students enrolled and the number of faculty employed in a given year. Organizational complexity is measured by the logarithm of the number of academic programs in the university in a given year. As Figure 2.3 in Chapter 2 shows, during the twentieth century, both size and complexity increased at Stanford, but with considerable fluctuation.

We have experimented with different measures of organizational size and complexity and with different functional forms of their effects in order to avoid multicolinearity problems associated with these variables. In the set of analyses reported in the following chapters, size and complexity are both defined in terms of the differences in their natural logarithms from t-2 to t-1 (where t is calibrated in years). Thus, in the models, we use the lagged *change* in logarithms of size and the lagged *change* in logarithms of complexity. We assume that the rule system responds to the magnitudes of changes in organizational size and complexity in the previous year.

Rule Histories

Past history variables are not defined for rule births since rules that are born have (within the scope of the present study) no prior histories. We use two variables to measure past histories in the study of rule changes. The first rule history variable is the historical plasticity of the rule, measured by the number of revisions a rule had experienced prior to the time of the current rule revision. This variable was updated whenever a change occurred.

The second rule history variable is the age of a rule at the time of the last previous revision. The most obvious measure of the age of a rule is the number of years that have passed from the time the rule was created to the time under consideration, but there are two reasons for preferring the age of the rule at the time of the last previous revision. The first reason is statistical. Because we use the information on the duration between the current and the last revisions to model the instantaneous rate of rule change, rule age overlaps with the duration between rule changes. To avoid potential problems associated with such a time-varying measure, we use instead the age of the rule at the time of the most recent revision, that is, the number of years between the year the rule was first established and the year it was last revised. The age of a rule when it was last revised is highly correlated with the number of years since the rule was created, but it is updated only when a rule change occurs. Because it is not updated during the time a rule is at risk of being changed, it is less tainted by spurious negative duration dependence due to population heterogeneity.

The second reason for using rule age at the time of the last previous revision is substantive. Rule age at the time of last revision has a natural organizational learning interpretation. The age of a rule when it is revised is a rough measure of the knowledge base available to rule makers at the time of the revision. Thus it can be considered as a measure of the learning captured by the rule.

Rule Densities and Ecologies

We count the number of existing rules, rule births, rule suspensions, and rule revisions each year in each of two domains: (1) administrative rules (1961–1987); and (2) academic rules (1891–1987). The administrative rule data are further subdivided into six substantive subcategories of rules (two of which were merged for the analysis of rule revisions). The academic rule data are further subdivided into "student" rules and "faculty" rules. From these data we obtain the density of rules in each subpopulation each year, as well as all combinations of current changes in the "same" area, changes in the "same" area in the previous year, changes in "other" areas in the same year, and changes in "other" areas in the previous year.

CHARACTERISTICS OF THE COVARIATES

Tables 4.1, 4.2, 4.3, 4.4, 4.5, and 4.6 summarize the covariates included in model estimation and the basic descriptive statistics of those covariates, including their means, standard deviations, and first-order correlations with each other. Tables 4.1, 4.2, and 4.3 show the variables used in models examining *administrative* rules. Table 4.1 shows the variables involved in the nested models of rule birth. Table 4.2 shows the variables involved in the density models of rule birth. And Table 4.3 shows the variables used in hazard rate models of rule change.

In a similar fashion, Tables 4.4, 4.5, and 4.6 show the variables used in models examining *academic* rules. Table 4.4 shows the variables involved in the nested models of rule birth. Table 4.5 shows the variables involved in the density models of rule birth. And Table 4.6 shows the variables used in hazard rate models of rule change.

TABLE 4.1

Administrative rules: Means, standard deviations, and first-order correlations for variables used in the nested models of rule births

	Mean	s. d.	1	2	3	4	5	6	7	8	9	10	11	12
1 Administrative rule births per year	7.233	10.855												
2 Administrative Guide regime age	84.500	8.680	-.48											
3 Change in number of programs (log)	0.013	0.041	-.11	-.08										
4 Change in number of students (log)	0.012	0.017	.60	-.55	-.10									
5 Change in number of faculty (log)	0.028	0.031	.44	-.63	-.22	.62								
6 Percent government funding (wt. avg.)	0.419	0.019	.00	-.43	.12	.36	.31							
7 No. of higher educ. laws (wt. avg.)	2.536	1.176	-.12	.12	-.14	-.25	-.17	-.35						
8 No. of suspensions, t-1	2.767	4.361	-.18	-.29	-.02	-.02	.10	.13	.15					
9 No. of revisions, t-1	14.633	9.012	-.16	-.45	.20	.07	.20	.03	.22	.34				
10 No. of changes in academic area, t-1	9.000	5.398	-.20	-.04	.24	-.36	-.32	-.06	.23	.33	.08			
11 No. of suspensions, t	3.033	4.428	.15	-.25	.02	.37	.16	.05	.09	.01	.17	-.17		
12 No. of revisions, t	16.133	10.133	.06	-.32	.10	.08	.15	-.27	.23	.25	.28	.37	.38	
13 No. of changes in academic area, t	9.148	5.369	-.23	-.07	-.07	-.20	-.20	-.13	.29	.01	.49	.08	.32	.05
			1	2	3	4	5	6	7	8	9	10	11	12

TABLE 4.2

Administrative rules: Means, standard deviations, and first-order correlations for variables used in the density models of rule births

		Mean	s.d.	1	2	3	4	5	6	7	8	9	10	11	12	13
1	Rule birthrate (local)	0.983	2.263													
2	Organization charts	0.167	0.374	-.08												
3	Personnel rules	0.167	0.374	.16	-.20											
4	Accounting rules	0.167	0.374	-.06	-.20	-.20										
5	External property rules	0.167	0.374	-.06	-.20	-.20	-.20									
6	Procurement rules	0.167	0.374	.07	-.20	-.20	-.20	-.20								
7	Service rules	0.167	0.374	-.03	-.20	-.20	-.20	-.20	-.20							
8	Global suspensions	3.033	4.428	.17	.00	.00	.00	.00	.00	.00						
9	Local suspensions (joint)	0.506	1.555	.55	-.03	.04	-.06	-.03	.13	-.05	.47					
10	Susp. organization charts	0.067	0.894	.07	.17	-.03	-.03	-.03	-.03	-.03	.32	.55				
11	Susp. personnel rules	0.106	0.766	.56	-.06	.31	-.06	-.06	-.06	-.06	.10	.46	-.01			
12	Susp. accounting rules	0.050	0.265	.01	-.08	-.08	.42	-.08	-.08	-.08	.09	.11	-.01	-.03		
13	Susp. external property rules	0.067	0.456	-.03	-.07	-.07	-.07	.33	-.07	-.07	.07	.25	-.01	-.02	-.03	
14	Susp. procurement rules	0.161	0.898	.43	-.08	-.08	-.08	-.08	.40	-.08	.24	.54	-.01	-.02	-.03	-.03
15	Susp. services rules	0.056	0.392	-.02	-.06	-.06	-.06	-.06	-.06	.32	.26	.21	-.01	-.02	-.03	-.02
16	Global density	95.500	20.786	-.31	.00	.00	.00	.00	.00	.00	-.13	-.06	-.07	-.06	-.03	.06
17	Local density (joint)	15.917	8.262	-.09	-.34	.78	.10	-.21	-.13	-.20	-.05	.02	-.01	.16	.05	-.04
18	Density organization charts	1.617	3.801	-.06	.95	-.19	-.19	-.19	-.19	-.19	.02	.03	.26	-.06	-.08	-.06
19	Density personnel rules	5.056	11.815	.06	-.19	.96	-.19	-.19	-.19	-.19	.03	.01	-.03	.24	-.08	-.06
20	Density accounting rules	2.961	6.765	-.09	-.20	-.20	.98	-.20	-.20	-.20	.00	-.06	-.03	-.06	.43	-.06
21	Density external property rules	1.994	4.687	-.10	-.19	-.19	-.19	.95	-.19	-.19	-.02	-.01	-.03	-.06	-.08	.36
22	Density procurement rules	2.244	5.252	.02	-.19	-.19	-.19	-.19	.96	-.19	-.02	.12	-.03	-.06	-.08	-.06
23	Density services rules	2.044	4.821	-.04	-.19	-.19	-.19	-.19	-.19	.95	.01	-.04	-.03	-.06	-.08	-.06
24	*Administrative Guide* regime age	84.500	8.680	-.25	.00	.00	.00	.00	.00	.00	-.25	-.12	-.10	-.08	-.05	.06
25	Global density academic rules	185.857	57.365	-.26	.00	.00	.00	.00	.00	.00	-.35	-.17	-.10	-.08	-.07	-.06
26	Change in number of programs (log)	0.013	0.041	.00	.00	.00	.00	.00	.00	.00	.02	.01	-.05	.08	-.02	.06
27	Change in number of students (log)	0.012	0.017	.28	.00	.00	.00	.00	.00	.00	.37	.18	.19	.04	.12	-.07
28	Percent government funding (wt. avg.)	0.419	0.019	.02	.00	.00	.00	.00	.00	.00	.05	.02	.08	.05	-.05	-.14
29	No. of higher educ. laws (wt. avg.)	2.536	1.176	-.02	.00	.00	.00	.00	.00	.00	.09	.04	-.06	.13	.14	.08
30	No. of revisions	14.633	9.012	.01	.00	.00	.00	.00	.00	.00	.17	.08	.04	.04	.13	.00
				1	2	3	4	5	6	7	8	9	10	11	12	13

TABLE 4.2 (continued)

Administrative rules: Means, standard deviations, and first-order correlations for variables used in the density models of rule births

	14	15	16	17	18	19	20	21	22	23	24	25	26	27	28	29
15 Susp. services rules	-.03															
16 Global density	.02	-.06														
17 Local density (joint)	-.06	-.05	.42													
18 Density organization charts	-.08	-.06	.04	-.28												
19 Density personnel rules	-.08	-.06	.11	.86	-.18											
20 Density accounting rules	-.08	-.06	.06	.13	-.19	-.19										
21 Density external property rules	-.08	-.06	.12	-.15	-.18	-.18	-.19									
22 Density procurement rules	.38	-.06	.11	-.08	-.18	-.18	-.19	-.18								
23 Density services rules	-.08	.32	.10	-.13	-.18	-.18	-.19	-.18	-.18							
24 *Administrative Guide* regime age	-.01	-.11	.93	.39	.05	.10	.05	.11	.10	.11						
25 Global density academic rules	-.01	-.13	.91	.37	.03	.10	.05	.11	.11	.08	.97					
26 Change in number of programs (log)	.03	-.09	.08	.03	-.03	.02	.00	.02	.02	-.02	-.08	.03				
27 Change in number of students (log)	.03	.12	-.68	-.28	.03	-.09	-.05	-.09	-.08	-.05	-.55	-.58	-.10			
28 Percent government funding (wt. avg.)	-.01	.03	-.35	-.15	-.02	-.03	.00	-.04	-.03	-.08	-.43	-.13	.12	.36		
29 No. of higher educ. laws (wt. avg.)	-.08	.08	.21	.09	-.06	.01	.04	.04	.03	.04	.12	-.02	-.14	-.25	-.35	
30 No. of revisions	-.01	.09	-.27	-.11	-.05	-.02	.00	-.03	-.04	-.03	-.45	-.47	.20	.07	.03	.22
	14	15	16	17	18	19	20	21	22	23	24	25	26	27	28	29

TABLE 4.3

Administrative rules: Means, standard deviations, and first-order correlations for variables used in the hazard rate models of rule changes

	Mean	s.d.	1	2	3	4	5	6	7	8	9	10	11
1 Spell duration	0.477	0.083											
2 Rule age	4.858	5.453	.05										
3 Number of previous changes	2.075	2.560	-.02	.70									
4 Rule regime age	14.725	7.540	.15	.48	.22								
5 General organizational rules	0.098	0.298	-.03	.10	.18	-.04							
6 Accounting rules	0.188	0.391	.00	.14	.13	-.03	-.16						
7 Procurement rules	0.144	0.351	.01	-.21	-.07	.01	-.14	-.20					
8 Service and external property rules	0.242	0.429	.02	-.10	.00	.02	-.19	-.27	-.23				
9 Change in number of programs (log)	0.013	0.042	-.04	-.09	.00	-.18	-.02	.01	.01	-.03			
10 Change in number of students (log)	0.011	0.016	-.05	-.23	-.16	-.48	.06	.03	-.01	.01	-.01		
11 Change in number of faculty (log)	0.028	0.029	-.07	-.26	-.17	-.53	.07	.01	-.02	-.01	-.16	.56	
12 Percent government funding (wt. avg.)	0.194	0.041	-.11	-.34	-.10	-.68	-.04	.03	-.01	-.02	.32	.00	.25
13 No. of higher educ. laws (wt. avg.)	2.579	1.157	-.04	.02	.03	.05	-.05	.00	.00	.03	-.19	-.20	-.08
14 Rule changes, same area, t-1	3.619	4.305	-.02	-.10	-.07	-.28	-.10	-.02	-.10	-.36	.14	-.01	.16
15 Rule changes, other areas, t-1	14.190	9.459	-.10	-.28	-.09	-.60	.04	.04	.03	.15	.15	.14	.34
16 Rule changes, Senate rules, t-1	9.120	5.354	-.03	-.06	.03	-.12	-.03	.00	.00	-.02	.24	-.29	-.26
17 Rule changes, same area, t	3.325	4.037	-.16	-.15	-.11	-.29	-.07	-.01	-.12	-.37	.12	.04	.11
18 Rule changes, other areas, t	14.162	9.308	-.10	-.31	-.14	-.62	.04	.04	.03	.17	.03	.26	.34
19 Rule changes, Senate rules, t	9.225	5.258	-.03	-.08	.01	-.14	-.05	.00	-.01	.01	-.09	-.20	-.16
			1	2	3	4	5	6	7	8	9	10	11

TABLE 4.3 (continued)

Administrative rules: Means, standard deviations, and first-order correlations for variables used in the hazard rate models of rule changes

	12	13	14	15	16	17	18
13 No. of higher educ. laws (wt. avg.)	.24						
14 Rule changes, same area, t-1	.31	.09					
15 Rule changes, other areas, t-1	.53	.19	.12				
16 Rule changes, Senate rules, t-1	.25	.21	.14	.16			
17 Rule changes, same area, t	.29	.12	.35	.08	.10		
18 Rule changes, other areas, t	.45	.22	.03	.52	.08	.07	
19 Rule changes, Senate rules, t	.31	.30	.15	.25	.10	.11	.16
	12	13	14	15	16	17	18

TABLE 4.4

Academic rules: Means, standard deviations, and first-order correlations for variables used in the nested models of rule births

	Mean	s.d.	1	2	3	4	5	6	7	8	9	10	11
1 Academic rule births per year	3.546	4.284											
2 Faculty rule births	1.485	2.923	.87										
3 Student rule births	2.062	2.249	.77	.36									
4 Council regime age	48.000	28.145	.32	.40	.08								
5 Senate regime age	1.959	4.675	.19	.17	.15	.63							
6 Senate regime intercept	0.206	0.407	.60	.61	.36	.70	.83						
7 Change in number of programs (log)	0.014	0.058	.03	.07	-.04	.07	-.05	.03					
8 Change in number of students (log)	0.033	0.129	-.10	-.09	-.07	-.15	-.09	-.11	.04				
9 Change in number of faculty (log)	0.032	0.058	-.02	-.02	-.01	-.01	-.11	-.11	.19	-.05			
10 Percent government funding (wt. avg.)	0.099	0.092	.37	.47	.09	.87	.35	.54	.13	-.06	.03		
11 No. of higher educ. laws (wt. avg.)	0.993	1.229	.54	.59	.27	.77	.52	.68	-.02	-.06	-.02	.76	
12 No. of suspensions, t-1	0.887	1.492	.38	.28	.35	.23	.12	.28	-.01	-.01	-.09	.18	.29
13 No. of revisions, t-1	7.526	4.619	.37	.33	.27	.19	.07	.25	.08	.00	.13	.13	.21
14 No. of changes in administrative area, t-1	19.500	11.931	.44	.40	.30	-.59	-.65	-.27	.12	.17	.25	.54	.20
15 No. of suspensions, t	0.897	1.489	.49	.36	.47	.22	.10	.29	-.03	-.01	.01	.20	.30
16 No. of revisions, t	7.629	4.561	.45	.32	.45	.17	.06	.27	-.06	-.10	-.13	.14	.22
17 No. of changes in administrative area, t	19.370	11.718	.44	.51	.11	-.58	-.63	-.39	.10	.16	.25	.56	.25
18 Rule agenda, student area, t-1	9.412	5.669	.37	.26	.37	.12	.04	.22	.06	-.03	.18	.07	.14
19 Rule agenda, faculty area, t-1	3.351	5.670	.71	.77	.35	.42	.25	.65	.06	-.08	-.08	.42	.48
20 Other agenda, student area, t-1	6.289	7.214	.44	.43	.27	.76	.68	.81	.04	-.01	-.08	.66	.65
21 Other agenda, faculty area, t-1	9.660	12.481	.56	.55	.35	.76	.68	.87	.04	-.10	-.05	.66	.71
22 Rule agenda, student area	7.979	5.648	.57	.38	.60	.28	.14	.32	.03	-.12	.01	.25	.33
23 Rule agenda, faculty area	3.371	5.661	.84	.90	.43	.41	.18	.63	.03	-.13	-.05	.44	.57
24 Other agenda, student area	6.567	7.485	.53	.55	.29	.77	.69	.83	.04	-.13	-.01	.68	.71
25 Other agenda, faculty area	9.887	12.570	.63	.64	.36	.76	.64	.87	.01	-.12	-.03	.69	.73
			1	2	3	4	5	6	7	8	9	10	11

TABLE 4.4 (continued)
Academic rules: Means, standard deviations, and first-order correlations for variables used in the nested models of rule births

	12	13	14	15	16	17	18	19	20	21	22	23	24
13 No. of revisions, t-1	.58												
14 No. of changes in administrative area, t-1	.38	.17											
15 No. of suspensions, t	.25	.18	.37										
16 No. of revisions, t	.23	.31	.37	.58									
17 No. of changes in administrative area, t	.27	.25	.43	.38	.17								
18 Rule agenda, student area, t-1	.60	.89	.28	.29	.33	.17							
19 Rule agenda, faculty area, t-1	.39	.43	.43	.27	.33	.31	.35						
20 Other agenda, student area, t-1	.24	.23	-.13	.21	.25	-.46	.21	.58					
21 Other agenda, faculty area, t-1	.41	.32	.00	.23	.25	-.31	.28	.66	.84				
22 Rule agenda, student area	.30	.40	.21	.57	.83	.24	.42	.33	.26	.32			
23 Rule agenda, faculty area	.32	.37	.47	.39	.43	.43	.28	.81	.56	.64	.39		
24 Other agenda, student area	.33	.28	-.09	.23	.22	-.15	.24	.65	.78	.83	.34	.54	
25 Other agenda, faculty area	.41	.28	.17	.39	.31	.00	.29	.70	.80	.89	.38	.67	.84
	12	13	14	15	16	17	18	19	20	21	22	23	24

TABLE 4.5

Academic rules: Means, standard deviations, and first-order correlations for variables used in the density models of rule births

		Mean	s.d.	1	2	3	4	5	6	7	8	9	10	11	12	13	14
1	Rule birthrate (local)	1.773	2.617														
2	Faculty rules by Council	0.385	0.488	-.37													
3	Student rules by Senate	0.115	0.320	.24	-.29												
4	Student rules by Council	0.385	0.488	-.04	-.63	-.29											
5	Faculty rules by Senate	0.115	0.320	.41	-.29	-.13	-.29										
6	Global suspensions	0.897	1.486	.40	-.12	.20	-.12	.20									
7	Local suspensions (joint)	0.448	1.018	.44	-.32	.22	.14	.07	.73								
8	Susp. faculty rules	0.086	0.438	.43	-.06	.22	-.16	.43	.39	.36							
9	Susp. student rules	0.355	0.945	.27	-.30	-.07	.23	-.14	.60	.90	-.08						
10	Susp. Council rules	0.260	0.765	.07	-.22	.27	.38	-.12	.45	.70	-.01	.75					
11	Susp. Senate rules	0.180	0.729	.55	-.20	-.12	-.20	.22	.54	.65	.51	.46	-.09				
12	Susp. student rules by Council	0.240	0.758	.07	-.25	.43	.40	-.11	.41	.69	-.06	.77	.98	-.08			
13	Susp. faculty rules by Council	0.020	0.140	-.04	.18	-.11	-.11	-.05	.21	.08	.30	-.05	.14	-.04	-.05		
14	Susp. student rules by Senate	0.112	0.604	.33	-.15	-.05	-.15	-.07	.41	.54	-.04	.59	-.06	.82	-.06	-.03	
15	Susp. faculty rules by Senate	0.066	0.417	.47	-.13	-.06	-.13	.47	.34	.35	.95	-.06	-.05	.55	-.05	-.02	-.03
16	Global density	99.918	67.117	.27	-.37	.58	-.37	.58	.22	.16	.16	.09	-.11	.33	-.10	-.03	.26
17	Local density (joint)	37.102	24.813	-.04	-.65	.58	.49	.34	.00	.14	-.03	.16	.26	-.09	.28	-.08	-.10
18	Density faculty rules	13.212	21.174	.02	.15	-.23	-.50	.79	.06	-.14	.20	-.24	-.18	.00	-.20	.07	-.12
19	Density student rules	23.515	28.275	-.05	-.67	.09	.81	-.30	-.04	.23	-.17	.32	.37	-.08	.40	-.12	.00
20	Density Senate rules	9.857	22.467	.21	-.35	.32	-.35	.80	.11	.04	.16	-.04	-.15	.21	-.14	-.06	.11
21	Density Council rules	26.700	25.541	-.22	-.30	-.38	.79	-.38	-.09	.10	-.17	.20	.39	-.27	.40	-.02	-.20
22	Density student rules by Council	20.080	28.544	-.09	-.56	-.25	.89	-.25	-.06	.18	-.14	.26	.41	-.18	.43	-.10	-.13
23	Density faculty rules by Council	6.620	10.237	-.28	.82	-.23	-.51	-.23	-.05	-.25	-.02	-.25	-.16	-.16	-.21	.24	-.12
24	Density student rules by Senate	3.232	10.600	.13	-.24	.89	-.24	-.11	.07	.12	-.06	.16	-.10	.28	-.10	-.04	.37
25	Density faculty rules by Senate	6.525	20.752	.16	-.25	-.11	-.25	.92	.08	-.02	.21	-.12	-.11	.09	-.10	-.05	-.06
26	Acad. Council regime age	49.500	28.939	.26	-.32	.48	-.32	.48	.22	.16	.18	.07	-.10	.32	-.10	-.02	.23
27	Change in number of programs (log)	0.014	0.058	.02	-.01	.02	-.01	.02	-.03	-.02	-.01	-.02	-.02	-.01	-.01	-.07	-.01
28	Change in number of students (log)	0.031	0.125	-.08	.05	-.08	.05	-.08	-.01	-.01	-.01	.00	.05	-.06	.04	.05	-.05
29	Percent government funding (wt. avg.)	0.302	0.156	.15	-.17	.26	-.17	.26	.26	.19	.14	.14	.07	.19	.06	.09	.14
30	No. of higher educ. laws (wt. avg.)	1.023	1.230	.45	-.29	.46	-.29	.46	.30	.22	.33	.08	-.11	.42	-.13	.08	.28
31	Global density admin. rules (Senate regime)	24.600	45.471	.45	-.43	.65	-.43	.65	.27	.19	.24	.07	-.18	.46	-.17	-.08	.32
32	No. of revisions	6.530	3.996	.23	-.05	.08	-.05	.08	.12	.09	.05	.08	.10	.02	.09	.06	.00
				1	2	3	4	5	6	7	8	9	10	11	12	13	14

TABLE 4.5 *(continued)*

Academic rules: Means, standard deviations, and first-order correlations for variables used in the density models of rule births

	15	16	17	18	19	20	21	22	23	24	25	26	27	28	29	30	31
16 Global density	.18																
17 Local density (joint)	-.01	.48															
18 Density faculty rules	.18	.53	.25														
19 Density student rules	-.13	.03	.69	-.53													
20 Density Senate rules	.19	.85	.42	.73	-.17												
21 Density Council rules	-.17	-.28	.60	-.38	.82	-.47											
22 Density student rules by Council	-.11	-.20	.68	-.44	.93	-.31	.93										
23 Density faculty rules by Council	-.10	-.14	-.39	.28	-.54	-.29	-.11	-.46									
24 Density student rules by Senate	-.05	.60	.01	-.19	.16	.38	-.32	-.22	-.20								
25 Density faculty rules by Senate	.24	.61	.45	.88	-.27	.88	-.33	-.22	-.21	-.10							
26 Acad. council regime age	.19	.90	.51	.44	.09	.64	-.09	-.08	.00	.44	.44						
27 Change in number of programs (log)	.01	.03	.01	.01	.00	-.01	.01	.01	.01	-.02	.00	.07					
28 Change in number of students (log)	-.03	-.13	-.07	-.06	-.01	-.09	.01	.01	.01	-.06	-.06	-.14	.04				
29 Percent government funding (wt. avg.)	.12	.68	.53	.33	.20	.34	.20	.11	.20	.23	.24	.81	.09	-.09			
30 No. of higher educ. laws (wt. avg.)	.32	.70	.26	.34	-.02	.52	-.21	-.16	-.07	.37	.38	.77	-.02	-.05	.55		
31 Global density admin. rules (Senate regime)	.27	.90	.22	.42	-.16	.88	-.57	-.38	-.35	.59	.60	.74	.02	-.11	.40	.68	
32 No. of revisions	.03	.19	.06	.07	.02	.09	.01	.01	.01	.06	.08	.08	.10	.02	.25	.13	.09
	15	16	17	18	19	20	21	22	23	24	25	26	27	28	29	30	31

TABLE 4.6

Academic rules: Means, standard deviations, and first-order correlations for variables used in the hazard rate models of rule changes

		Mean	s.d.	1	2	3	4	5	6	7	8	9	10	11
1	Spell duration	0.933	0.267											
2	Rule age	11.331	18.990	.11										
3	Number of previous changes	2.448	4.067	.10	.82									
4	Council regime age	62.836	27.026	.04	.06	-.03								
5	Senate regime age	4.722	6.430	.07	-.09	-.13	.75							
6	Senate regime intercept	0.446	0.497	-.03	-.09	-.14	.82	.82						
7	Area (faculty=1)	0.392	0.488	-.03	-.26	-.26	.32	.28	.34					
8	Change in number of programs (log)	0.015	0.052	-.02	.03	.02	.01	-.15	.02	.01				
9	Change in number of students (log)	0.021	0.106	.01	.00	.01	-.14	-.10	-.13	-.05	-.01			
10	Change in number of faculty (log)	0.028	0.045	-.02	.04	.04	-.11	-.18	-.19	-.06	.05	-.09		
11	Percent government funding (wt. avg.)	0.132	0.086	-.03	.13	.02	.83	.35	.61	.25	.15	-.06	-.01	
12	No. of higher educ. laws (wt. avg.)	1.512	1.331	-.05	.02	-.06	.77	.56	.70	.27	-.07	-.07	-.08	.74
13	No. of rule changes, same area, t-1	4.902	4.071	-.07	.12	.12	-.17	-.20	-.10	-.53	.08	.04	.10	-.11
14	No. of rule changes, other area, t-1	3.378	3.886	-.05	-.16	-.17	.27	.17	.35	.64	.06	-.03	-.05	.28
15	No. of rule changes, same area	4.939	4.108	-.04	.11	.12	-.18	-.21	-.11	-.55	-.02	.00	-.04	-.11
16	No. of rule changes, other area	3.408	3.893	-.06	-.16	-.17	.27	.18	.36	.65	-.04	-.09	-.11	.26
17	Rule agenda, student area, t-1	10.166	6.036	-.11	-.04	-.04	.03	-.05	.16	.05	.07	-.01	.11	.09
18	Rule agenda, faculty area, t-1	5.083	6.877	-.14	-.04	-.07	.37	.11	.56	.20	.15	-.09	-.14	.47
19	Other agenda, student area, t-1	9.999	8.326	-.02	-.03	-.10	.79	.68	.84	.30	.03	-.04	-.20	.65
20	Other agenda, faculty area, t-1	16.173	14.677	-.04	-.03	-.10	.79	.66	.87	.31	.03	-.11	-.11	.66
21	Rule agenda, student area	9.200	5.838	-.10	-.02	-.03	.16	.07	.27	.08	-.04	-.08	-.03	.22
22	Rule agenda, faculty area	4.890	6.675	-.16	-.02	-.06	.35	.05	.53	.18	.09	-.12	-.07	.49
23	Other agenda, student area	10.441	8.650	-.03	-.02	-.10	.80	.71	.86	.30	.05	-.13	-.11	.67
24	Other agenda, faculty area	16.293	14.671	-.06	-.03	-.10	.78	.62	.86	.30	-.05	-.09	-.09	.68
				1	2	3	4	5	6	7	8	9	10	11

TABLE 4.6 (continued)

Academic rules: Means, standard deviations, and first-order correlations for variables used in the hazard rate models of rule changes

		12	13	14	15	16	17	18	19	20	21	22	23
13	No. of rule changes, same area, t-1	-.08											
14	No. of rule changes, other area, t-1	.32	-.28										
15	No. of rule changes, same area	-.07	.49	-.36									
16	No. of rule changes, other area	.35	-.35	.58	-.31								
17	Rule agenda, student area, t-1	.14	.55	.50	.17	.21							
18	Rule agenda, faculty area, t-1	.39	.13	.38	.05	.31	.29						
19	Other agenda, student area, t-1	.64	-.10	.32	-.08	.35	.16	.51					
20	Other agenda, faculty area, t-1	.67	-.04	.38	-.11	.31	.24	.58	.80				
21	Rule agenda, student area	.37	.18	.25	.47	.49	.41	.26	.18	.22			
22	Rule agenda, faculty area	.48	.11	.35	.12	.36	.26	.80	.51	.55	.30		
23	Other agenda, student area	.72	-.07	.35	-.11	.33	.18	.57	.76	.82	.27	.46	
24	Other agenda, faculty area	.68	-.06	.36	-.06	.37	.27	.62	.77	.84	.31	.57	.79
		12	13	14	15	16	17	18	19	20	21	22	23

FIVE

Explaining Patterns of Rule Birth

In this chapter and the next, we report our empirical studies of the evolution of the rule system at Stanford University.[1] We distinguish three types of vital events: rule births, rule suspensions, and rule revisions. For most of the analyses reported here, rule suspensions and revisions are combined into a larger category of events that we call rule changes. Throughout these analyses, our focus is on examining and assessing how statistical regularities in rule dynamics relate to the theoretical ideas about organizational structure, environmental changes, rule histories, rule ecology, and organizational attention discussed previously in Chapter 3 and associated with specific observable covariates in Chapter 4. Rule births are considered in this chapter. Chapter 6 deals with rule changes.

Rule births are important events in the evolution of an organizational rule system. They add new elements to the rule system and thus are directly linked to the growth of the rule system. We focus on patterns of rule births in two main areas of the rule system at Stanford: (1) academic rules from 1891 to 1987; and (2) administrative rules from 1961 to 1987. The cumulated numbers of rule births in these two areas are displayed in Figure 5.1. Both academic and administrative rule collections grew considerably throughout their histories. The

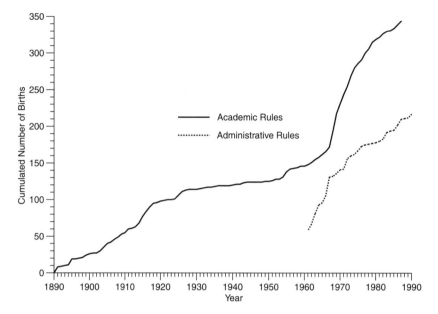

Figure 5.1   Cumulated rule births of administrative and academic rules,
1891–1987

growth in the number of academic rules was at a relatively steady, modest rate
between the 1920s and the 1960s. After the mid-1960s, however, the number
of both academic and administrative rules grew at a much faster pace. During
the latter period, the patterns in the two areas appear to parallel each other.

Effects of Covariates

To elaborate how the theoretical ideas developed in the previous chapters
might provide clues to understanding the rule production patterns displayed
in Figure 5.1, we first estimate a set of nested models that assess the contribution of several sets of covariates to patterns of rule births within the administrative and academic rule populations at Stanford. The models are described in
the following section and the results are presented immediately afterward, first
for administrative rules, then for academic rules, and then for the two academic rule regimes separately. To explore further the effects of attention, his-

torical contexts, and distinctive rule populations, we then focus on the history of rule growth in the academic area alone, using explicit measures of attention and disaggregating the data into four historical periods and into two subpopulations of academic rules. These results are presented in a section entitled "Exploring Effects of Attention, Historical Contexts, and Subpopulations of Rules on Academic Rule Production." Finally, the effects of rule density and rule suspensions on births in both administrative and academic rule populations are discussed.

MODELING RULE BIRTH

Our analytical focus is on the rate of changes in the number of rule births over time. Since the number of rule births each year is relatively small, we treat births as event count data, which often follow a Poisson process, i.e., they are assumed to be "independently" and "randomly" generated over a time span. The Poisson model as originally developed assumes that the rate of event occurrence is independent of the history of previous events and the current state of the system. In recent applications in social science, this assumption has often been relaxed and the Poisson model has been generalized to take time-varying covariates and time dependency into consideration (Spilerman 1970, 1971; Hannan and Freeman 1984, 1989; Hannan and Carroll 1992; Hausman, Hall, and Griliches 1984). The Poisson model is specified as follows:

$$Pr(B=b_t) = \frac{\exp(-\lambda)\, \lambda^{b_t}}{b_t!}$$

where b_t is the number of events (rule births) that occur in a specified time interval t.

Following common practice, we model the effects of the covariates on the rate of changes in rule birth. Since the birthrate can either increase or decrease, but never become negative, the rate is estimated in the form:

$$\log \lambda = \boldsymbol{\beta}'\mathbf{X}_t$$

where λ is the rate of rule birth under study, $\mathbf{X}_t$ is the set of the covariates related to our theoretical interests, and $\boldsymbol{\beta}$ is the column of corresponding coefficients to be estimated. That is, we estimate the linear effects of the covariates on log λ, the logarithm of the birthrate. We choose "year" as the time interval. This results in ninety-six time intervals for academic rules and twenty-six time intervals for administrative rules.

The Poisson model assumes that the mean, λ, of the dependent variable equals its variance. When the variance exceeds the mean significantly, an over-dispersion problem is present. Violation of this assumption leads researchers to a different set of models, most commonly the negative binomial model to take overdispersion into consideration. In most of the analyses reported in this chapter, overdispersion is not a problem, and we estimate the Poisson model. In some analyses where overdispersion is evident, we adopt alternative models to be described later.

RESULTS

Because of the distinctive histories and population characteristics of the two areas, we analyze administrative rules (1961–1987) and academic rules (1891–1987) separately. We also estimate separate models for the two academic rule regimes to assess if rule production followed different processes under the Academic Council (1891–1967) and Faculty Senate (1968–1987) regimes, and to compare administrative and academic rule production in comparable historical time periods.

Administrative Rule Births, 1961–1987

We first consider patterns of administrative rule birth. We estimate a set of nested models, introducing one set of the covariates at a time. In so doing, we hope to assess the distinctive effects of groups of covariates that measure the roles of rule regime history, organizational structure, environmental changes, and rule ecology.

Table 5.1 shows the results from five nested models of administrative rule birth. The analyses are based on the 210 observed administrative rule births between 1961 and 1987.

Rule Regime History. Model 1 (M1) includes only rule regime age as a co-variate. Rule regime age is used here to capture the effects of increasing competencies at making and using rules within a rule regime. In the case of the administrative rules, the only rule regime covered in these data begins in 1961

TABLE 5.1

Estimated coefficients for five nested models of administrative rule births, 1961–87

	M1	M2	M3	M4	M5
Constant	2.357***	2.074***	3.481***	4.454***	5.211***
	(0.136)	(0.293)	(0.923)	(1.062)	(1.169)
Administrative Guide regime age	-0.054***	-0.040**	-0.073***	-0.103***	-0.099***
	(0.011)	(0.016)	(0.023)	(0.028)	(0.029)
Change in number of programs (log)		0.204	3.132	2.955	0.058
		(2.026)	(2.173)	(2.198)	(2.679)
Change in number of students (log)		15.540***	10.967	3.645	-21.130**
		(5.992)	(6.704)	(7.475)	(10.560)
Change in number of faculty (log)		-3.129	-0.864	-3.568	-3.386
		(3.809)	(3.949)	4.428)	(4.960)
Percent government funding (wt. avg.)			-9.078**	-8.960**	-12.609***
			(3.891)	(4.098)	(4.515)
Number of higher education laws (wt. avg.)			0.281***	0.328***	0.271***
			(0.087)	(0.092)	(0.096)
Number of suspensions admin. rules at t-1				-0.064**	-0.103***
				(0.026)	(0.033)
Number of revisions admin. rules at t-1				-0.012	0.028
				(0.014)	(0.020)
Number of changes acad. rules at t-1				-0.025	-0.013
				(0.20)	(0.024)
Number of suspensions admin. rules at t					0.112***
					(0.030)
Number of revisions admin. rules at t					0.000
					(0.017)
Number of changes acad. rules at t					-0.074**
					(0.030)
Log likelihood	-88.915	-85.519	-80.415	-72.909	-63.680
LR–chi-square	23.527***	6.792*	10.209***	15.012***	18.458***
d.f.	1	3	2	3	3
Number of births	210	210	210	210	210

NOTE: Estimations were done with Limdep. All models are Poisson regression models. Inclusion of the rule regime clock reduced dispersion to a level consistent with the Poisson model. The LR–chi-square statistic gives the improvement of fit of a given model (M_i) over the preceding model (M_{i-1}). For Model 1 the LR statistic gives the improvement of the fit of Model 1 over a model which includes only the intercept. *=p<0.1; **=p<0.05; ***=p<0.01.

with the establishment of the *Administrative Guide*. The estimated parameter is negative and highly significant, indicating that the rate of rule birth declines as the rule regime matures. This effect continues to be negative and highly significant in subsequent models. That is, the effect of rule regime age is robust, independent of the effects of other covariates in the models.

Organizational Structure. Model 2 (M2) of Table 5.1 adds covariates reflecting changes in the size and complexity of the university. As the log-likelihood ratio test (reported at the bottom of Table 5.1) indicates, these structural dimensions improve the fit of the model only marginally. The estimated parameter for change in the (log) number of students is positive and highly significant. However, the parameter becomes nonsignificant in subsequent models. It even turns significant and negative in Model 5 (M5), possibly due to multicolinearity or to confounding effects stemming from external pressures. Neither change in the (log) number of faculty nor change in the (log) number of academic programs has any significant effect. Overall, the rate of rule growth is less sensitive to changes in organizational size and complexity than a simple Weberian model of bureaucracy would predict.

Environmental Changes. We suspect that rule systems in a university are especially sensitive to changes in the political and legal system. For this reason, Model 3 (M3) adds two covariates measuring levels of federal government funding and the number of legislative acts related to higher education. Lagged three-year moving averages are used to capture trends in these variables. Both external variables have strong, significant effects in this model, as well as in all subsequent models; and the improvement in fit due to including these variables is highly significant. The parameter for the federal government share of all higher education funding is negative, indicating that administrative rule production increases when the relative contribution of federal funding decreases. Although the results presented below suggest that this effect may be partially confounded with other processes indicated by other covariates in the subsequent models, this finding provides a multivariate explanation for the observation that, since the 1960s, the proportion of federal funding in all U.S. institutions of higher learning followed a decreasing trend (see Figure 2.4), whereas the number of administrative rules increased during the same period (Figure 5.1). On the other hand, the parameter for the number of federal laws enacted in the area of higher education is positive, indicating that administrative rule production responds positively to legislative involvement.

Rule Ecologies. In Models 4 and 5 (M4, M5), we examine the spatial and temporal context of rule production. Model 4 considers the temporal context by introducing three lagged variables of the temporal ecology. The first variable is the number of suspensions of administrative rules in the previous year. Its parameter estimate is highly significant and negative. That is, a large number of rule suspensions in one year leads to a low rate of rule births in the following year. In separate analyses (not reported here), we tested if this effect reflects last year's births, but including the number of births in the previous year does not diminish the negative, significant parameter for the number of suspensions in the previous year. On the other hand, neither the number of revisions of administrative rules in the previous year nor the number of changes in academic rules in the previous year has any significant effect on administrative rule production. It appears that rule production in the administrative area is largely uncoupled from rule change activities in the immediately previous year.

Model 5 (M5) adds three contemporaneous variables of the rule ecology. Several results are worth noting. First, contemporaneous suspensions of administrative rules have a strong, positive effect on the rate of administrative rule production. This effect is not due to links with specific predecessor rules since the coding procedures excluded defining such events as "births." Rather, it appears to be true that the suspension of rules frees some "regulatory space" for new rules, although such an interpretation does not explain the lagged negative effect of suspensions very well. We return to this possibility when we consider density effects below. Second, contemporaneous revisions of administrative rules have no observable effect on the rate of rule births. Third, contemporaneous changes (suspensions plus revisions) in the academic area have a significant, negative effect on administrative rule births. This suggests that changes in the academic area in some way impede administrative rule birth. One explanation consistent with our discussion about the role of organizational attention is that rule activity in other areas (e.g., the academic area) may direct attention away from the administrative area and thereby decrease the rate of administrative rule birth.

In general, the results of Models 1 through 4 are sustained as additional variables are added in Model 5. In particular, the negative effects of rule regime age and changes in the proportion of revenue coming from government funding as well as the positive effects of the number of federal laws are still significant in Model 5. The exception is the effect of changes in the size of the student body, which is positive and significant in Model 2, insignificant in Models 3 and 4, and becomes negative and significant in Model 5. This pattern has no easy explanation.

Academic Rule Births, 1891–1987

The history of academic rules examined here covers a substantially longer time span than does the history of administrative rules and involves a major change of rule regime in 1968. Primary responsibility for academic rule making shifted in 1968 from the Academic Council to the Faculty Senate. We analyze patterns of academic rule birth using a set of nested models parallel to those for administrative rules. Table 5.2 shows parameter estimates for five nested models of academic rule production. The analyses are based on 344 observed rule births between 1891 and 1987.

Rule Regime History. Model 1 (M1) includes the rule regime variables. All the parameters are significant. The parameters estimated for both Academic Council regime age and Faculty Senate regime age are significant and negative. These results are similar to those observed in the administrative area. That is, as a rule regime matures, rule production declines. Moreover, the strong and significant effect of Faculty Senate regime age indicates that rule production during the Faculty Senate regime declined much faster than during the Academic Council regime. The significant and positive intercept term for the Faculty Senate regime indicates that the rate of academic rule production shifted dramatically upward after the regime change. After this initial regime change peak, academic rule production declined rapidly and approached pre-senate levels. The rule regime effects appear quite robust. The parameter estimates for the regimes retain their signs and (for the most part) their significance as more covariates are added in subsequent models.

Organizational Structure. In Model 2 (M2) measures of changes in organizational size and complexity are added. Although these variables improve the overall fit of the model and the likelihood statistics show that the set of covariates as a whole are statistically significant, the individual parameters are not significant here and remain nonsignificant in subsequent models. At least as they are measured by these variables, year-to-year changes in organizational structure have only minor effects on academic rule production. These patterns are similar to those observed in the administrative area.

TABLE 5.2

Estimated coefficients for five nested models of academic rule births, 1891–1987

	M1	M2	M3	M4	M5
Constant	1.071***	1.011***	1.069***	0.959***	0.558**
	(0.141)	(0.161)	(0.190)	(0.205)	(0.241)
Academic Council	-0.007**	-0.006*	-0.008	-0.014*	-0.018**
regime age	(0.003)	(0.004)	(0.007)	(0.008)	(0.008)
Faculty Senate	-0.104***	-0.105***	-0.091***	-0.066**	-0.019
regime age	(0.015)	(0.015)	(0.024)	(0.026)	(0.029)
Intercept Faculty	2.509***	2.491***	2.163***	1.886***	1.347***
Senate regime	(0.204)	(0.206)	(0.247)	(0.263)	(0.294)
Change in number of		-1.375	-0.477	-0.510	0.206
programs (log)		(1.143)	(1.170)	(1.169)	(1.168)
Change in number of		-0.564	-0.713	-0.760	-0.906
students (log)		(0.628)	(0.634)	(0.619)	(0.645)
Change in number of		0.903	0.358	0.107	0.069
faculty (log)		(1.135)	(1.158)	(1.164)	(1.253)
Percent government			-1.193	0.225	1.813
funding (wt. avg.)			(1.901)	(1.975)	(2.055)
Number of higher education			0.209***	0.218***	0.182***
laws (wt. avg.)			(0.070)	(0.070)	(0.070)
Number of suspensions				0.040	0.039
acad. rules at t-1				(0.029)	(0.030)
Number of revisions				0.027*	0.043***
acad. rules at t-1				(0.015)	(0.016)
Number of suspensions					0.090**
acad. rules at t					(0.035)
Number of revisions					0.043***
acad. rules at t					(0.015)
Log likelihood	-211.368	-203.034	-198.764	-195.453	-187.857
LR–chi-square	213.312***	16.668***	8.540**	6.621**	15.192***
d.f.	3	3	2	2	2
Number of births	344	344	344	344	344

NOTE: Estimations were done with Limdep. All models are Poisson regression models. Inclusion of the rule regime clock reduced dispersion to a level consistent with the Poisson model. The LR–chi-square statistic gives the improvement of fit of a given model (M_i) over the preceding model (M_{i-1}). For Model 1 the LR statistic gives the improvement of the fit of Model 1 over a model which includes only the intercept. *=p<0.1; **=p<0.05; ***=p<0.01.

Environmental Changes. Model 3 (M3) adds measures of the involvement of the political and legal structure. Change in the proportion of revenue that comes from government funding has no significant effect on the birthrate, but change in the number of federal laws dealing with higher education does. The rate of academic rule births increases with increases in federal legislation in the area of higher education. This effect stays positive, strong, and significant in subsequent models. Consistent with our findings in administrative rule birth, rule growth at Stanford appears to be especially sensitive to federal legislative attention to higher education.

Rule Ecologies. In Model 4 (M4) we add two lagged measures of the ecology of rules. The first measure is the number of suspensions of academic rules in the previous year. It is not significant here, nor is it significant in subsequent models. The second measure is the number of academic rule revisions in the previous year. This parameter is positive and significant at the 0.1 level. It becomes stronger and its significance level improves in subsequent models. That is, revisions of academic rules in the previous year are associated with a higher rate of rule births in the academic area. In the last model of Table 5.2 (Model 5, or M5) we add measures of contemporaneous rule changes. Both are positive and significant. The positive effect of contemporaneous suspensions is consistent with our results in the administrative area. In both rule populations, contemporary suspension of rules frees some "regulatory space" for new rules, giving rise to new rules. The positive effect of contemporaneous revisions parallels the lagged effect of revisions on academic rule production. The contemporaneous and lagged effects of revisions stand in interesting contrast to the results in the administrative area where we found no significant effect of rule revisions on rule birth.

Academic Rule Births in Two-Rule Regimes

As we noted before, there were two distinctive rule regimes in the academic area, with different historical contexts, different rhythms of rule changes, as well as different rule-making processes. Thus, it is useful to assess whether there are significantly different patterns of rule birth across these two regimes. Tables 5.3 and 5.4 show parameter estimates for five nested models of academic rule production in each of the two rule regimes. The first rule regime covers the period from 1891 to 1967; the second rule regime covers the period from 1968 to 1987. Dividing academic rule births in this way allows us to consider these

TABLE 5.3

Estimated coefficients for five nested models of academic rule births during the Academic Council regime, 1891–1967

	M1	M2	M3	M4	M5
Constant	1.071***	1.017***	1.069***	0.828***	0.453
	(0.141)	(0.162)	(0.196)	(0.232)	(0.280)
Academic Council	-0.007**	-0.006*	-0.009	-0.014*	-0.020**
regime age	(0.003)	(0.004)	(0.008)	(0.008)	(0.009)
Change in number of		-0.757	-0.258	-0.203	0.045
programs (log)		(1.136)	(1.359)	(1.344)	(1.362)
Change in number of		-0.499	-0.698	-0.695	-0.722
students (log)		(0.618)	(0.646)	(0.618)	(0.674)
Change in number of		0.554	0.491	-0.080	0.917
faculty (log)		(1.238)	(1.247)	(1.337)	(1.400)
Percent government			-2.067	-0.333	1.085
funding (wt. avg.)			(2.164)	(2.278)	(2.366)
Number of higher education			0.305***	0.276**	0.298***
laws (wt. avg.)			(0.113)	(0.117)	(0.115)
Number of suspensions				0.107*	0.084
acad. rules at t-1				(0.057)	(0.061)
Number of revisions				0.041*	0.017
acad. rules at t-1				(0.023)	(0.025)
Number of suspensions					0.126**
acad. rules at t					(0.056)
Number of revisions					0.071***
acad. rules at t					(0.023)
Log likelihood	-165.943	-158.442	-155.129	-150.886	-142.747
LR–chi-square	4.610*	15.002***	6.627**	8.486**	16.279***
d.f.	2	3	2	2	2
Number of births	172	172	172	172	172

NOTE: Estimations were done with Limdep. All models are Poisson regression models. Inclusion of the rule regime clock reduced dispersion to a level consistent with the Poisson model. The LR–chi-square statistic gives the improvement of fit of a given model (M_i) over the preceding model (M_{i-1}). For Model 1 the LR statistic gives the improvement of the fit of Model 1 over a model which includes only the intercept. *=p<0.1; **=p<0.05; ***=p<0.01.

TABLE 5.4

Estimated coefficients for five nested models of academic rule births during the Faculty Senate regime, 1968–87

	M1	M2	M3	M4	M5
Constant	3.011***	3.015***	1.740	-0.097	-1.041
	(0.118)	(0.198)	(1.419)	(2.283)	(2.661)
Faculty Senate	-0.111***	-0.106***	-0.074*	-0.022	0.008
regime age	(0.015)	(0.017)	(0.039)	(0.066)	(0.077)
Change in number of		-2.653	-1.422	-1.201	1.345
programs (log)		(2.413)	(2.531)	(2.590)	(3.206)
Change in number of		-14.583*	-14.644*	-13.450	-20.350*
students (log)		(7.895)	(7.871)	(8.547)	(11.730)
Change in number of		2.910	-0.815	-4.331	1.570
faculty (log)		(3.406)	(4.579)	(6.503)	(7.860)
Percent government			3.232	8.247	9.401
funding (wt. avg.)			(5.690)	(7.437)	(8.695)
Number of higher education			0.154	0.197*	0.147
laws (wt. avg.)			(0.102)	(0.114)	(0.156)
Number of suspensions				0.037	0.046
acad. rules at t-1				(0.047)	(0.057)
Number of revisions				0.013	0.014
acad. rules at t-1				(0.034)	(0.040)
Number of changes				0.008	-0.003
admin. rules at t-1				(0.015)	(0.018)
Number of suspensions					0.019
acad. rules at t					(0.081)
Number of revisions					0.059
acad. rules at t					(0.045)
Number of changes					0.004
admin. rules at t					(0.016)
Log likelihood	-45.425	-42.633	-41.287	-40.694	-39.623
LR–chi-square	62.988***	5.583	2.693	1.185	2.142
d.f.	2	3	2	3	3
Number of births	172	172	172	172	172

NOTE: Estimations were done with Limdep. All models are Poisson regression models. Inclusion of the rule regime clock reduced dispersion to a level consistent with the Poisson model. The LR–chi-square statistic gives the improvement of fit of a given model (M_i) over the preceding model (M_{i-1}). For Model 1 the LR statistic gives the improvement of the fit of Model 1 over a model which includes only the intercept. *=p<0.1; **=p<0.05; ***=p<0.01.

two regimes separately. It also provides us (with the results from the second rule regime) with a period drawn from the academic rule system that is comparable with the period covered by the administrative rule data. The obvious statistical cost of the division is to reduce the database for each regime significantly. The number of academic rule births in the first rule regime is 172; in the second it is also 172.

Estimates for the first rule regime (see Table 5.3) are quite consistent, both in direction and magnitude, with estimates for the whole period (Table 5.2), but the same cannot be said with confidence for estimates from the second rule regime (Table 5.4). Although there are no coefficients that indicate an effect opposite to the effects observed throughout the whole period, no consistently significant coefficients are observed in the results from the second rule regime. This result is undoubtedly partly attributable to the shortness of the time period covered and to the reduction in number of observations, but it must also be viewed as a warning that some regularities in rule-creating processes may have been swamped by external pressures during the second academic rule regime. Our descriptive statistics show that there was a fourfold increase in the annual number of rule births from the first to the second regime, and the change was quite abrupt. We suspect that major changes in internal governance structure (the role of the Faculty Senate and the associated rule-making structures) and especially in the environment (active student and faculty involvement and the increasing role of government and legal system) may have generated contextual turbulence to which the rule system responded, rendering the internal dynamics (organizational structure, rule ecology) less salient.

EXPLORING EFFECTS OF ATTENTION, HISTORICAL CONTEXTS, AND SUBPOPULATIONS OF RULES ON ACADEMIC RULE PRODUCTION

The findings reported above show significant history dependence in both rules and rule regimes and some evidence of the contagion and competition effects of rule ecology. That analysis also suggests that birthrates in the academic and administrative rule populations are different and respond somewhat differently to the variables we have considered. In this section, we address these issues more explicitly by taking another look at academic rule histories.

Data and Models

We introduce three sets of new data or disaggregations of data: data on organizational attention; disaggregation of the data into specific historical time periods; and disaggregation of the data into two distinct rule subpopulations.

Organizational Attention. We construct an explicit measure of attention by rule-making bodies, a coding of agenda items for meetings of the Academic Council and Faculty Senate and examine how the distribution of agenda attention affects the rate of rule birth. Although we have used competition and contagion of attention (in a rule ecology) as explanatory mechanisms in the previous analyses, we have not, in general, observed attention directly. Direct observations of attention are not readily available in archival data. In order to make a modest first step toward measuring attention explicitly, however, we code information on the agenda of Academic Council and Faculty Senate meetings during the period covered by the study. Although the measure is, at best, only a rough approximation, these agendas provide clues to the distribution of organizational attention over time. Since a majority of academic rules are made by the Academic Council or Faculty Senate, attention in the academic areas is to some extent indexed by the agenda of these meetings.

We make two distinctions with respect to items on the agenda. First, we distinguish rule-related from rule-unrelated agenda. The former refers to agenda items that deal with organizational rules, such as proposing, discussing, or making decisions on rules. They include discussing, confirming, proposing, or making rule revisions. They are measured as the number of items on the agenda at each meeting of the Faculty Senate or Academic Council and aggregated on a yearly basis. Rule-unrelated agenda refer to those agenda items that do not focus on the rule system, such as committee appointments, budgetary reviews, or annual reports from various committees. They are measured as the number of items on the agenda of the Faculty Senate or Academic Council meetings and aggregated on a yearly basis. Second, we distinguish agenda items concerning student-related rules from items concerning faculty-related rules. The former refer to items such as degree requirements and grading policies. The latter include items such as those related to faculty appointment and promotion, benefits, and housing.

Historical Contexts. Organizational problems arise because of changes in the environment, especially those in the political and legal environment, or because of the accumulation of problems to a level above some "turn-off" threshold. Therefore, we would expect that external shocks will produce episodes of intensified problem-solving processes and rule dynamics, rather than a continuous process of incremental learning. To explore these features of rule making, we use the same measures of the legal and political environment described in Chapter 4 and used in previous sections. In addition, we take into consideration the role of specific historical contexts. In the analysis reported above, we considered two historical periods, divided by a change of the academic rule regime in 1968. In the present section, we introduce a finer-grained periodization by incorporating a set of dummy variables that measure historical period effects. On the basis of an examination of the patterns of environmental and university changes in these years, and in keeping with earlier work by Zhou (1993), we divide the historical context into the following four periods:

1889–1915. The first period comprised the "early" years. During this period major decisions at Stanford, including rule making, were made largely by the president. There was little consultation with the faculty (Mirrielees 1959).

1916–1945. The second period can be labeled as the "years of external crises," including the Great Depression and two world wars. These external events tended to disrupt the normal processes in the university.

1946–1965. The third period includes the "years of expansion." Both American higher education in general and Stanford University grew rapidly during this period.

1966–1987. The last period can be labeled as the "years of crisis and re-adjustment." This period includes the challenge of student protests in the late 1960s and financial and institutional pressures on institutions of higher education after 1970.

Following Hannan and Freeman (1989, 210), we create a set of dummy variables for these historical periods. The first period is the baseline. The second period is coded as one for the years 1916 to 1987; the third period as one from 1946 to 1987; the fourth period as one from 1966 to 1987.[2]

Subpopulations of Rules. We examine population heterogeneity by disaggregating academic rule histories into two substantive areas. We distinguish rules regulating student conduct from rules regulating faculty conduct. As in our earlier analyses, we used Poisson models to estimate the effects of the covariates on the rate of rule births. The standard errors of the estimates are adjusted for possible overdispersion problems.[3]

Results

Table 5.5 reports the results of three separate Poisson models for the rate of rule birth. In the first model, all birth events are included in the analysis. The second and the third models analyze births in the student and faculty areas separately, treating them as distinctive populations.

Organizational Attention. Based on our speculations about competition for attention in the rule-making processes, we might expect to find that the rate of rule birth would be positively related to rule-related organizational agendas, but inversely related to rule-unrelated agendas. And we might expect to find that the rate of rule birth would be positively related to rule agendas in the same area, but inversely related to rule-related agendas in other areas.

The expectations are only partly confirmed. The overall model indicates that a high number of rule-related agenda items in both student and faculty areas in a particular year has a positive effect on aggregate rule production. This effect is consistent with the general idea that the allocation of organizational attention to rule-related themes intensifies rule making. The subpopulation specific models indicate that attention to rule-related items intensifies rule making within each area, and partially also across areas (attention to faculty rule items intensifies student rule production). Rule-unrelated agenda variables have no statistically significant effect on rule production in any of the rule populations (although most of the signs are negative, consistent with a competition of attention effect).

The attention dependence in the subpopulations of student and faculty rules is consistent with the positive effect of revisions on academic rule births (presented in Table 5.2). Yet, the absence of "rule-unrelated agenda" effects indicates that many rules come into existence regardless of the level of attention paid to rule-unrelated items. Rules are made even in the presence of distracting agenda items. In addition, these findings indicate that attention to rule making can spread to neighboring areas and stimulate rule production there. Our results indicate that this occurs when a strong presence of faculty rule-related items on the agenda intensify rule production in the student area. Yet, this does not occur in the opposite direction; student rule-related agenda items do not affect faculty rule production. This suggests that contagion of attention is not symmetric, but rather unidirectional. New rules for the faculty entail new rules for students. But student rule production is not similarly consequential for faculty rule production.

TABLE 5.5
Estimated coefficients for academic rule births, 1891–1987, by subpopulations, using period effect dummies

	Overall	Student	Faculty
Constant	1.725***	1.608*	-0.287
	(0.552)	(0.874)	(0.732)
Change in number	0.271	0.096	0.723
of programs (log)	(1.484)	(1.802)	(2.416)
Change in number	0.788	1.032	0.275
of faculty (log)	(1.401)	(1.658)	(2.429)
Change in number	-0.191	-0.182	-0.588
of students (log)	(0.823)	(0.993)	(1.369)
Percent government	-4.117	-7.181**	2.949
funding (wt. avg.)	(2.533)	(3.211)	(4.162)
Number of higher education	-0.111	-0.158	-0.035
laws (wt. avg.)	(0.105)	(0.143)	(0.156)
Rule agenda, student area, t	0.084***	0.113***	0.029
	(0.013)	(0.016)	(0.021)
Rule agenda, faculty area, t	0.063***	0.038**	0.073***
	(0.011)	(0.018)	(0.014)
Other agenda, student area, t	0.003	-0.015	0.017
	(0.013)	(0.021)	(0.016)
Other agenda, faculty area, t	-0.011	-0.003	-0.010
	(0.009)	(0.014)	(0.012)
Period 2 (1916–45)	-0.366	-0.315	-0.885*
	(0.234)	(0.271)	(0.464)
Period 3 (1946–65)	0.861*	1.255**	0.207
	(0.451)	(0.607)	(0.717)
Period 4 (1966–87)	0.962***	0.826*	1.120**
	(0.345)	(0.487)	(0.509)
Deviance	104.35	102.90	88.46
LR–chi-square	293.5	120.8	330.2
d.f.	12	12	12
Number of observations	94	94	94

NOTE: All models are Poisson regression models. LR–chi-square tests of improvement of fit over model with intercept only. *=p<0.1; **=p<0.05; ***=p<0.01.

Overall, attention effects are not as clear-cut as might be anticipated. The weak agenda effects are undoubtedly partly due to inadequacies in the measure of attention. The number of rule-related agenda items is a crude measure of attention spent on a rule-making process. A more substantive interpretation of the results would focus on the dual effects of attention. Attention to rules can result in new rules, or, alternatively, it can result in rule changes. Either a rule change or a rule birth is a potential outcome of decision maker attention to rules. In this sense, rule births compete with (or substitute for) rule change, and neither alone is well predicted simply from attention. We will examine this issue further in the next chapter, when we consider the role of attention in rule changes.

Historical Contexts. Several of the historical period variables in Table 5.5 are significant. The positive effects of the dummy variables in the overall model for the third and fourth periods indicate that the birthrate accelerated after World War II. To be more specific, for the "overall model," the rate in the third period (1946–1965) is more than twice that of the second period and the rate in the fourth period (1966–1987) is about 2.5 times that of the third period (the acceleration pattern is similar within the subpopulations, although the timing of maximum acceleration seems to differ across subpopulations). On the basis of the models set forth above, we noted a strong negative effect of regime age on rule production, punctuated by a big increase when rule regimes change. The model in this section indicates a similar trend, but the interpretations implied by the two different models are somewhat different.

Within the present model, one might construe the results as supporting a view that emphasizes the tendency of organizational rules to proliferate in response to environmental changes in the larger social context, as reflected in the period effects. Within the model specified above, on the other hand, one might construe the results as supporting the view that changes in rule regimes produce upward shifts in rule births followed by decline. It is hard to imagine distinguishing decisively between these two interpretations by using the present data. We are inclined to believe that each captures some of the reality of rule birth production, but that neither tells the whole story. However, in the following section we will explore the relation between rule regime age effects and density effects in rule births and will conclude that apparent rule regime age effects are largely, but not entirely, eliminated when one controls for density.

Subpopulations of Rules. Student rules might reasonably be expected to respond to external shocks that are different from those affecting faculty rules.

The types of problems that arise in the student area are different from those in the faculty area. The student body is significantly more transient than the faculty. The authority structure governing the two areas differs. For all of these reasons, one would not be surprised to discover differences between the two subpopulations. The differences we observe are, however, rather modest.

As columns 2 and 3 of Table 5.5 show, few of the individual variables, other than the time periods, make a significant difference for both faculty and student rules. None of the organizational structure variables has significant effects. The percent of funding for higher education that comes from the federal government is negatively associated with the rate of rule birth in the student area, but is not significantly related to rule births in the faculty area. A cross-population effect of rule-related agenda is found for student rules, but not for faculty rules. However, there are notable differences in rule birthrates and in the effect of historical periods between the faculty and student areas. For the student area, the rate is significantly higher in the last two periods. On the other hand, the birthrate in the faculty area varies nonmonotonically over time: the second period has a decrease in the birthrate as compared with the first period. The birthrate in the third period does not differ significantly from that of the second period. The birthrate in the fourth period is significantly greater than that of the third period.

A possible explanation for the above findings is that academic rule births, particularly those in the faculty area, are more responsive to crisis or external shocks and less responsive to either cumulative learning or institutionalization processes. That is, the rate of rule birth is situation oriented and context bound. This interpretation is supported by the findings that neither organizational size and structure nor external intervention by the federal government showed significant or consistent effects on the birthrate during the period studied. The interpretation has to be qualified by the competing speculation that regime age effects will account for a significant fraction of the results interpreted here as period effects.

Effects of Rule Density and Rule Suspensions

The analyses above identified some aspects of the ecological contexts of rule births, particularly the ways rule revision and suspension at one time and place affect rule production at another time and place. As we noted, there is some indication that rules occupy "regulatory" or "knowledge" space, thereby inhibiting the creation of new rules. In this section we examine this idea further, drawing from Schulz (1998b).

THEORETICAL ISSUES

We explore the two alternative sets of predictions presented in Chapter 3 with regard to the effects of rule density on the birth of new rules (see Table 3.2). The first set of predictions is generally consistent with theories of bureaucratic proliferation and argues that creation of rules improves the capabilities and stimulates the activity of rule-making bodies. As a result, rules breed rules with increasing intensity. The second set of predictions is generally consistent with theories of organizational problem solving and learning. As the organization accumulates experience (knowledge) and expands its rule apparatus, it increasingly responds to problems in a routinized fashion by applying existing rules. Thus, as an organizational bureaucracy expands, the organization encounters fewer and fewer problems that are not yet covered by existing rules. Bureaucracies breed rules, but, at the same time, by expanding the range of problems to which they respond automatically, they also reduce opportunities for generating new knowledge and creating new rules. Especially in situations of environmental stability, the supply of organizational problems which is amenable to regulation is reduced, and this exhaustion of the problem space results in a decline in organizational rule production. Thus, viewed from the perspective of organizational learning, rules breed rules with decreasing intensity. To compare these alternative views with our observations, we first describe the data and models used and then present and discuss empirical models of rule density.

DATA AND MODELS

For the most part, the analysis uses the same set of independent variables listed in Chapter 4 and involved in the analyses reported above. These include organizational growth (change in the log of student[4] enrollment from t-2 to t-1), growth in complexity (change in the log of number of degree programs from t-2 to t-1), government funding (average proportion of total higher education revenue provided by federal and state funding during the previous three years), legislation (three-year moving average of the annual number of laws enacted in the United States in the area of higher education), regime age, and the number of rule revisions per year.

In addition, we consider another organizational factor—the role of university presidents—in the rule-making process. We specify a set of dummy variables for different university presidents in Stanford history to capture possible effects of changes in administration on the rule production process.[5] All independent variables except the suspension variables are lagged.[6] As we did earlier in this chapter, we here analyze administrative and academic rules separately. We assume that both parts are sufficiently decoupled to allow separate treatment. To test this assumption, some of the models presented below test for interactions between academic and administrative rules. The empirical analyses of this section are based on a total of 344 academic rule births and 177 administrative rule births (the number of administrative rule births is reduced from 257 due to missing values of covariates and exclusion of the founding version of the *Guide*).

Problems can be more or less widely shared between different parts of the rule system. Problem absorption and recycling might affect rule production only locally (e.g., only within accounting rules), or more globally (e.g., among all administrative rules). In order to explore problem absorption and recycling systematically, we disaggregate both administrative and academic rules into more refined subpopulations. Administrative rules are sorted into six main problem areas: personnel, accounting, procurement, general organization (e.g., organization charts), services (such as printing and so forth), and rules regarding external property (e.g., government property, gifts). Each of these administrative areas is treated here as an administrative rule subpopulation. The total numbers of births in the various administrative subpopulations are: organization charts—18; personnel rules—53; accounting rules—21; external property rules—20; procurement rules—40; and service rules—25.

Academic rules are sorted into two main problem areas: student rules (e.g., grading rules) and faculty rules (e.g., tenure rules). As noted earlier, there are also two academic rule regimes, the Academic Council regime (1891–1967) and the Faculty Senate regime (1968–1987). Each of the four combinations of rule-making regime and problem area is treated here as an academic rule subpopulation. The total numbers of births in the academic subpopulations

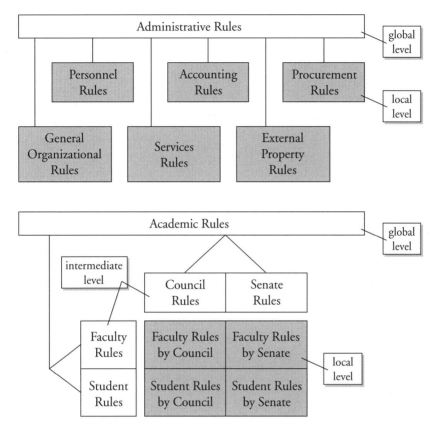

Figure 5.2   Subpopulations of academic and administrative rules

are: student rules made by the Academic Council—127; faculty rules made by the Academic Council—45; student rules made by the Faculty Senate—73; and faculty rules made by the Faculty Senate—99.

The overall structure of the rule areas for this set of analyses is shown in Figure 5.2. For administrative rules, we distinguish two levels of aggregation. The global level aggregates across all rule areas. At the local level, the administrative rule areas define six administrative subpopulations. For academic rules, we distinguish a global level, a local level, and an intermediate level. The global level aggregates across all rule areas and regimes. The intermediate level distinguishes two kinds of aggregation: faculty and student rules (aggregating across areas); and Academic Council and Faculty Senate rules (aggregating across regimes). At the local academic level, four subpopulations exist: student rules made during the Academic Council regime; faculty rules made during the Academic Council regime; student rules made during the Faculty Senate regime; and faculty rules made during the Faculty Senate regime.

In this set of analyses, we adopt the Poisson model described earlier. We also incorporate recent elaborations of Poisson model methodology that attempt to address population heterogeneity problems in models of birth processes (e.g., Brannas and Rosenqvist 1994; Lomi 1995). The main strategy of these approaches is to disaggregate populations into subpopulations and to allow baselines as well as parameters to vary across subpopulations. Since the number of subpopulations involved in this study is moderate, fixed effects models are used. The models specify different baseline rates for different subpopulations. These different baseline effects serve as base points for the mixing distribution used in the Poisson model.[7]

Time series of the birthrate for each of the six administrative rule subpopulations and each of the four academic rule subpopulations are computed. These subpopulation specific birthrates are the dependent variables of the analysis. Next, time series of the covariates are computed and added to the subpopulation specific birthrate time series. Finally, the data for the six administrative rule subpopulations are pooled, as are the data for the four academic rule subpopulations. This procedure yields two pooled cross-sectional data sets—one for academic rules and one for administrative rules.

To test if baselines differ among subpopulations, models with a common intercept are compared with models specifying different intercepts for each subpopulation. Because the multibaseline models are derived from the single baseline models by adding the subpopulation dummy variables, likelihood ratio statistics can be computed to test the improvement of fit.

In order to analyze global and local effects, densities and suspensions are computed for the local level and the global level (see Figure 5.2). Models are specified that allow density and suspension parameters to differ among subpopulations.[8] Models that include the joint terms assume a single slope for all subpopulations. Models that include the separate terms allow the slopes to differ among subpopulations.[9]

There are two tables of parameter estimates for administrative rules and two tables for academic rules. The first tables in each subsection (i.e., Tables 5.6 and 5.8) report analyses that constrain the slopes of density and suspension parameters to be equal across subpopulations (although intercepts are allowed to differ). The models in these first tables are nested and therefore permit the use of likelihood ratio tests (included in the tables in the row called LR–chi-square). The rho-squared statistic is also reported at the bottom of these tables. The second table in each subsection (i.e., Tables 5.7 and 5.9) reports analyses that allow slopes of density and suspension variables to differ among subpopulations. Those models are not nested for the most part, and thus only the rho-squared statistic is reported at the bottom of the tables.

RESULTS

The results[10] are reported separately for administrative and academic rule populations. Differences between the two are noted in the discussion of academic rules and in subsequent chapters.

Administrative Rule Births, 1961–1987

Table 5.6 shows five models of administrative rule production. Model 1 (M1) in Table 5.6 includes the effects of the control variables only. Growth in the student population and growth in the number of academic programs increase the birthrate. An increased level of government funding seems to retard administrative rule production. None of the presidential tenure variables has a significant effect in this model. Nor do the number of rule revisions in the preceding year. The effects of these control variables change to some degree in subsequent models as density and suspension variables are added.

Global Density and Suspension Effects. Model 2 (M2) explores the effects of global density and suspension measures. Both parameters are highly significant. Global density has a strong negative effect, and global suspensions a strong positive effect. These results indicate that the rate of administrative rule production declines with the number of administrative rules already in the system and increases in years in which many rules are suspended. Thus, these results are congruent—on the global level—with problem absorption and recycling. Inclusion of local-level variables in subsequent models modifies these global effects.

Variations among Administrative Rule Areas. Differences among administrative rule areas are revealed in Model 3 (M3). Model 3 adds five area dummy variables and thereby allows the baseline rates for the six administrative rule

TABLE 5.6

Estimated coefficients for joint slopes of subpopulations, administrative rule births, 1961–87

	M1	M2	M3	M4	M5	M6
Global density admin. rules		-0.079***	-0.079***	-0.041**	-0.082***	-0.087***
		(0.017)	(0.017)	(0.018)	(0.031)	(0.031)
Global suspensions admin. rules		0.112***	0.112***	-0.012	0.030	0.032
		(0.024)	(0.024)	(0.030)	(0.039)	(0.039)
Local density (joint slope)				-0.063***	-0.060***	-0.060**
				(0.023)	(0.023)	(0.023)
Local suspensions (joint slope)				0.322***	0.312***	0.311***
				(0.036)	(0.036)	(0.036)
Admin. Guide regime age					0.175*	0.295
					(0.105)	(0.208)
Global density acad. rules						-0.016
						(0.024)
Organization charts			-0.856***	-0.935***	-0.916***	-0.899***
			(0.290)	(0.309)	(0.307)	(0.308)
Accounting rules			-0.693**	0.030	0.008	0.017
			(0.274)	(0.311)	(0.311)	(0.312)
External property rules			-0.744***	-0.354	-0.361	-0.349
			(0.279)	(0.292)	(0.292)	(0.293)
Personnel rules			0.223	0.883**	0.810**	0.823**
			(0.212)	(0.359)	(0.361)	(0.363)
Service rules			-0.511**	-0.106	-0.115	-0.097
			(0.258)	(0.272)	(0.272)	(0.274)
Constant	9.485***	8.620**	8.965***	6.157*	8.480**	9.219**
	(3.263)	(3.422)	(3.424)	(3.480)	(3.876)	(4.110)
Δ Number students	22.782***	-15.631	-15.631	3.980	-8.847	-7.648
	(7.789)	(10.940)	(10.940)	(11.420)	(13.810)	(13.870)
Δ Number programs	5.314**	9.215***	9.215***	6.647**	7.563***	8.018***
	(2.271)	(2.604)	(2.604)	(2.610)	(2.702)	(2.795)
Government funding	-22.346***	-8.975	-8.975	-7.766	-7.834	-5.282
	(7.931)	(8.561)	(8.561)	(8.929)	(9.350)	(10.190)
Legislation	0.057	0.209**	0.209**	0.069	-0.034	-0.095
	(0.072)	(0.083)	(0.083)	(0.086)	(0.108)	(0.142)
Presid. Period 5	-0.600	-0.408	-0.408	0.119	-0.525	-0.260
	(0.468)	(0.498)	(0.498)	(0.527)	(0.670)	(0.775)
Presid. Period 6	-0.103	1.331**	1.331**	0.653	0.568	0.709
	(0.523)	(0.591)	(0.591)	(0.615)	(0.637)	(0.655)
Presid. Period 7	-0.219	1.755***	1.755***	1.061**	0.147	-0.116
	(0.309)	(0.522)	(0.522)	(0.494)	(0.745)	(0.854)
Number of revisions	-0.012	0.025	0.025	0.018	0.036*	0.032
	(0.013)	(0.018)	(0.018)	(0.017)	(0.020)	(0.021)
Log likelihood	-273.756	-258.812	-243.845	-193.810	-192.362	-192.136
LR–chi-square	83.254***	29.888***	29.933***	100.070***	2.897*	0.452
d.f.	8	2	5	21	1	1
#Parameters	8	10	15	17	18	19
Rho-Sq.	0.107	0.148	0.179	0.332	0.333	0.331

NOTE: The LR–chi-square statistic gives the improvement of fit of a given model (M_i) over the preceding model (M_{i-1}). For Model 1 the LR–chi-square statistic gives the improvement of the fit of Model 1 over a model which includes only the intercept. *=p<0.1; **=p<0.05; ***=p<0.01.

subpopulations to differ. The sixth area, procurement rules, is used as the reference category. Adding these area intercepts significantly improves the fit (p<0.01 according to the likelihood ratio test). The parameter estimates indicate that personnel rules have the highest rate of rule production, whereas organization charts have the lowest. The other rules exhibit intermediate levels of rule production. These parameters change to some degree in subsequent models as more variables are added to the model.

Most of these differences in the baseline of rule production can be interpreted as stemming from differential problem supply. Personnel and procurement rules, located at the interface between the organization and its environment, presumably face many problems (e.g., agency problems and an ever-expanding legal environment) and thus have a high rule birthrate. Accounting rules and organization charts, very close to the core of the organization, are presumably well shielded from external turbulence and indeed have a very low birthrate. External property rules are located in a very narrow, specialized area (rules regarding government property and rules regarding donations). They show a comparatively low level of rule production. Overall, it appears that the rate of administrative rule production is larger in those subpopulations that might be expected to have relatively large supplies of problems.

Local Density and Suspension Effects. Model 4 (M4) adds measures of local density and suspensions. Both have highly significant effects on administrative rule production. Local density has a negative effect. Local suspensions have a positive effect. The improvement of fit is very large.[11] The parameter estimates of Model 4 indicate that the effects are stronger within rule subpopulations (local density) than in the global population of all administrative rules (global density). The predominance of local effects is even more salient for suspensions. Local suspensions have a highly significant and positive effect on the birthrate. The global suspension effect disappears after local suspensions are included. This result is consistent with the idea that problems are recycled mainly within rule areas and less among other areas.

Regime Age Effects. Model 5 (M5) tests effects of regime age (the age of the *Administrative Guide*). The regime age parameter is marginally significant and is positive (although it becomes nonsignificant in the next model). This result is interesting in two respects. First, it deviates from our earlier results in Chapter 5, where we found a consistent negative effect of regime age. The apparent reason for this difference is that we now assess the effect of regime age controlling for density. Including density in the models renders the regime age parameter positive. This suggests that the negative regime age effect found earlier may be primarily a result of negative density dependence of administrative rule births. Thus, it is not the passing of regime time, but rather the cumulated rule output of regimes (within specific problem areas) that drives the birthrate down. Second, the fact that negative density dependence is still evident in this model lends credence to the possibility that the negative density dependence of administrative rule birthrate is genuine and not spurious.

Cross-population Effects. In order to test if administrative rule births are independent of academic rule births, the global density of academic rules is added in Model 6 (M6). The improvement of fit is not significant. This indicates that academic and administrative rules are sufficiently independent to be analyzed separately.

Varying Effects of Density across Areas. The models explored so far presuppose that the slopes of the density and suspension effects are equal across administrative subpopulations. Yet, density effects could easily differ in strength across subpopulations, depending as they might on the level of turbulence in the area. The models in Table 5.7 address this issue directly. These models allow the slopes of the density and suspension effects to differ across the six administrative rule subpopulations.

The models in Table 5.7 exclude those variables that showed no significant effects in Model 6 above. Thus the global suspension effect is excluded, as are measures of government funding, organizational growth, revisions, administrative time clock, and academic rule density. Model 1 in Table 5.7 is equivalent to Model 4 in Table 5.6, except for the excluded variables (their exclusion does not significantly alter the parameters of the remaining variables). It serves as a baseline model for the other models presented in the table.

Model 2 replaces the single slopes for density and the number of suspensions with six density and six suspension slopes for the administrative subpopulations. This substantially increases the number of parameters of the model (from 13 to 23). The corresponding rho-squared statistic (which takes into account the increase in the number of parameters) is 0.37, slightly better than the one for Model 1. Of the six local density parameters in Model 2, three are statistically significant. All the significant density parameters are negative. The significant parameters pertain to the areas of accounting, procurement, and external property rules (i.e., rules regarding government property

TABLE 5.7   133

Estimated coefficients for separate slopes of subpopulations, administrative rule births, 1961–87

	M1	M2	M3
Global density admin. rules	-0.040***	-0.036***	-0.036***
	(0.009)	(0.010)	(0.010)
Local density (joint slope)	-0.065***		
	(0.023)		
Local suspensions (joint slope)	0.315***		
	(0.027)		
Density organization charts		0.109	0.109
		(0.107)	(0.146)
Density personnel rules		-0.037	-0.037
		(0.025)	(0.023)
Density accounting rules		-0.132**	-0.132**
		(0.060)	(0.056)
Density external property rules		-0.123*	-0.123*
		(0.074)	(0.071)
Density procurement rules		-0.126*	-0.126*
		(0.065)	(0.075)
Density services rules		0.018	0.018
		(0.082)	(0.085)
Suspensions organization charts		0.114	0.114
		(0.073)	(6.586)
Suspensions personnel rules		0.250***	0.250*
		(0.046)	(0.135)
Suspensions accounting rules		0.594	0.594*
		(0.386)	(0.358)
Suspensions external property rules		0.260	0.260
		(0.307)	(0.250)
Suspensions procurement rules		0.580***	0.580***
		(0.068)	(0.128)
Suspensions services rules		-0.111	-0.111
		(0.284)	(0.396)
Alpha			0.063
			(0.103)
Constant	3.115***	2.632***	2.632***
	(0.438)	(0.680)	(0.817)
Organization charts	-0.974***	-1.958	-1.958
	(0.300)	(1.301)	(1.566)
Accounting rules	0.030	1.093	1.093
	(0.309)	(0.861)	(0.972)
External property rules	-0.384	0.378	0.378
	(0.290)	(0.753)	(0.851)
Personnel rules	0.881**	0.643	0.643
	(0.350)	(0.697)	(0.837)
Services rules	-0.129	-0.599	-0.599
	(0.270)	(0.893)	(1.047)
Δ Number programs	7.397***	6.970***	6.970***
	(2.509)	(2.684)	(2.673)
Legislation	0.099	0.174*	0.174*
	(0.074)	(0.089)	(0.089)
Presid. Period 5	0.429	0.245	0.245
	(0.406)	(0.429)	(0.340)
Presid. Period 6	0.187	-0.192	-0.192
	(0.388)	(0.419)	(0.347)
Presid. Period 7	1.085***	1.124***	1.124***
	(0.325)	(0.355)	(0.414)
Log likelihood	-194.673	-176.555	-175.055
# Parameters	13	23	24
Rho-sq.	0.342	0.367	0.369

NOTE: *=p<0.1; **=p<0.05; ***=p<0.01.

and gifts). The density coefficients are negative but not significant in personnel rules, organization charts, and service rules.

The strong density effect of accounting rules can be seen as a result of low
turbulence. Accounting rules are located close to the core of administrative activities and presumably face a comparatively low level of environmental turbulence (their level of rule production is comparatively low: 0.7 rules per year
in the average). The situation is similar for external property rules, a very narrow rule area that should be able to reach regulatory closure easily. The absence of a significant density effect in personnel rules can be seen as a result of
high turbulence (their average birthrate is the highest among administrative
subpopulations: 1.7 rules per year). Thus accounting, personnel, and external
property rules seem to confirm the idea that high levels of turbulence weaken
sorting and absorption mechanisms. Still, the turbulence idea finds only partial support in administrative rules. Procurement rules show a significant negative effect of density, even though one would expect the level of turbulence to
be considerable (the average level of procurement rule production is corre-
spondingly high: 1.3 rules per year).

Of the six local suspension parameters, only the suspensions in the personnel and procurement areas are significant (indeed, highly significant). They are
both positive, consistent with local recycling. One interpretation, although not
the only one, of these results is that organizational relationships to external
vendors and employees are subject to large agency problems and thus require
intense and immediate recycling of problems of suspended rules.[12]

Academic Rule Births, 1891–1987

Academic rules are analyzed in a way that is parallel to the analysis for administrative rules. Model 1 in Table 5.8 shows the baseline model for academic
rules. It includes effects of the control variables only. The control variables are
the same as in Table 5.6, except that they are measured over a different time
period here (1891 to 1987 for academic rules). Noteworthy effects of the control variables include the highly significant and positive effect of legislation, a
mildly significant and positive effect of revisions, and widely fluctuating, significant effects of the presidential tenure periods. The effects of the control
variables change somewhat in subsequent models as density and suspension
variables are added to the model.

Global Density and Suspension Effects. Both the density and the suspension

TABLE 5.8   135
Estimated coefficients for joint slopes of subpopulations, academic rule births, 1891–1987

	M1	M2	M3	M4	M5	M6
Global density acad. rules		-0.015***	-0.016***	0.004	0.019	0.019
		(0.004)	(0.004)	(0.007)	(0.014)	(0.014)
Global susp. acad. rules		0.224***	0.172***	0.045	0.016	0.016
		(0.037)	(0.045)	(0.066)	(0.068)	(0.068)
Local density (joint slope)				-0.035***	-0.034***	-0.035***
				(0.010)	(0.010)	(0.010)
Local suspensions (joint slope)				0.188***	0.193***	0.193***
				(0.068)	(0.069)	(0.069)
Acad. Council regime age					-0.039*	-0.039*
					(0.021)	(0.022)
Faculty Senate regime age					-0.063	-0.076
					(0.082)	(0.144)
Global density admin. rules						0.007
						(0.062)
Student rules by Council			0.995***	2.095***	2.057***	2.059***
			(0.176)	(0.391)	(0.391)	(0.391)
Student rules by Senate			1.527***	-0.855	-0.907	-1.548
			(0.469)	(0.805)	(0.843)	(5.804)
Faculty rules by Senate			1.832***	0.409	0.352	-0.289
			(0.465)	(0.602)	(0.643)	(5.773)
Constant	0.071	0.483**	-0.133	-0.861**	-0.796*	-0.795*
	(0.176)	(0.230)	(0.264)	(0.362)	(0.407)	(0.407)
Δ Number students	-1.067	-1.649*	-1.364	-1.525*	-1.764**	-1.753**
	(0.877)	(0.864)	(0.872)	(0.871)	(0.851)	(0.857)
Δ Number programs	0.038	0.501	0.210	0.260	0.125	0.115
	(1.200)	(1.214)	(1.217)	(1.219)	(1.230)	(1.234)
Government funding	0.064	1.310	1.619	1.712	0.904	0.924
	(1.080)	(1.240)	(1.234)	(1.238)	(1.490)	(1.499)
Legislation	0.329***	0.275***	0.156*	0.151*	0.219**	0.216**
	(0.059)	(0.063)	(0.083)	(0.083)	(0.089)	(0.092)
Presid. Period 2	-0.443	-0.275	-0.225	-0.183	0.148	0.144
	(0.337)	(0.367)	(0.361)	(0.363)	(0.439)	(0.440)
Presid. Period 3	-1.994***	-1.938***	-1.845**	-1.866**	-1.205	-1.206
	(0.733)	(0.737)	(0.738)	(0.739)	(0.831)	(0.831)
Presid. Period 4	2.028***	2.229***	2.158***	2.157***	2.445***	2.444***
	(0.726)	(0.731)	(0.730)	(0.732)	(0.751)	(0.751)
Presid. Period 5	1.218***	1.052***	0.518	0.855**	0.743*	0.792
	(0.218)	(0.292)	(0.353)	(0.382)	(0.392)	(0.586)
Presid. Period 6	-0.639***	1.150***	0.878**	0.613	0.200	0.189
	(0.204)	(0.388)	(0.408)	(0.419)	(0.478)	(0.488)
Presid. Period 7	-0.777***	-0.087	-0.002	-0.078	0.115	0.151
	(0.252)	(0.315)	(0.316)	(0.316)	(0.485)	(0.582)
Number of revisions	0.037**	0.030*	0.031*	0.032*	0.034*	0.033*
	(0.016)	(0.018)	(0.018)	(0.018)	(0.018)	(0.019)
Log likelihood	-326.631	-308.032	-285.101	-273.507	-271.669	-271.663
LR–chi-square	218.396***	37.199***	45.861***	23.189***	3.676	0.012
d.f.	11	2	3	2	2	1
# Parameters	11	13	16	18	20	21
Rho-sq.	0.225	0.263	0.309	0.331	0.331	0.328

NOTE: *=p<0.1; **=p<0.05; ***=p<0.01.

parameters are highly significant (p<0.01) in Model 2. Global density has a strong negative effect, and global suspensions have a strong positive effect.

Variations among Academic Rule Areas. In order to explore variations among subpopulations, the intercepts of the four academic subpopulations are allowed to differ in Model 3. Three dummy variables are added (representing student rules created by the Academic Council, student rules created by the Faculty Senate, and faculty rules created by the Faculty Senate). The omitted reference category consists of faculty rules created under the Academic Council. The improvement of fit is highly significant, and all three parameters are highly significant as well (p<0.01). Some of these effects disappear (or fluctuate widely) in subsequent models, but some (such as the effect of student rules made by the Academic Council) persist. Thus this result provides mild support for the idea of differential problem supply across subpopulations.

Local Density and Suspension Effects. In Model 4, the improvement of fit due to adding local density and local suspensions is highly significant. Both parameters are highly significant (p<0.01). Local density has a strong, negative effect on academic rule production. Suspensions have a positive effect on academic rule production. The global parameters for density and suspensions turn nonsignificant after including the local measures. This result suggests that, in partial contrast to the administrative rules, density effects among academic rules are mainly localized (i.e., confined to the individual subpopulations). One should note, however, that the temporal segregation of Academic Council populations from Faculty Senate populations logically exclude interactions between council and senate populations and thus might limit global effects.

Regime Age Effects. Model 5 explores regime age dependence. The parameter estimates provide only weak support for effects of regime age. Although both are negative, only one of them (the Academic Council regime age) is mildly significant (p<0.1). The joint slope for local density is not affected by including regime age, suggesting that density dependence is not confounded by age dependence. Moreover, more complex models (presented below) show consistently nonsignificant regime age effects.

Cross-population Effects. In Model 6, the global density of administrative rules is added to the covariates already included in the preceding model. The improvement of fit is not significant. This suggests that academic rule production is substantially independent from administrative rule density.

Varying Effects of Density across Areas. The models in Table 5.8 assume homogeneity in the density and suspension parameters. That assumption is relaxed in the models in Table 5.9 where differences in the slopes of the density and the suspension effects across academic subpopulations are examined. As before, those variables that showed no significant effects (i.e., global density and suspensions, the number of programs, and the Faculty Senate regime age) are excluded. Model 1 in Table 5.9 is equivalent to Model 5 in Table 5.8, except for the excluded variables. Model 1 functions as the baseline model for Table 5.9.

Model 2 in Table 5.9 replaces the single slopes for density and the number of suspensions with separate slopes for student and faculty rules. The two density parameters are highly significant and negative. Numerically, they are essentially equal. In contrast, the suspension parameters are quite different. The parameter for student rule suspensions is highly significant, whereas for faculty rules it is not significant. This suggests that density mechanisms do not differ between student and faculty rules, but that recycling does differ.

An alternative direction of disaggregation of rules on an intermediate level is explored in Model 3. Model 3 allows slopes to differ for the Academic Council regime and the Faculty Senate regime. Both density parameters are highly significant and negative, and both suspension parameters are significant and positive. It is noteworthy that the parameters are fairly similar in strength, suggesting that the two subpopulations experience density and recycling effects in approximately the same way.

We now proceed to the lowest level of aggregation of academic rules. In Model 4 different slopes for each of the four academic rule subpopulations are allowed. Of the four density parameters, three are negative, but only one of them is significant—the density of faculty rules under the Faculty Senate regime. Student rules are not density dependent in either of the subpopulations. Of the four suspension parameters in Model 4, two are significant ($p<0.01$). Both pertain to the student subpopulations and both are positive. This result reaffirms the earlier result from Model 2 of Table 5.9. Recycling plays a larger role in student rules than it does in faculty rules.

Overall, it seems that Model 4 is not a better model than the simpler Models 1, 2, and 3. Disaggregating the overall slope for academic rules into subpopulation specific slopes is unrewarding in terms of numerical parameter differences and improvement of fit.[13]

TABLE 5.9

Estimated coefficients for separate slopes of subpopulations, academic rule births, 1891–1987

	M1	M2	M3	M4	M5
Local density (joint slope)	-0.027***				
	(0.007)				
Local susp. (joint slope)	0.214***				
	(0.047)				
Density student rules		-0.033***			
		(0.009)			
Density faculty rules		-0.030***			
		(0.008)			
Suspensions student rules		0.253***			
		(0.050)			
Suspensions faculty rules		0.046			
		(0.114)			
Density Acad. Council rules			-0.040***		
			(0.013)		
Density Faculty Senate rules			-0.023***		
			(0.008)		
Suspension Faculty Senate rules			0.202***		
			(0.068)		
Suspension Acad. Council rules			0.234***		
			(0.067)		
Density student rules by Council				-0.018	-0.011
				(0.019)	(0.022)
Density faculty rules by Council				0.024	0.037
				(0.043)	(0.047)
Density student rules by Senate				-0.002	-0.004
				(0.017)	(0.022)
Density faculty rules by Senate				-0.022***	-0.024**
				(0.009)	(0.012)
Susp. student rules by Council				0.214***	0.214**
				(0.070)	(0.094)
Susp. faculty rules by Council				0.298	0.266
				(0.559)	(0.838)
Susp. student rules by Senate				0.307***	0.327**
				(0.079)	(0.151)
Susp. faculty rules by Senate				-0.053	-0.060
				(0.124)	(0.221)
Alpha					0.071
					(0.070)
Constant	-0.418	-0.590*	-0.686*	-0.848**	-0.812*
	(0.283)	(0.358)	(0.371)	(0.413)	(0.415)
Student rules by Council	1.773***	2.027***	2.215***	2.206***	2.101***
	(0.298)	(0.425)	(0.471)	(0.510)	(0.508)
Student rules by Senate	-0.144	0.147	-0.550	1.717	2.156
	(0.664)	(0.621)	(0.767)	(1.408)	(2.118)
Faculty rules by Senate	0.911*	1.416**	0.408	3.505**	4.000*
	(0.527)	(0.628)	(0.686)	(1.455)	(2.129)
Δ Number students	-1.595*	-1.640**	-1.730**	-1.733**	-1.717
	(0.821)	(0.826)	(0.835)	(0.832)	(1.247)
Government funding	2.056*	2.303*	2.394*	1.440	1.148
	(1.209)	(1.217)	(1.252)	(1.394)	(1.414)
Legislation	0.190**	0.185**	0.194**	0.168*	0.160
	(0.085)	(0.086)	(0.085)	(0.088)	(0.112)

TABLE 5.9 *(continued)*

	M1	M2	M3	M4	M5
Presid. Period 2	0.094	0.029	0.148	0.148	0.103
	(0.409)	(0.408)	(0.418)	(0.430)	(0.457)
Presid. Period 3	-1.598**	-1.720**	-1.770**	-1.336	-1.180
	(0.771)	(0.775)	(0.784)	(0.837)	(1.091)
Presid. Period 4	2.335***	2.275***	2.299***	2.408***	2.398***
	(0.741)	(0.742)	(0.742)	(0.747)	(0.908)
Presid. Period 5	0.931**	0.345	0.805**	-0.157	-0.247
	(0.369)	(0.468)	(0.385)	(0.521)	(1.373)
Presid. Period 6	0.567**	0.648**	0.364	0.367	0.482
	(0.287)	(0.283)	(0.337)	(0.370)	(0.734)
Presid. Period 7	0.005	0.081	-0.141	-0.096	-0.005
	(0.283)	(0.288)	(0.303)	(0.331)	(0.431)
Acad. Council regime age	-0.018	-0.010	-0.008	-0.031	-0.036
	(0.014)	(0.014)	(0.016)	(0.022)	(0.029)
Number of revisions	0.023	0.023	0.030*	0.032*	0.034
	(0.017)	(0.017)	(0.018)	(0.018)	(0.024)
Log likelihood	-279.793	-278.031	-278.975	-274.817	-274.010
# Parameters	16	18	18	22	23
Rho-sq.	0.337	0.337	0.335	0.335	0.335

NOTE: *=p<0.1; **=p<0.05; ***=p<0.01.

Rule Births in Summary

Rule births are major events in the evolution of an organizational rule system. They signal the addition of new knowledge, retention of experience, solution of problems, or absorption of environmental changes over time. They are also regulated by organizational processes both within and outside the rule system. The main results of the empirical analysis of rule births are the following: first, rule births are responsive to internal and external problems. Among administrative rules, decreases in government funding, increases in legislation, increases in the number of students, and increases in the number of academic programs all result in increases in administrative rule births. Academic rule births are less sensitive to these environmental and organizational factors, but increases in legislation lead to increases in rule births.

Second, the birthrates of both administrative and academic rules are strongly affected by the density of rules in the area and the rate of rule suspension in the area. The higher the density of rules, the lower the birthrate. The higher the suspension (death) rate, the higher the birthrate. These density and suspension effects tend to be local. Effects of the number of rules and the rate of suspension within a given subpopulation are greater on that subpopulation than they are on other subpopulations. The effects of density and suspensions on birthrates vary from one subpopulation to another. They are stronger in administrative rules than in academic rules and vary more significantly among administrative subpopulations than among academic subpopulations. Some, but not all, of these latter variations can be attributed to differences in environmental turbulence in the subareas.

Third, we find little support for the hypothesis that the birthrate of rules is affected by regime age independent of environmental changes and ecological effects that are correlated with it. To be sure, rule regime age has an apparent negative effect on both administrative and academic rule births. Over the history of a rule regime, rule births decline. This effect appears, however, to be largely a consequence not of regime age per se but of the timing of historical pressures and of two internal variables—the density of rules and the death (suspension) rate. The regime age effect loses significance or is reversed when density and suspension variables are introduced. Thus we find support for those conceptions of problem solving and learning that associate the birthrate of rules not with the number of problems or amount of knowledge previously gained but with the number of problems or amount of knowledge still remaining (see Table 4.2).

SIX

Explaining Patterns of Rule Change

The previous chapter examined the production of new rules. This chapter considers changes in existing rules.[1] Rule changes include both suspensions of rules and revisions of them. In this chapter, the two separate kinds of events have been treated as belonging to a common category of change. We pool the two events partly because of the small number of suspensions and partly because although revisions and suspensions have, as we have seen in Chapter 5, different effects on the rate of births, the theoretical predictions about the incidence of the two kinds of events are virtually indistinguishable.

Rule changes are different from rule births in at least two respects: first, transformations of a population of rules through rule changes seem more consistent with an incremental kind of organizational change than do transformations through rule births. A rule birth generates a new element in the rule system, whereas a rule change takes place within the framework of existing rules. It affects a preexisting rule. Second, the processes affecting rule births and those affecting rule changes are likely to be different. In particular, because rule changes take place within the framework of existing rules, the prior history of a rule emerges as a possible factor in its change. Whereas any one rule has only one birth, it can have a number of revisions in its lifetime. Thus

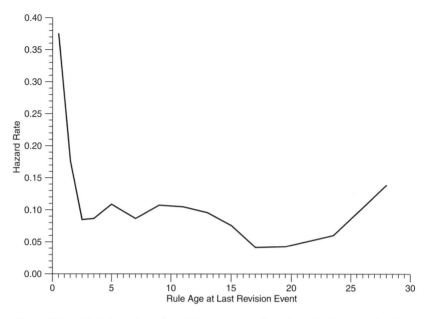

Figure 6.1   Administrative rule revision rate as a function of rule age at the last revision event

a rule can accumulate a history of revisions, and that history can affect its subsequent development.

As in the analysis of rule birth, our analytical focus is on explaining what factors affect the rate of rule change over time and in what ways. We analyze longitudinal data recording changes of administrative rules from 1961 to 1987 and of academic rules from 1891 to 1987. Figures 6.1 and 6.2 show estimates of the hazard of rule change[2] as a function of rule age at the time of the last previous revision for administrative rules and academic rules respectively. The graphs represent average change hazards in the respective rule populations.

As the figures show, rules that experienced their last revision early in their lives have relatively high rates of change. As the age at the time of last revision increases, rules are less prone to changes. In the case of administrative rules, the decline in change rate is apparently ended and even reversed after about sixteen years. In the case of academic rules, the decline is steady with the exception of some nonmonotonic fluctuations in the early years. In the following sections we explore a number of factors specific to individual rules and their contexts which might produce this pattern of rule change.

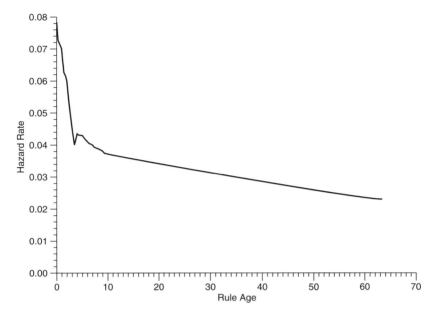

Figure 6.2   Academic rule revision rate as a function of rule age

Effects of Covariates

Following an approach parallel to our treatment of rule births, we estimate a
set of models to explore the distinctive contribution of each set of covariates to
the history of rule changes within the administrative and academic rule populations at Stanford. However, the possible role of prior history in affecting rule
changes leads us to adopt analytical strategies that differ from those used to
consider rule births.

MODELING RULE CHANGES

Since rule changes can occur at any time, and the covariates of theoretical interests may also change over time, we use event history models to model the
processes of rule changes (Tuma and Hannan 1984). Event history models have
the advantage of using full information on the timing of events, treating the
prior history of each rule, and accommodating time-varying covariates. Wher-
ever appropriate, we use time-varying covariates in the models we estimate. Information on organizational size and complexity, governmental funding, leg-

islative acts, and rule ecology is updated annually, while the covariates regarding past rule history use the information when the event occurred. One of the strongest features of event history methodology is its ability to deal with right-censoring problems. This is particularly important in this study since rules still alive at the end of 1987 are right-censored.

We treat the dynamics of rule changes as a continuous-time and discrete-state stochastic process, defining the rule change rate as the instantaneous transition rate, as proposed by Tuma and Hannan (1984). The hazard rate λ is defined as,

$$\lambda(t\,|\,\omega_{n-1}) = \lim_{\Delta t \to 0} \frac{p(t,\,t+\Delta t\,|\,\omega_{n-1})}{\Delta t}$$

where p is the transition probability, and ω_{n-1} is the prior history of the rule.

For the statistical analyses, we assume that the observed waiting times t are draws from a distribution with exponential density

$$f(t) = \lambda e^{-\lambda t}$$

where λ is the hazard rate of rule change. The basic exponential model assumes a constant hazard rate over time. We generalize this model to allow the hazard rate to depend on constant and dynamic covariates. Thus the hazard rate is constant only within levels of those covariates. In particular, if the covariates contain linear functions of time, the hazard rate follows a step function[3] that can approximate any arbitrary functional form of the hazard rate. To ensure that the parameter estimates yield nonnegative predictions for the hazard rate, we estimate linear effects of the covariates on the logarithm of λ, thus

$$\log \lambda = \beta' X_t$$

where X_t represents a vector of constant and time-varying covariates and β a vector of coefficients to be estimated.

The models assume that each successive event is independent, conditional on the covariates included in the model. In our data, a rule may be revised more than once. Repeated events are likely to violate the assumption of statistical independence. On the other hand, repeated events provide critical information about rule dynamics and the evolution of the rule system over time. Clearly, ignoring them will seriously undermine the effort to understand the dynamics of rule change. In order to capture interdependencies among repeated events, we adopt the strategy of incorporating identifiable prior information explicitly into the model (Tuma and Hannan 1984; Allison 1984). In particular, the two variables of rule age at the time of last previous revision and number of prior revisions serve this purpose.

RESULTS

We analyze the data for administrative and academic rules separately.

Administrative Rule Changes, 1961–1987

As in the case of rule birth data, we estimate a set of nested models, entering different sets of covariates incrementally. Comparisons among nested models allow us to assess the distinctive contribution of a specific set of covariates of theoretical interest. Table 6.1 shows the maximum likelihood estimates from six nested models of administrative rule changes (revisions plus suspensions). This set of analyses is based on the histories of administrative rules from 1961 to 1987. There were 659 rule changes observed during this period.

Rule History. Model 1 (M1) includes two variables: the number of previous revisions of the rule, and rule age at the time of last revision. These two variables measure the history of a particular rule. The number of previous revisions captures the plasticity of the rule, its past record of modification. Rule age at the time of last revision can be seen as a proxy for how long the rule has existed in the rule system. The proxy mitigates some statistical problems associated with using contemporaneous rule age. At the same time, rule age at the time of last revision has an important substantive interpretation. It reflects the knowledge captured by the rule, knowledge that existed at the time of the last revision. Thus it can be seen as measuring the learning content of a rule.

The estimated parameter for rule age at the time of last revision is negative and significant. The estimated parameter for the number of previous revisions is positive and significant. That is, the rate of rule change decreases with rule age at the time of last previous revision and increases with the number of prior revisions. These results are maintained throughout subsequent models. Clearly, the rate of rule change depends on the prior history of the rule, independent of other organizational processes considered in these models. Past revisions increase the hazard of subsequent change, and increases in rule age at the time of last revision decrease the hazard. Thus each revision of a rule

TABLE 6.1

Estimated coefficients for six nested models of administrative rule changes, 1961–87

	M1	M2	M3	M4	M5	M6
Constant	-1.435***	4.535***	4.878***	5.908***	6.180***	5.011***
	(0.056)	(0.602)	(0.855)	(1.341)	(1.539)	(1.690)
Rule age	-0.112***	-0.045***	-0.045***	-0.045***	0.047***	-0.036**
	(0.014)	(0.017)	(0.017)	(0.017)	(0.017)	(0.017)
Number of previous changes	0.149***	0.115***	0.113***	0.113***	0.110***	0.128***
	(0.021)	(0.024)	(0.024)	(0.024)	(0.025)	(0.024)
Rule regime age		-0.073***	-0.076***	-0.085***	-0.087***	-0.079***
		(0.008)	(0.010)	(0.013)	(0.014)	(0.016)
General organizational rules		0.091	0.100	0.110	-0.150	0.382**
		(0.142)	(0.143)	(0.144)	(0.154)	(0.166)
Accounting rules		-0.151	-0.149	-0.155	-0.353***	0.137
		(0.127)	(0.127)	(0.127)	(0.134)	(0.146)
Procurement rules		-0.110	-0.110	-0.115	-0.431***	0.338*
		(0.141)	(0.141)	(0.141)	(0.159)	(0.176)
Service and external property rules		-0.333***	-0.330***	-0.339***	-0.749***	0.206
		(0.125)	(0.125)	(0.125)	(0.155)	(0.186)
Change in number of programs (log)			-0.043	1.414	1.682	-0.412
			(1.138)	(1.248)	(1.275)	(1.365)
Change in number of students (log)			-0.904	-1.500	-2.904	1.032
			(3.170)	(3.693)	(4.360)	(4.391)
Change in number of faculty (log)			-0.768	0.176	1.365	-2.830
			(2.073)	(2.103)	(2.242)	(2.603)
Percent government funding (wt. avg.)				-3.461	-2.559	-4.394*
				(2.134)	(2.231)	(2.299)
Number of higher educ. laws (wt. avg.)				0.154***	0.151***	0.081
				(0.050)	(0.052)	(0.054)
Rule changes, same area, t-1					-0.065***	-0.053***
					(0.015)	(0.015)
Rule changes, other areas, t-1					0.005	0.008
					(0.006)	(0.006)
Rule changes, Senate rules, t-1					0.006	0.007
					(0.010)	(0.011)
Rule changes, same area, t						0.121***
						(0.011)
Rule changes, other areas, t						0.000
						(0.007)
Rule changes, Senate rules, t						-0.005
						(0.010)
Log likelihood	-2196.114	-2133.580	-2133.408	-2128.461	-2117.393	-2059.061
LR–chi-square	74.886***	125.069***	0.345	9.892***	22.137***	116.664***
d.f.	2	5	3	2	3	3

NOTE: The LR–chi-square statistic gives the improvement of fit of a given model (M_i) over the preceding model (M_{i-1}). For Model 1 the LR–chi-square statistic gives the improvement of the fit of Model 1 over a model which includes only the intercept. *=p<0.1; **=p<0.05; ***=p<0.01.

produces contradictory effects on the likelihood of future changes, a negative effect associated with the increased age at the time of the revision and a positive effect associated with plasticity.

Rule Regime History and Area Differences. Model 2 (M2) of Table 6.1 adds rule regime age, that is, the number of years (at the beginning of the spell) since 1961. The estimated parameter is negative and highly significant. It continues to be negative and highly significant in subsequent models. That is, the rate of rule change declines as the rule regime matures. The model also adds dummy covariates that divide the sample of rules into four subsamples defined by the subject matter of the rules. In this model and subsequent ones there is indication of some heterogeneity among the various subsamples, although the differences are not entirely consistent in direction or magnitude over all models.

Organizational Structure. Model 3 (M3) of Table 6.1 adds covariates reflecting changes in the size and complexity of the university. These structural dimensions are insignificant here and in all subsequent models. These findings are similar to those in the analyses of rule birth, indicating that the link between organizational structure and modifications in the rule system (both births and changes) is either weak or so complex that it is not well captured with the kinds of covariates and models we use. For example, it is possible that structure affects rule changes with considerable and variable lags, or that the effects of structural growth are captured in the intercept terms which represent a constant baseline of changes for each rule area.

Environmental Changes. Model 4 (M4) adds two covariates reflecting the involvement of the political and legal system with the university. The parameter for the three-year moving average of the federal government share of all higher education funding is negative but not significant. It becomes marginally significant in Model 6. The parameter for the three-year moving average of the number of federal laws enacted in the area of higher education is positive and highly significant, although it loses significance in Model 6. It appears that both governmental intervention variables have some effects on the rate of rule change, but they are confounded with the contemporaneous rule activity variables introduced in Model 6.

Rule Ecology. An individual organizational rule does not change in isolation from the rest of a rule system. Rather, any particular rule is connected with other rules and rule changes. Thus we expect that rule changes at one time and in one part of the rule system affect changes at other times and places. Model 5 considers these effects with one-year lags. The results indicate that the number of changes in the same subarea of administrative rules in the previous year affects the change rate. Its parameter estimate is highly significant and negative. Rule change activity in a particular domain in one year reduces activity in that domain in the following year. On the other hand, neither the number of changes of administrative rules in other areas in the previous year nor the number of changes in academic rules during the previous year has any significant effect on administrative rule change.

Model 6 adds three contemporaneous measures of the rule ecology. Contemporaneous changes of administrative rules in the same area have a strong, positive effect on the rate of administrative rule change. Contemporaneous changes of administrative rules in other administrative rule areas, as well as in the academic rule area, have no statistically significant effect on the rate of administrative rule change.[4] Thus rule change activities appear to be decoupled across areas. Among rules within the same area, on the other hand, there is evidence for a strong contagion (positive) effect in the same year and a strong competitive (negative) effect from one year to the next.

In general, most of the results of Models 1 through 5 are sustained as additional variables are added in Model 6. In particular, the negative effects of rule age at last revision, rule regime age, and last year's changes in the same area are maintained, as are the positive effects of the number of previous revisions of the rule and contemporaneous changes in other rules in the same area. The positive significant effect of the number of laws dealing with higher education is found in Models 4 and 5 but not in Model 6. For the sets of the covariates as a whole, we find that, except for the three variables measuring changes in organizational structure, all other sets of covariates—those measuring rule histories, rule regime age, governmental intervention, and rule ecology—significantly improve the model fit.

Academic Rule Changes, 1891–1987

Table 6.2 reports the maximum likelihood estimates of six nested models of academic rule changes.

Rule History. Model 1 includes only the intercept and the two variables measuring the prior history of the rules: the age of the specific rule at the time of the most recent revision event and the number of prior revisions experi-

TABLE 6.2

Estimated coefficients for six nested models of
academic rule changes, 1891–1987

	M1	M2	M3	M4	M5	M6
Constant	-2.394***	-1.475***	-1.450***	-1.363***	-1.484***	-2.301***
	(0.046)	(0.099)	(0.100)	(0.123)	(0.138)	(0.167)
Rule age	-0.015***	-0.012***	-0.012***	-0.012***	-0.012***	-0.011***
	(0.003)	(0.004)	(0.004)	(0.004)	(0.004)	(0.004)
Number of previous changes	0.117***	0.093***	0.093***	0.094***	0.094***	0.088***
	(0.012)	(0.013)	(0.013)	(0.013)	(0.013)	(0.012)
Acad. Council regime age		-0.012***	-0.011***	-0.016***	-0.017***	-0.021***
		(0.002)	(0.002)	(0.004)	(0.005)	(0.005)
Faculty Senate regime age		-0.095***	-0.099***	-0.084***	-0.086***	-0.041*
		(0.014)	(0.014)	(0.018)	(0.020)	(0.021)
Faculty Senate regime		0.970***	0.969***	0.816***	0.905***	0.407*
		(0.159)	(0.160)	(0.188)	(0.215)	(0.140)
Area (faculty = 1)		-0.930***	-0.928***	-0.927***	-0.614***	-0.131
		(0.111)	(0.111)	(0.111)	(0.150)	(0.178)
Change in number of programs (log)			-1.219*	-1.049	-1.086	0.088
			(0.707)	(0.716)	(0.707)	(0.710)
Change in number of faculty (log)			-1.023	-1.107	-1.409**	-0.942
			(0.682)	(0.680)	(0.697)	(0.759)
Change in number of students (log)			-0.203	-0.277	-0.326	-0.636*
			(0.308)	(0.308)	(0.314)	(0.357)
Percent government funding (wt. avg.)				0.747	0.971	1.962*
				(1.081)	(1.102)	(1.160)
Number of higher educ. laws (wt. avg.)				0.063	0.067	0.092*
				(0.056)	(0.056)	(0.055)
Rule change, same area, t-1					0.026**	0.0004
					(0.011)	(0.012)
Rule change, other area, t-1					-0.041**	-0.010
					(0.019)	(0.020)
Rule change, same area, t						0.132***
						(0.010)
Rule change, other area, t						-0.005
						(0.020)
Log likelihood	-2276.2	-2148.4	-2145.4	-2144.3	-2139.1	-2054.2
LR–chi-square	109.82***	255.41***	6.17*	2.18	10.26***	169.96***
d.f.	2	6	9	11	13	15
Number of events	726	726	726	726	726	726

NOTE: The LR–chi-square statistic gives the improvement of fit of a given model (M_i) over the preceding model (M_{i-1}). For Model 1 the LR–chi-square statistic gives the improvement of the fit of Model 1 over a model which includes only the intercept. *=p<0.1; **=p<0.05; ***=p<0.01.

enced by that rule. Model 1 reveals that a rule's age at the time of its last revision significantly decreases the rate of rule change, and the number of prior revisions significantly increases the rate. Compared with a baseline model with no covariates, the two rule history variables significantly increase the fit of the model. These results are consistent in both their direction and their significance with the results observed in the administrative area.

Rule Regime History and Area Differences. Rule-making processes in the academic area changed in a major way in 1968 when primary rule-making authority was shifted from the Academic Council to the Faculty Senate. We ask whether the regime changes (together with changes in rule-making agents, processes, and frequencies) affected the rate of rule change. Model 2 considers the effect of the two rule regimes. We include the ages of the rule regimes in this model. Academic Council regime age is the length of the period between 1891 and the beginning of the spell, and Faculty Senate regime age is the length of the period between 1968 and the beginning of the spell. We also include a dummy variable allowing the baseline intercept for the second regime to have a level different from that of the first, and a second dummy variable indicating whether the rule is in the faculty (coded as 1) or the student area.

All four parameter estimates are significant (and remain significant in most subsequent models). The parameters for the two regime age variables are negative, indicating that the rate of rule change decreases with the ages of both rule regimes. The decline is much stronger for the Faculty Senate regime. The positive parameter for the Faculty Senate regime intercept indicates that the overall rate of rule change increased sharply after the start of the Faculty Senate regime. This result is identical to the patterns found for rule births, where the rate declined on a moderate slope over the time of the Academic Council regime, jumped up when the Faculty Senate regime was initiated, and declined sharply thereafter (see Figure 4.3). There is also clear indication that the rate of rule change in the faculty area is significantly lower than that in the student area (the omitted category). The area effect in the last model is weakened because it is captured by the contemporaneous effects of rule ecology. Overall, the rule regime and rule area variables significantly improve the model fit.

Organizational Structure. Model 3 introduces the three variables on organizational structure. Only changes in the number of programs has a (marginally) significant effect (which disappears in subsequent models). Thus, overall, changes in organizational structure with respect to both size and complexity have no systematic or significant effects on rule changes in either the administrative or the academic areas.

Environmental Changes. Model 4 adds the two variables measuring governmental involvement. Adding these two variables does not improve the model significantly. However, both the number of laws concerning higher education and the proportion of higher education funding contributed by the federal government show marginally significant and positive effects in Model 6. That is, there is some evidence that rule changes are in part responsive to increasing intervention of government and legal systems into the higher education sector. These influences, as measured in our model, are not striking.

Rule Ecology. Model 5 adds two lagged measures of the rule ecology. The first variable is the number of changes in the same subarea of academic rules in the previous year. The second variable is the number of changes in the other subarea of academic rules in the previous year.[5] Adding this set of the covariates improves the fit of the model. Rule changes in the same area in the previous year have a significant contagious (positive) effect on the rate. Rule changes in the other area in the previous year, on the other hand, have a significant competitive (negative) effect on the rate. Both of these effects differ from those found in administrative rules. Both disappear in Model 6 (when contemporaneous changes are added).

Model 6 adds two contemporaneous measures of the rule ecology. Contemporaneous changes of academic rules in the same area have a strong, positive effect on the rate of academic rule change. Contemporaneous changes of academic rules in the other area have no statistically significant effect on the rate of administrative rule change. Including the current rule events in Model 6 leads to improvement in the fit of the model. These findings are consistent with the patterns in the administrative areas. Rule changes within the same area are highly contagious within a given year. On the other hand, rules across areas are decoupled. There are no observable contagion effects across areas or across time.

Regime Effects. The previous analyses indicated that there are significant differences between the two rule regimes in the baselines and the regime age dependencies of rates of rule change. To examine if the processes of rule change also differ across these two regimes, separate models have been estimated for academic rule changes during each of the two rule regimes—the first regime from 1891 to 1967 and the second regime from 1968 to 1987. The results are not reported here in detail here but can be summarized: the two rule regimes appear to differ in their aggregate levels of rule activity but to exhibit similar structures of factors contributing to variations from their individual bases. The estimates for each of the rule regimes are quite consistent, both in direction and magnitude, with the estimates for the whole period (as reported in Table 6.2). Rule histories, the age of rule regime, and rule activities in the previous and current years all improve the fit of the model significantly in both regimes. The only conspicuous exceptions are that the effect of the share of funding that comes from the federal government is significant and positive during the first rule regime but insignificant in the second rule regime, and the covariates measuring organizational structure improve the fit only in the second rule regime.

EXPLORING EFFECTS OF ATTENTION, HISTORICAL
CONTEXTS, AND SUBPOPULATIONS OF RULES
ON ACADEMIC RULE CHANGE

As we did in the analysis of rule births, we explore how organizational attention, specific historical contexts, and rule subpopulations affect rule changes. Because the attention variables are available only for the academic rule-making process, we restrict the analysis to that rule population.

Analyses

We report two sets of analyses. The first analysis is a comparison between the determinants of rule changes in the faculty and in the student area. The second analysis is an examination of patterns of rule changes across four historical periods. Our intent is to explore the existence and causes of differences between the two rule sectors and across historical periods in the evolution of organizational rules.

Our primary focus is on the role of organizational attention. Organizational attention is measured by the annual number of Academic Council or Faculty Senate agenda items related to student or faculty rules, and the number of items unrelated to such rules. To examine the role of historical context, we focused on the four-period scheme as defined in Chapter 5: 1889–1915; 1916–1945; 1946–1965; and 1966–1987. Other covariates are the same as used in the previous model estimations. Similar to our earlier analysis, we used an exponential event history model in the estimation.

Results

We first compare the determinants of the rate of rule changes across the faculty and the student areas. The results are shown in Table 6.3. In the first model, all academic rules are included in the analysis. The second and the third models analyze changes in the student and faculty areas separately, treating them as distinct populations. In addition to the set of organizational attention (agenda) variables, we also include a set of dummy variables of historical periods to assess nonlinear changes in the rate of change across time. Overall, this alternative analysis confirms the major findings of the earlier one.

Organizational Attention. We included rule-related agenda and rule-unrelated agenda in the same year (t) and the previous year ($t\text{-}1$) to examine the effect of organizational attention on the rate of rule change. Overall, attention allocation in the previous year has no systematic and significant effect on the rate of rule change, as indicated by the nonsignificant effects of the agenda items at $t\text{-}1$. An exception is the marginally significant and negative effect of lagged rule-related agenda in the faculty area. The weak effects of lagged agenda variables indicate that organizational attention across years is well compartmentalized and decoupled across consecutive years.

In contrast, concurrent agenda variables have strong effects on the rate of rule change. Especially the allocation of attention to rule-related agenda items has significant and positive effects on rule change in the overall population and within subpopulations. That is, large numbers of faculty rule-related agenda items in a given year are associated with high rates of change in faculty rules and large numbers of student rule-related agenda items are associated with high rates of change in student rules. Cross-subpopulation effects are absent, however, as allocation of attention to rule-related items in one area has no significant effect on the rate of change in the other area. Organizational attention in one area appears to be decoupled from attention in other areas. Allocation of attention to rule-unrelated items has comparatively weak effects on the rate of rule change. Only the attention to agenda items unrelated to student rule making shows any effects, moderately impeding student rule changes and stimulating faculty rule changes.

These effects are not surprising, but they provide some elaboration of key theoretical ideas. First, it seems clear that the allocation of attention matters. Formalized attention of decision makers to rules in a given area is associated with rule change activities in the same rule area, suggesting that rule change

154

TABLE 6.3
Estimated coefficients for academic rule changes,
1891–1987, by subpopulations

	Overall	Student	Faculty
Constant	-2.449***	-2.294***	-2.900***
	(0.121)	(0.129)	(0.355)
Rule age	-0.007**	-0.012***	-0.034***
	(0.003)	(0.004)	(0.009)
Number of previous changes	0.091***	0.075***	0.294***
	(0.012)	(0.013)	(0.036)
Change in number of programs (log)	-0.613	-0.368	-3.548
	(0.760)	(0.786)	(2.653)
Change in number of faculty (log)	-1.329*	-1.138	-3.323
	(0.768)	(0.818)	(2.267)
Change in number of students (log)	0.043	0.072	-2..039
	(0.342)	(0.358)	(1.284)
Percent government funding (wt. avg.)	1.613	1.363	5.969
	(1.404)	(1.513)	(4.157)
Number of higher educ. laws (wt. avg.)	0.007	0.051	-0.065
	(0.077)	(0.085)	(0.201)
Rule agenda, student area, t-1	0.009	0.011	0.002
	(0.008)	(0.009)	(0.025)
Rule agenda, faculty area, t-1	0.006	0.018	-0.063*
	(0.012)	(0.014)	(0.035)
Other agenda, student area, t-1	0.009	0.004	0.031
	(0.010)	(0.013)	(0.020)
Other agenda, faculty area, t-1	-0.005	-0.008	0.012
	(0.007)	(0.008)	(0.012)
Rule agenda, student area, t	0.066***	0.074***	0.026
	(0.007)	(0.008)	(0.023)
Rule agenda, faculty area, t	0.028**	-0.007	0.122***
	(0.012)	(0.014)	(0.028)
Other agenda, student area, t	-0.016	-0.024	0.051**
	(0.011)	(0.013)	(0.025)
Other agenda, faculty area, t	0.001	0.002	0.010
	(0.007)	(0.009)	(0.015)
Period 2 (1916–45)	-0.467***	-0.388***	-1.294***
	(0.133)	(0.143)	(0.416)
Period 3 (1946–65)	-0.444*	-0.157	-2.554***
	(0.273)	(0.303)	(0.831)
Period 4 (1966–87)	-0.778***	-0.465	-0.969
	(0.264)	(0.304)	(0.766)
Log likelihood	2155.32	1684.16	3704.68
LR–chi-square	351.50***	192.07***	175.46***
d.f.	18	18	18
Number of events	726	615	111

NOTE: All models are event history regression models. LR–chi-square tests of improvement of fit over model with intercept only. *=p<0.1; **=p<0.05; ***=p<0.01.

processes involve a substantial amount of formal recognition of rule problems by rule-making bodies. This strengthens notions both of rule change as stemming from explicit organizational attention to problems and of rule change processes as formally celebrated rituals.

Second, rule domains appear to be relatively autonomous. The effects of attention are strong within areas and virtually nil across areas. Similarly, the effects of rule changes on other rule changes are strong within areas and absent across areas. To some degree, this is the result of differences in distance among rules. Rules in the same area are closer to each other in terms of thematic relatedness. Changes of some rules in an area are likely to require changes of related rules in the same area—an instance of functional interdependence. But rules in the same area are also closer to each other in terms of rule change processes—an instance of procedural interdependence. Changes in rules involve allocation of attention to the rules by rule makers. Changing some rules of an area apparently increases the readiness of members of the rule-making body to change other rules. This supports a general notion of attention partitioning. Within rule-making bodies, attention to a particular rule spreads to related rules within the jurisdiction of the rule-making body, while it does not spill over to other bodies. In this way, an organizational division of labor between different rule-making bodies partitions organizational attention into partially independent subsystems.

Third, rule changes are independent across different time periods, suggesting that rule change processes are procedurally independent over time. Although rule change processes do have temporal extension, it is likely that they are too brief to extend over several time periods and thus lack the ability to influence other rule change processes at other times—an instance of diachronic procedural independence. It is also possible that most implications of rule changes for other rules show up quickly or are anticipated by participants soon enough, resulting in contemporaneous adjustments of the affected rules, and less in delayed adjustments—an instance of functional diachronic independence of rule changes.

Thus organizational attention on rules appears to be focused, rather than diffuse. Rule changes within one area during one time period increase the likelihood of rule changes for other rules in that area during that time period, but there are few contagion effects that extend beyond the immediate sector and time. The structures of the rule-making bodies—Academic Council and Faculty Senate—contribute strongly to this focus. During the period covered by the data, they were organized into area-based attention agents, such as a committee for undergraduate studies, a committee for faculty affairs, and so forth. The presence of these attention agents and the routinization of organizational attention focused attention and localized the contagion of rule change in time and space.

Subpopulations of Rules. Columns 2 and 3 of Table 6.3 show the coefficients for rule changes in the faculty and the student area separately. The effects are fairly consistent across areas. For the most part, the differences are differences in the magnitudes of effects, rather than in their sources. In both areas, increases in the age of a rule at the time of its last previous revision decreases the rate of current revision, while the cumulative number of prior revisions increases the rate. Magnitudes of effects vary somewhat, e.g., prior revisions have a stronger effect in the faculty area. Structural variables and environmental variables have consistently weak effects in both populations. In both populations, the rate of revision declined over historical periods, although the decline is not significant in period 3 of the student rules. In general, rules in both areas show similar patterns despite the differences in their respective technologies and environments.

Historical Contexts. The period variables in Table 6.3 indicate that there is considerable variation over the historical periods, both in the overall rate of rule change and in area-specific rates. This suggests that the mechanisms affecting rule births and changes may be sensitive to particular historical periods. Period variables by themselves, however, do not do a good job of capturing the underlying mechanisms of historical change (Isaac and Griffin 1989). In order to explore these issues we estimated several models for different cohorts of rules and examined how the effects of covariates varied across the historical periods. We divided academic rule event data into the same four historical cohorts discussed in Chapter 5. The periods are: 1889–1915; 1916–1945; 1946–1965; and 1966–1987. As discussed in Chapter 5, these periods conform to a plausible qualitative disaggregation of Stanford history. We estimated a set of models for each period similar to those reported in Table 6.3, except that in this case the covariates of periods were dropped. Since a preliminary analysis of agenda effects showed no differences between the impact of agenda items in the student and faculty areas, we aggregated the two types of agenda for model parsimony in this analysis.

TABLE 6.4

Estimated coefficients for academic rule change
during four historical periods

	1891–1915	1916–1945	1946–1965	1966–1987
Constant	-1.950***	-2.789***	-2.941**	-4.877***
	(0.249)	(0.300)	(1.264)	(0.789)
Rule age	0.006	-0.016*	-0.007	-0.006
	(0.026)	(0.008)	(0.007)	(0.005)
Number of previous changes	0.115***	0.117***	0.068***	0.044*
	(0.038)	(0.021)	(0.025)	(0.025)
Change in number of programs (log)	-5.864***	0.693	0.269	-2.037
	(1.796)	(1.304)	(1.743)	(2.444)
Change in number of faculty (log)	-1.124	0.518	1.394	—ᵃ
	(1.126)	(2.051)	(3.927)	
Change in number of students (log)	5.537***	-0.124	0.245	—ᵃ
	(1.632)	(0.547)	(1.045)	
Percent government funding (wt. avg.)	—	-1.443	1.797	6.165*
		(2.982)	(3.119)	(3.414)
Number of higher educ. laws (wt. avg.)	—	0.054	-0.093	0.069
		(1.747)	(0.190)	(0.125)
Rule agenda, t-1	-0.055**	0.009	-0.004	-0.004
	(0.022)	(0.015)	(0.022)	(0.011)
Other agenda, t-1	0.075*	-0.006	-0.014	0.009
	(0.043)	(0.026)	(0.022)	(0.006)
Rule agenda, t	0.020	0.065***	0.071***	0.031***
	(0.018)	(0.013)	(0.020)	(0.011)
Other agenda, t	-0.041	0.008	0.003	0.002
	(0.035)	(0.020)	(0.032)	(0.007)
Area (faculty = 1)	-0.129	-1.077***	-2.156***	-0.844***
	(0.280)	(0.221)	(0.461)	(0.157)
Log likelihood	-326.55	-710.80	-359.09	-686.76
LR–chi-square	46.4***	131.9***	91.0***	124.5***
d.f.	10	12	12	10
Number of events	131	265	126	204

NOTE: All models are event history regression models. The four periods are estimated separately.
LR–chi-square tests improvement of fit over model with intercept only. O.S.C., p. 41 in tables.
ᵃ This category is not estimated because of multicollinearity problems.

Table 6.4 reports the coefficient estimates for the four periods. Splitting
data into the four smaller cohorts yields some noticeable variations in the parameter estimates across periods. The intercepts across the four periods indicate an overall declining trend of rule change rate over the historical periods,
net of the effects of the covariates included in the models. This finding is consistent with observations drawn from earlier analyses. Rule age at the time of
last revision is insignificant in most historical periods. We believe that this re-

sult is mainly an artifact of treating rules in the four periods as distinctive populations. Rule age at last revision is updated only at revision events, which occur relatively infrequently. When the whole history is divided into periods, the measurement of rule history by rule age at last revision is attenuated—only those records that fall within a specific period are included in the analysis for that period. It is possible that the proportion of rules that are never revised increases. This may cause the reduction of the variance of rule age at last revision within some periods, which results, in turn, in reduced statistical power and thus weaker effects. The cumulative number of previous rule revisions has positive effects in all periods, although the significance levels vary.

Changes in organizational size and complexity appear to be relatively unimportant to rule change. Organizational structure, as measured by academic programs and the sizes of the faculty and students, has significant effects in the first period, but its contribution to the rate of rule change becomes insignificant in subsequent periods. The effects of environmental changes—measured by governmental funding and legislative acts—are even less pronounced. The only marginally significant coefficient (a positive one) is shown by governmental funding in the last period.

The effects of organizational attention as measured by agenda distribution show similar patterns as the findings before: the rate of rule change is largely related to organizational attention to rule-making activities in the current year (rule-related agenda at t). In most cases, the rate is decoupled from attention to rule-unrelated items and from the distribution of attention in the previous year.

Overall. The effects displayed in Table 6.3 are generally consistent with the results of Table 6.2, discussed above. For example, the effects of the period variables in Table 6.3 are roughly consistent with the earlier finding of a negative effect of regime age. The effects of rule history on rule changes within areas are highly significant and consistent with the previous findings. Increases in rule age at the time of last revision significantly decrease the rate of change, while the cumulative number of rule revisions increases the rate of change. Attention distribution has highly consistent effects in models of rule change in the whole population, within areas, and within historical time periods. Baseline rates of rule change vary noticeably across subpopulations and historical periods. Variations in the strength of effects across historical time periods suggest that underlying mechanisms have fluctuated somewhat over historical periods, although most effects are markedly stable across models of rule change in subpopulations and (with some exceptions) historical periods.

Rule Changes in Summary

Structural and environmental effects on rule changes exist, but they tend to be relatively weak and relatively inconsistent. Structural changes of the university, for the most part, play little role in determining the rate of rule change. The number of legislative acts concerning education passed by the federal government has a positive effect on the rate of rule change of administrative rules (but not academic rules).

Attention variables give a somewhat more complicated picture. There are clear symptoms of the contemporaneous contagion of attention for both administrative and academic rules, only a few signs of contemporaneous attention competition. The rate of change in other rules in the same area of rules in the same year has a positive effect on the rate of change in the focus rule. Explicit attention (in terms of agenda items) in a particular area of academic rules increases the rate of change in that area.

By far the more consistent and conspicuous effects stem from rule histories. The effects of their histories on rule changes are robust across different models, different areas, and different historical periods. The longer a rule regime endures and the later a specific rule has been revised, the less the likelihood of rule change. The more a particular rule has been revised in the past, the greater the likelihood of its being revised again. These effects are strong, consistent, and cumulative. Variations in their magnitudes across models seem more likely to reflect differences in model specifications than differences in the underlying phenomena.

The patterns of rule changes reported here reveal some dynamics that contrast with the dynamics of rule births inferred from the patterns of rule births in Chapter 5. The rate of rule birth seems to be more sensitive than the rate of rule change to historical context. Organizational attention to rule birth events also seems to be more interrelated across areas than it is in the case of rule changes, as indicated by the significant effect of rule agenda in the faculty area on rule birth in the student areas. It appears that organizations create rules in response to problems produced by such things as environmental complexity, external shocks, and changes in their constituencies. As organizations absorb those problems into rules, rule production slows. On the other hand, once rules are created they become strongly regulated by an internal dynamic. The rate of rule change decreases with a rule's age at the time of last revision and increases with the number of prior revisions. Rule births and rule changes create a rule system, but they respond to somewhat different pressures and in somewhat different ways.

SEVEN

Regularities in Rule Dynamics

Our studies indicate that organizational rule histories have regularities that might not be obvious either from focusing on increases in organizational size or complexity, or from assuming an efficient historical match between rules and their environments, or from the usual telling of detailed contextual stories about rule adoption. The regularities we observe can be grouped within two sets of observations. First, rule sets are the cumulated residue left by a history of dealing with political and technical problems. Rules record solutions to old problems and thus become the basis for organizational competence in new ones. Second, rules are the result of an internal dynamic within a collection of rules. There is learning around rules, learning that changes the vulnerability of rules. Rules are located in an ecology of rules, and changes in any particular rule lead to subsequent changes in the same or other rules.

The two sources of rule development are far from independent. Changes in the external environment stimulate internal complications and disagreements, and problems inside an organization stimulate external pressures. The orchestration of rule change often confounds any simple causal order. Nevertheless, the distinction may have some value as a basis for organizing observations drawn from these quantitative studies of rule production. And it may illuminate some issues in the organizations literature on organizational learning and change, issues connected to ideas of structural inertia (Hannan and Freeman 1984; Amburgey, Kelly, and Barnett 1993), and to the relation between efficiency and adaptability (March 1991, 1994b; Weick 1982).

Rules as Residue of Problem Solving

In part, rules are solutions to problems and pressures. Organizations adapt to their environments by adopting rules that solve problems and respond to the pressures of critical constituents and participants. As those pressures and problems change, rules change. However, solutions (rules) are likely to endure after the problems have disappeared and the pressures have waned. As a result, the collection of rules found at any particular time does not reflect the problems and pressures of that time alone. It is a cumulated residue left by a history of problem solving and responding to pressures on the organization. To the degree that the residue fits the environmental problems and pressures of subsequent times, the organization survives, but the sporadic and indeterminate nature of those problems and pressures makes the array of rules better understood as a collection of traces of history than as a precise matching to current conditions.

In the present studies, we have considered the environmental creation of organizational problems and pressures in two ways: first, by looking at differences among historical periods involving different kinds of political, social, and economic issues; and second, by relating changes to specific aggregate measures of governmental involvement in higher education.

EFFECTS OF HISTORICAL CONTEXTS

Our analytical strategy of focusing on the entire history of an organizational rule system, the longitudinal data we collected, and the associated models help us identify causal connections among variables that vary over time. One important set of variables includes those that reflect environmental pressures on rule systems. This impact of the social, economic, and political environments on social institutions is mediated by the rationing of scarce attention. The social definition of institutional problems and mobilization of attention to them are subject to the difficulties of attending to everything at once. Consequently, external attention to problems in particular institutions (e.g., families, business firms, educational institutions) tends to focus on a few institutions at a time, and the amount of general social and political attention to any specific major institution tends to vary from one historical period to another.

When an institution, such as a single university or a system of higher education, becomes normatively and economically more central to the society in which it is embedded, attention to the institution is mobilized. The mobilization is reflected in media coverage, governmental policies, public opinion, and judicial intervention. When an institution becomes less central, the attention wanes. Since these drifts in centrality tend to be slow, there are long cycles of attention and inattention (Downs 1972). Within the long cycles, there tend to be shorter local cycles of fadlike attention. The focus of attention in one part of the social and political system tends to spread to other parts (Hilgartner and Bosk 1988). Similar fashions in attention affect the mass media and social consciousness. As a result, short-term attention pulses are added to the longer-run cycles.

The combination of short and long cycles of attention affects particular rule systems (e.g., those of universities) by producing variation in external pressures across historical periods. Insofar as we could, we have measured environmental pressures directly; but both the measured forms of pressure and those that are not measured tend to cluster within historical periods. The clustering makes it difficult to disaggregate period effects into their distinctive dimensions of pressures. We have considered two overlapping definitions of natural historical periods for Stanford University. The first divides both administrative and academic rule histories into what we have called rule regimes. In the case of the administrative rules, we identified only one rule regime. In the case of academic rules, we identified two. The second definition of historical periods divides the whole academic rule history at Stanford into four separate historical periods.

Rule Regimes

Historical contexts are associated with rule regimes. By a rule regime, we mean the system by which rules are created, revised, and maintained, as well as the rule-making agents and processes. Major reconstitutions of rule regimes occur infrequently. They are not predictable within the present framework but can be observed as distinct historical events. We have used historical descriptions of the rule systems at Stanford to establish the periods associated with particular rule regimes. In the case of administrative rules, the period studied (1961–1987) is viewed as a single rule regime. It begins with the establishment of the *Administrative Guide* and the procedures for modifying it. In the case of academic rules, the period studied (1891–1987) is divided into two rule regimes with 1968 as the first year in the second regime. The first regime begins with the founding of the university. The second regime begins with the establishment of the Faculty Senate and the rule-making procedures connected to it. The shift is associated with major changes in American universities in the late 1960s and early 1970s. The historical processes that established these rule regimes are not studied directly.

Changes in rule regimes make a difference. When, in 1968, the Academic Council was replaced as the principal academic rule-making body by the Faculty Senate, academic rule making intensified and was put on a new basis (including a shift of focus from student issues toward faculty issues). At the same time, old rules were abolished at an unprecedented level. In fact, the rate of academic rule suspension tripled during the first two decades of the Faculty Senate regime. The fact that the shift in rule-making bodies had such strong influence on rule suspension and rule production at this university signals how powerful large-scale interventions can be for the development of bureaucratic systems.

Distinguishing the effects of a new rule regime from the effects of the historical setting that led to its creation is difficult within the context of this study, but we believe the effects are substantial. Newly constituted rule regimes reflect changed rule environments. They also introduce new procedures for making and changing rules. Consequently, when a rule regime is reconstituted, two things happen: first, the base rates of rule births and rule changes are altered. When a new regime is created, there is a flurry of rule making. It seems likely that this flurry stems both from the energy of newness and from the mixture of external pressures and internal problems that have stimulated regime change.

In the present case, the second academic rule regime has a substantially higher rate of rule production and change than did the first one. The average annual number of academic rules created between 1891 and 1967 was 2.2; the comparable number for the period from 1968 to 1987 was 8.6. Second, the regime "clock" is reset. The age of a rule regime affects rules (see below), and that age is measured not from the start of the organization but from the date of transformation to a new regime. Perhaps more importantly, rule-making processes as well as the structure of organizational attention in the rule areas are being transformed along with shifts across rule regimes.

Although the effects of regime baselines and regime clocks reflect the impact of the current environment on the rule system, they also capture the interaction between past imprints on the rule system and current conditions. Changes in rule regimes involve shifts in internal political processes, changes in rule-making routines, and adjustment of perspectives regarding the appropriateness of old rules for the demands of the current environment. New rule regimes "discover" and emphasize new inconsistencies between old rules and current conditions, resulting in enhanced rates of rule making and rule changing. From that perspective, rule regimes act as organizational filters that emphasize specific kinds of fit between historical traces and current conditions.

Finally, it seems likely that "problems" are not simply given but are shaped by the existence of rules. The agents of problems are problem instigators—individuals and groups that gain reputations and other rewards for identifying and posing problems for and to institutional rule systems. Since the rewards are greater for discovering problems in domains for which there are few rules and modest experience, the accumulation of rules and experience reduces the attractiveness of a domain to problem instigators. The classical example is the deflection of legal inventors from domains where extensive legal experience exists to domains where it does not. Examples in recent years include the deflection of legal problem instigators from traditional domains of real property and human rights into areas of intellectual "property" and animal "rights." In this study, it is likely that new regimes attract problem instigators because they provide fresh arenas for status and power enhancement. As a regime ages and accumulates rules, problem opportunities diminish and the attractiveness of the regime for instigators declines, resulting in a reduced discovery of problems and less rule making.

Four Historical Periods

Historical contexts can also be associated with specific historical periods. In the present study, we have considered academic rule birth and change during four distinct historical periods: 1889–1915, 1916–1945, 1946–1965, and 1966–1987. These periods were defined by a consideration of standard histories of universities in general and of Stanford University in particular. For academic rules, the historical periods so defined refine somewhat the definition of context tied exclusively to rule regime. The first three periods divide what has been called above the Academic Council regime into three separate periods. The last period is largely coterminus with the Faculty Senate regime.

When academic rule birth and rule revision data are disaggregated into these separate periods and analyzed separately, some effects that are significant in the aggregate data become statistically insignificant, partly presumably because of reduction in sample size but also partly because some effects are specific to specific periods. In particular, it appears to be true that the basic rate of rule birth and revision and the impact of governmental interventions and organization structure variables are somewhat different in the final period from what they were earlier.

The pattern of changes in the rate of academic rule birth over historical periods is quite different from the pattern of changes in the rate of academic rule revision. The overall rate of academic rule births increased across historical periods, especially after World War II. In contrast, the rate of rule revision in the academic area decreased over the same historical periods. These results indicate that environmental changes, insofar as they are measured by period effects, have impacts on rule births that are different from their impacts on rule changes. Increasing governmental pressures and social movements forced the university to create new rules to comply with the environmental demands; on the other hand, once a rule was created, it tended to follow a different dynamic and to become stable over time, thereby forming a relatively invariant historical residue.

A related finding is that there are noticeable differences in period effects across subpopulations of academic rules. For instance, rules in the student area exhibit a higher birthrate after 1946, whereas faculty rules had a significantly higher birthrate only after 1966. With regard to rule changes, we find that the rate of change of faculty rules decreased more rapidly over time than did the rate of change of student rules, indicating, perhaps, that the former became more insulated from environmental changes. These findings caution that it would be simplistic to treat all rules as belonging to a homogeneous population. The dynamics associated with different kinds of rules and the processes that generate those dynamics result in different paths and rates of change.

These historical context effects, whether measured by regime or by the more detailed historical periods, cannot be ignored. They indicate that there may be a number of unmeasured features of the environment (as well as organizational processes in response to them) that affect the results and that those unmeasured features may be so tightly interlinked as to make an effort to untangle them an exercise in futility. Despite this complication, however, most of the key results of the study are maintained even when historical context effects are controlled in the statistical analysis.

EFFECTS OF GOVERNMENT ACTIONS

The connection between the reconstitution of rule regimes and the environmental context is ordinarily conspicuous. Other effects of external environments on rule histories are somewhat less transparent. They are buried in the details of responses to less dramatic exogenous pressures. We speculated that shorter run exogenous pressures on rules in American universities would be particularly likely to come from the federal government, which has expanded its involvement in higher education throughout the twentieth century.

The data show that the funding and legislative activities of the federal government have important effects on rule births and revisions. These effects are fairly general but not universal. We measured year-to-year changes in the proportion of governmental funding and in the number of legislative acts (three-year moving average). These measures capture organizational responses to *changes* in governmental intervention. We find that, in general, the rates of *academic* rule births are not sensitive to changes in funding. In mild contrast, there is some modest evidence that changes in the proportion of federal funding may have increased the rate of revision in the academic area since the mid-1960s. The rates of *administrative* rule births and revisions, on the other hand, are negatively (but not always significantly) associated with increases in the proportion of funding that comes from the federal government. The greater the increase in the proportion of higher education revenues coming from the federal government, the fewer the new administrative rules and the fewer the administrative rule revisions. The effects of federal pressures on rules may well depend on the involvement of the federal government in the funding of universities, but the creation of new administrative rules at Stanford is more associated with periods of declining funding than with periods of increasing funding. It appears to be the tightening of funds that focuses attention on administrative procedures.

Changes in the number of higher education laws at the federal level have somewhat more consistent and more directly interpretable effects. Changes in the number of laws generally affect the rate of rule births positively in both the administrative and the academic areas. The effects on rule revisions are less consistent and significant but usually in the same direction. Rule systems are shaped not only by grand reconstitutions when a rule regime changes but also by more modest, continuing pressures arising from their social and political environments.

RULES AND THE PROBLEM SPACE

Environmental problems and pressures do not translate directly into bursts of rule production. The effects are mediated by the relation between new problems and residues left by old ones, in particular by the capability of existing rules to absorb new problems. When new, unprecedented problems are made salient by environmental pressures, by the creation of new rule regimes, or when old problems are recycled by the suspension of old rules, opportunities for new rules increase. The problem space expands. New problems are available for solution, and new rules are forged to deal with them. When new rules are created, the problem space contracts until it is expanded again by new pressures. Bursts of new rules occur when new, unprecedented external pressures emerge.

Over time, rules accumulate. The population of rules grows through additions. By comparison, the elimination of rules plays a much smaller role; births considerably exceed suspensions. Rules are produced in response to problems emerging at specific times, and they are retained subsequently, even if the problems that led to their creation do not recur. In this way, the evolution of a population of rules appears to be somewhat like the development of a field of knowledge or a technology. The population of rules reflects cumulated capabilities developed over an extended history and thus tends to grow indefinitely, particularly if the organization has gone through several new challenges along the way. The growth of rules is not, however, exponential. Rules do not produce rules. Problems produce opportunities for rules. Rules and experience with them reduce those opportunities. As a result, as we note more fully below, the density of rules in a particular problem area is negatively related to the likelihood of the birth of a new rule.

The creative handling of problems through existing rules makes it unlikely that rules precisely match current conditions. When old rules are stretched to deal with new problems, pressures for new rule production are reduced, and the explicit match between current rules and current conditions is attenuated. As a result, predicting current rules from current environmental pressures is difficult. The difficulty becomes especially profound if old rules become taken for granted, or if competencies with old rules make it relatively easy for rule users to solve new problems through skillful application and reinterpretation of old rules. Whatever the combination of causes, the results indicate that written rules tend to survive after the conditions that led to their adoption change, resulting in a retention of historical residues in the rule system.

The Internal Dynamics of Rules

Organizational rule systems are products of their environments, but they are also products of their own internal processes. Rule births and changes are regulated by learning and ecological interactions internal to the organization. Rule histories and the resulting rule densities, as well as the internal diffusion of problem attention all affect the transformation of a population of rules. We consider the effects of three clusters of internal factors: first, the effects of a few organizational variables; second, the effects of rule histories; and third, the effects of rule ecologies.

EFFECTS OF ORGANIZATIONAL VARIABLES

Most discussions of bureaucracy associate rule birth and change with problems stemming either from the environment or from organizational properties, such as age, size, or complexity (for an overview, see Donaldson 1996). In this section, we consider the effect of such variables on the rates of rule birth and revision.

Size and Complexity

Numerous writers on organizations have speculated that variations in the size and complexity of an organization produce variations in the intensity of rule construction and elaboration. The twentieth-century history of universities in the United States has been a history of growth brought on by a sharply rising demand for education and research. The long-run increases in students, faculty, programs, and research commitments have led to considerable elaboration of university structure. The first-order correlations between the total number of students, total number of faculty, and total number of programs, on the one hand, and cumulated numbers of rule births or rule revisions are positive. Because the size and complexity variables are correlated strongly with simple time clocks represented by the age of a rule regime, leaving both kinds of variables in the analysis would introduce serious multicollinearity problems. Rule regime age by itself would capture most of the explanatory power of that variable plus the size and complexity variables. In order to avoid such problems, we have used the year-to-year changes in size and complexity, rather than their observed levels, in the present models. This focuses attention on relatively short-run changes.

The results do not support an expectation that short-run changes in size and complexity in the organization will lead to parallel changes in rule elaboration. Although we observe occasional significant effects, they are relatively uncommon, relatively small, and often inconsistent. Changes in the number of programs and faculty size do not translate into any consistent changes in the rate of rule births or rule revisions. Changes in the number of students sometimes shows a significant effect, but it is usually a negative effect. If anything, increases in students lead to decreases, rather than increases, in the rates of rule births and revisions. Nor does introducing size and complexity change variables reliably improve model fits as a whole.

Although they need to be tempered by awareness of the special features of the Stanford locale and the present analysis, these findings raise questions about conventional views that changes in organizational rules are connected primarily to managing organizational complexity. We find very few size and program effects in any of our models of rule birth and rule change. It appears possible that past discussions of this subject have confused size effects with cumulated baseline effects. Because size generally increases (at least in organizations that survive and are studied when they are large), it may appear that size causes rule production (that is, "bureaucratic formalization"). The results here suggest that this may be a spurious relation.

Rule Regime Age

We ask whether the rates of rule birth and revision are modified by the simple passage of time since the beginning of a rule regime. The maturation of a rule regime differs from the maturation of an individual rule discussed below. Rule maturation is measured by the age of a particular rule, whereas the maturation of rule regime is measured by the age of a particular system of rules and rule making. The two ideas of aging capture two different clocks in the history of rules and two different forms of maturation.

It was not clear, a priori, what we should have expected to find with respect to the effects of regime age. The effects might well have been positive. Presumably, rule agencies improve their capabilities at rule making and thus are more likely to find tinkering with rules a satisfying activity and will seek to do it. From such a perspective, we would expect an accelerating propensity to engage in rule making as a rule regime ages. On the other hand, the effects also might well have been negative. The most natural explanation for a decline in rule births and revisions with duration of a rule regime lies in the mutual adjustment of regimes and rules. As a rule regime ages, organizational agencies for creating and modifying rules find themselves increasingly comfortable with rules that exist, perhaps because they have been responsible for shaping them already in the past.

The empirical results are clear. In administrative as well as academic rules, both the rate of rule birth and the rate of rule revision decrease with the age of the rule regime. Whatever attractions rule making and revision may have because of increased organizational self-assurance at it, the organization does less of both. Rules become more stable the longer a rule regime endures. In this sense, the passage of time within a particular regime stabilizes rules. Relatively high rates of birth and revision are observed immediately after a rule regime change, followed by a gradual decline.

The age dependence of the Academic Council regime is much smaller than that of the Faculty Senate regime. The rate of academic rule birth declined slowly as the Academic Council rule regime aged. In 1968 (when the Faculty Senate regime began), a sharp increase in birthrate occurred. The effects of "youth" combined with a general augmentation of rule production and revision to produce a major "spike" of rule activity at the beginning of the regime. Subsequently, the rate declined and the rate of academic rule production returned to a level close to that of the earlier regime.

As we noted before, regime age captures the time trajectory of the rule system. The declining rates of rule birth and revision point to an important feature of structural inertia in organizations. It is a common observation that as an organization ages, it becomes more resistant to change. This phenomenon has been attributed to such things as the pursuit of bureaucratic interests, the development of linkages to dense networks and structures, and external pressures for reliability and accountability. Our analysis suggests that these phenomena, insofar as they are mediated through rules, are intertwined with elements of learning both by organizations that learn to use existing rules, and by external problem instigators who learn to shun domains that are already crowded with rules. These elements of learning contribute to the increasing stability of organizational rules as a rule regime matures.

It is hard to ignore such a consistent and strong result. The longer a regime endures, the lower the rates of rule birth and rule revision. Nevertheless, there are reasons for caution. Since our data provide only three cases of rule regimes, the idea of rule regime may be inadequately tested here. It could be argued that the creation of a new academic rule regime in 1968 and the flurry of rules at the same time were both a direct consequence of external forces. It is also possible that rule regime age coincides with other time trends in the history of the organization. For instance, it may coincide with the first-order time trend of an organizational structure or organizational institutionalization.

On a more general level, one might speculate that although regime age shows a reliable negative coefficient, it does not capture the real mechanism of maturation. Stinchcombe's original account of the liability of newness (Stinchcombe 1965, 148–49) rests on the difficulty of inventing and learning new roles, of developing trust, and of establishing ties to relevant external actors in the early stages of organizational existence. Although all of these difficulties might continue with age, they are ameliorated by formal rules. Suppose that regime age is actually a proxy for the elaboration of rules to deal with organizational problems. Then, regime age by itself would be less important than the density of rules in an organization domain. This speculation led us to explore the effects of density and suspension rates of rules jointly with the effects of regime age. As we have indicated above and will discuss below, increases in density appear to be a significant explanatory factor for the observed regime age effect, at least with respect to rule birth.

EFFECTS OF RULE HISTORIES

Once it is created, a rule has a history. That history consists of various events that we have not observed. For example, we have no record of when, or with what effect, a rule has been invoked. Our record of a rule history consists of the date of its birth, the dates of any revisions of the rule that have occurred, and the date of its suspension if it has been suspended. With such a record, we are able to examine the effect of rule age and previous rule revisions on the likelihood of a new revision or suspension.

Rule Age at the Time of Last Revision

We measure rule age at the time of the most recent revision. As we have noted earlier, rule age at the time of last revision can be interpreted either as an index of the knowledge encoded in the rule or as a proxy for rule age. The interpretation as a proxy for rule age can be justified by the relatively high correlation with rule age and by the statistical advantages that such a proxy provides (see Chapter 3).

Newly created rules appear to be relatively vulnerable to revision and suspension, and rule age at the time of last revision significantly decreases that vulnerability. These findings are robust. They occur in both administrative and academic rules and in both rule regimes of the latter. Among academic rules, an increase of rule age at last revision by one year decreases the rate of rule change, on average, by 1.2%, compared with 4.6% for administrative rules (taking Model 5 estimates in Tables 6.1 and 6.2). These effects are smaller than the estimated effects of rule regime age, but they are clearly significant. Figure 7.1 shows the estimated effect of rule age at last revision on hazards of academic and administrative rule change. The hazards are steadily decreasing functions of rule age at the time of the last previous revision. For both kinds of rules the rate of change declines as the age of a rule at its last previous revision increases. The decline is faster for administrative rules than it is for academic rules.

If we interpret rule age at the time of last revision as a proxy for rule age, our results show a negative age dependence of rule changes. Negative age dependency is a quite characteristic outcome in hazard rate studies. Among possible interpretations of negative rule age dependence, two stand out particularly: the first is that the prospects for revision and suspension of individual rules change as the rules age. This "learning" hypothesis emphasizes the ways in which environments of rules adapt to rules. Rule users become accustomed to and develop competencies with rules, other rules are created that take prior rules as given and establish explicit or implicit links to them, external actors rely on unchanging expectations about the organization's behavior. These ad-

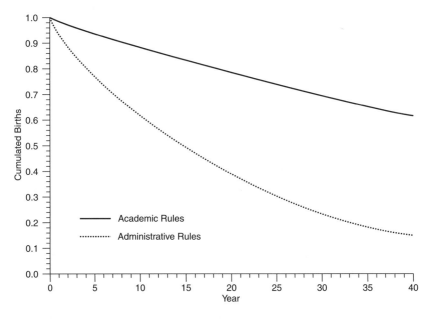

Figure 7.1   Effect of rule age at time of previous revision on the estimated rate
of administrative and academic rule change (Model 5)

justments also involve a certain amount of habituation. In this sense, rules become part of the scenery and are taken for granted (Berger and Luckmann
1967; Zucker 1983). If the adjustments of rule environments to rules improve
as rules age, then the rate of revisions and suspensions will decline. The second
interpretation of negative age dependence focuses on different, but unchanging, survival chances among individual rules. As is well known from other domains of duration studies, negative effects of duration on change can arise
from unmeasured heterogeneity in the population (Silcock 1954; Tuma and
Hannan 1984; Blossfeld, Hamerle, and Mayer 1989) or from sampling error
in performance sampling (March and March 1978). The complications that
these possibilities introduce into interpreting duration effects are notorious. In
the present case, it is possible for the data to show that (on average) the longer
a rule endures, the less likely it is to be revised even though there is no change
whatsoever in the vulnerability of individual rules.

    In order to explore the first interpretation while controlling for the second,
we have considered various potential sources of population heterogeneity in

our analyses. These include particularly heterogeneity associated with different types of academic (faculty or student) and administrative (five subareas) rules, and heterogeneity stemming from the prior revision history of rules. These variables capture important portions of the heterogeneity of the rules in the analysis, although not all. Moreover, we have defined rule age as age at the time of last revision, a measure that is not updated during the period in which a rule is at risk of being revised. This procedure eliminates the duration component from rule age and thereby minimizes the chance of a spurious result.

Still, some potential sources of spuriousness remain. The most noteworthy is a correlation between revisions and suspensions. If each rule has a likelihood of being revised that does not change over time, but varies from rule to rule, and if rules with high likelihoods of being revised also have high likelihoods of being suspended, then rules at high risk of being revised will be more likely to be suspended than rules at low risk. This heterogeneity story is complicated in the present case by its dependence on the covariation between rule suspension (which affects the changing population of rules) and rule revision and on the relative magnitudes of the suspension rates and the revision rates, but it is possible to introduce a spurious negative bias on the effect of rule age at the time of last revision on the hazard of rule change.

We thus cannot exclude the possibility that some fraction of the observed effect is due to unobserved heterogeneity. Nevertheless, it seems to us unlikely that these results could be due entirely to factors of unobserved heterogeneity. Our simulations of the survival and revision of rules under various assumptions regarding attrition and revision rates indicate that unobserved heterogeneity, if it exists, is by no means guaranteed to produce the results we observe. We are inclined to give credence to the speculation that rule environments adapt to individual rules as the rules mature.

However, it is likely that these adaptations are not a simple product of aggregate rule age. Rule age can be decomposed into two components: (1) age at the time of last revision; and (2) number of years since last revision. The first is a variable that measures the knowledge basis of a rule. Whenever a revision occurs, it reflects the cumulated experiences the organization has had with the rule up to that point. That knowledge is encoded in the new version of the rule. The longer a rule has existed at the time it is revised, the greater the breadth of experience captured by the revision. Thus age at the time of last revision is a measure of organizational knowledge associated with the rule and its application and is thereby a measure of organizational learning. The greater the learning encoded into the rule, the less the likelihood of subsequent revision.

The second component of rule age (number of years since last revision) is a measure of rule version obsolescence. As the environment changes, a rule version loses applicability. A previous analysis using the same data (limited to administrative rules) has shown that, controlling for the age of a rule at the time of last revision and for the number of previous revisions of that rule, there is a positive obsolescence effect (Schulz 1998a). That is, the greater the number of years since the last revision, the greater the rate of change.

The decomposition of rule age into its two components suggests that rule changes are driven by two separate kinds of aging effects—those stemming from cumulated experience captured in a rule and those stemming from cumulated experience not yet captured in a rule. The first effect decreases rule changes by increasing the knowledge reflected by the rule; the second increases rule changes by increasing the disparity between environmental needs and the rule. Together the two effects provide support for the idea that rules are repositories of knowledge. They provide less support for the idea that revision rates are affected by adaptations of rule environments to rules, although we cannot rule them out entirely. Thus our inclination is to consider rule age at last revision, not primarily as a proxy for rule age but as a variable in its own right, one that records the knowledge content of a rule.

Prior Revisions

The idea that rule maturation leads to an improved fit of a rule to its organizational setting suggests that such effects might be associated with the number of prior rule revisions. A rule that has been revised recently reflects cumulated knowledge, but predicting the cumulative effect of frequent revisions in the past (holding constant the recency of the latest revision) is complicated. On the one hand, it is possible that each additional revision might be seen as improving a rule and making it less likely to be revised again. Alternatively, revisions might be seen as introducing new untried features that increase the vulnerability of the rule.

The data unambiguously support the second idea more than the first. Prior revisions of a rule increase the rate of subsequent rule revision. This result is true both for administrative and for academic rules and for the two rule regimes of academic rules considered separately.

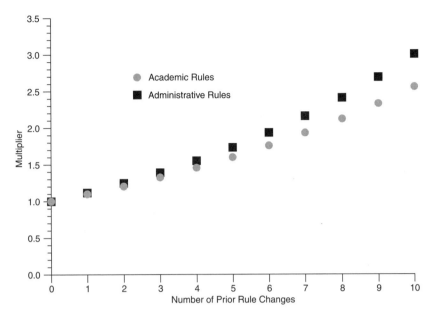

Figure 7.2   Effect of previous rule changes on the estimated rate of administrative and academic rule change (Model 5)

Like the results with respect to the negative dependence of rule change on rule age, the result of positive dependence of rule change on the number of previous revisions is subject to caution because of possible unobserved heterogeneity. Suppose each rule is characterized by a propensity to be changed that is stable over time. Further suppose that this propensity differs from one rule to another in a way not captured by observed covariates. Then hazard rate models of rule change will yield biased parameters with spurious positive occurrence dependence. A rule with a large change propensity would generate a rule history that is likely to contain many prior changes. Even if the propensity to change were constant over time for each rule, heterogeneity in propensities would yield results consistent with a world in which each previous revision increased the change of a subsequent one.

We cannot reject this possibility entirely. However, we believe that the positive occurrence dependence that we observe is at least partly a result of a genuine process of rule tinkering. Future research might find ways to disentangle genuine and spurious occurrence dependence in rule histories; but in the

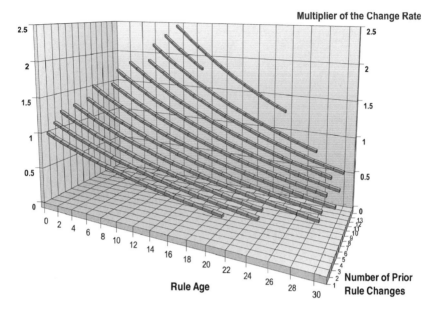

Figure 7.3   Combined effect of rule age and previous rule changes on the estimated rate of administrative and academic rule change for the sampling ranges of the variables (Model 5)

meantime, we think it is useful to speculate that the tendency for rules with previous revisions to experience increased rates of revision might be due to the destabilizing effects of previous revisions. In the present data, an increase in the number of previous revisions from 0 to 1 increases the hazard of academic rule revision (on average) by 9.9%, and for administrative rules by 11.6% (using estimates from Model 5 in Tables 6.1 and 6.2). And as Figure 7.2 shows, the number of prior revisions increases the rate of rule revision at an increasing rate, suggesting an accelerating introduction of complications.

These results in combination with the results with respect to rule age at last revision mean that events in a rule history may destabilize as well as stabilize organizational rules, depending on the nature of the learning experience. To demonstrate how rule age at last revision and the number of prior rule revisions affect the rate, we have estimated their effects in the form of a multiplier over the range of these two variables. The results are graphed in Figure 7.3. The figure shows the combined effect of rule age at last revision and the number of prior rule revisions on the rate of rule revision for administrative rules. The corresponding figure for academic rules is very similar. The figure shows twelve graphs, ranging from one previous rule revision to thirteen previous rule revisions. Combinations of rule age at last revision and number of previous revisions outside the sampling range are not plotted. The rate of rule revision is largest for rules that were last revised when they were young and that have a high number of previous revisions. It is smallest for rules that were last revised when they were old and that have experienced little previous revision.

EFFECTS OF RULE ECOLOGIES

Rule births and revisions in an organization are interconnected in an ecology of rules. One set of rules and revisions in them can affect another set of rules and revisions in them. The ecology is organized by two dimensions of "distance" that seem likely to affect the magnitude of ecological effects. Any particular revision in a rule is separated from any other revision by distances of both time and "space." Temporal distance between two rule revisions is simply the difference in their times of occurrence. Spatial distance between two rule revisions is a function of differences in the substantive concerns of the two rules involved. The closer the temporal or spatial connection, the greater the likely effect of change in one rule on change in another.

We have considered two clusters of ecological effects. The first is the effect of rule density and rule suspensions on rule birth. The second is the effect of rule revision in one temporal and spatial domain on rule revision in another domain. In addition, we also have explored the effects of agenda distribution in some analyses.

Density and Suspension Effects

The rule populations explored in this study expanded over time. In that sense, their histories are congruent with Weber's iron law of bureaucracy—at least with its moderate versions of constantly expanding bureaucracies (Weber 1978; Hall, Haas, and Johnson 1967; Blau and Schoenherr 1971). However, the rule histories studied here also suggest a second law of bureaucracy: the number of rules increases at a decreasing rate. Most rule populations analyzed in Chapter 5 grew in a way that supports this second law of bureaucracy. They exhibit a negative density dependence of the rule birthrate. The overall density

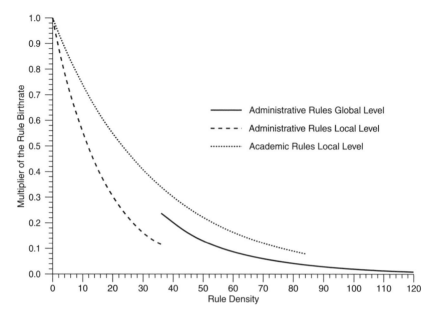

Figure 7.4   Density dependence of the rule birthrate: Computed effect of density on the birthrate, based on parameter estimates in Tables 5.7 and 5.9

dependence is plotted in Figure 7.4. The more rules there are in an area, the lower the birthrate.

The effects stemming from the density of rules in the immediate temporal and spatial neighborhood are stronger both numerically and in terms of statistical significance than are more global density effects. Especially in academic rules, the global effects vanish after the local effects are included. This result suggests that interrelations among rules are stronger within subpopulations than between them. The general implication is that, at least in this particular organization, the various rule populations are relatively independent. Each population follows a trajectory that is rather little affected by the trajectories of others. In this sense, at least, the separate rule domains are relatively loosely coupled.

The negative density effect is stronger in the more technical and formal administrative rules than in the more ambiguous, meaning-laden area of academic rules. Perhaps organizational rule production reaches organizational "carrying capacities" faster in systems of formal, technical rules than in systems of less formal rules. If we were willing to extrapolate this result to informal organizational rules, such as norms, beliefs, habits, and cultures, then we might speculate that rule proliferation in such informal rule systems would be even less inhibited. They might even display positive, rather than negative, density dependence.

Density effects are more variable among administrative rule subareas than among academic rule subareas. The academic area displays a comparatively coarse (and partially overlapping) functional differentiation that divides the rule population between one area focused on student issues and one focused on faculty issues. In contrast, the administrative area is more differentiated (six highly different problem areas). Some of the variations in density effects among administrative subareas might be attributable to differences in environmental turbulence. For example, accounting rules are probably subject to comparatively low levels of environmental turbulence. They show a strong negative density dependence. In contrast, personnel rules, located in a more turbulent environment, show no significant density dependence of the birthrate. In some other subpopulations, however, negative density dependence appears even in the presence of what might be assumed to be comparatively high levels of turbulence.

The results are generally consistent with the idea that the presence of rules in a particular area produces and indicates a reduced "problem space" in that area and thus leads to reduced rule birthrates. Such an interpretation is strengthened by the observed effect of rule suspensions on the birthrate of rules. If the suspension (death) of a rule frees problem space for new rules, then there should be a positive relation between suspensions and new births. This is, in fact, what is observed.

The notion that the existence of rules in an area reduces the possibilities for new rules in that area is further supported by an examination of the kinds of new rules generated over time. Not only did the rate of administrative rule births change over time but so also did the nature of those births. A comparison of the titles of rules created in 1963 with those created in 1983 reveals perceptible differences in content. The rules created in 1963 were likely to deal with recurrent issues of university administration relevant for many parts of the university, whereas the rules created in 1983 were more likely to deal with administrative niche issues such as stores procedures, surplus property sales, and so forth. By 1983 the rule-making process appears to have turned to comparatively rare problems (i.e., experienced by comparatively small numbers of participants in a comparatively small number of situations), resulting in the lower number of rules created in that year.

Comparisons of other years reveal a similar shift. This suggests that the rule-making process gradually shifts from frequently occurring problems to less likely ones, and finally to possible and potential contingencies. Since problems are confronted and absorbed in the order of their appearance, frequently occurring problems are likely to appear earlier in the organizational rule-making process and tend to be codified earlier than rare problems, which are likely to arrive and to be codified later. It takes longer and longer for this process to arrive at the next problem because the next problem is rarer than the preceding one (ceteris paribus). The result of this sorting by recurrence is a negative density dependence of rule births.

The density dependence results suggest that organizational learning produces its own obstacles to further learning and that returns to learning decline over time as rules (the products of learning) proliferate. Rules and routines help organizations to respond to problems in a programmed and efficient fashion. At the same time, rules create both a sense of familiarity with arriving problems, which reduces the likelihood that new problems will be seen as opportunities to draw new lessons, and a level of competence at dealing with usual problems, which makes exploration of new possibilities less rewarding in the short run (March 1991; Sagan 1993; Axelrod and Cohen 2000).

Contagion and Competition of Rule Revisions

A second kind of ecological effect is the impact of revisions in one temporal and spatial domain of the rule system on revisions in another domain. We have summarized several streams of theoretical ideas in this regard in Chapter 3 (see Table 3.1). These ecological effects might stem from functional interdependence. That is, the operation of one rule might have a functional impact on the operation of another. Alternatively, the effects might be produced by procedural interdependence and its consequences for the allocation of scarce attention in the process of rule making. As we observed earlier, theories of ecological effects across time and space provide contending speculations. On the one hand, we might speculate that functional interdependence makes a revision in one rule likely to stimulate revisions in other nearby rules. It is also possible to speculate that attention is contagious. Such speculations suggest that the relation between rule revision rates in one domain and rule revision rates in another will be positive, particularly when the two domains are relatively close in time and space. Alternatively, it is also possible to speculate that rules will substitute for each other or that attention will be competitive and subject to allocative rationing because of scarcity. Such speculations suggest that the relation between rule revision in one domain and revision rates in another will be negative, particularly when the two domains are relatively close.

The relations identified in the present data are not decisive with respect to these alternatives, but they suggest a tentative threefold resolution of the conflict. First, there is a consistent tendency for revisions to result in positive effects ("contagion" or "multiplication"), rather than negative effects ("competition" or "substitution"), on domains that are close in *both* time and space. Thus the likelihood that a rule will be revised is positively related to whether another rule in the same area is revised during the same time period, and the likelihood that a rule will be born at a particular time and in a particular area is positively related to whether other rules are being suspended or revised in that area at that time. This is true for both administrative and academic rules. All of the relations are statistically significant except the relation between revisions and births in the administrative rule data.

Second, although the effects are mixed and sometimes not significant, competition for attention and functional substitution (i.e., negative effects) seem to be more likely than contagion and multiplier effects (i.e., positive effects) to characterize the relation between revisions in domains that are close in *either* time or space, but not both. The main exception is the positive relation between the number of revisions of academic rules in one period and the number of births of academic rules in the next period. We also analyzed the agenda of the Faculty Senate in our analysis of the effects of attention allocation on the rate of change in the academic areas. We found some evidence of attention competition between the faculty and the student areas (see also Zhou 1993).

Third, there is no perceptible sign of ecological effects among domains that are close in *neither* time *nor* space. There are no significant results and the signs of the coefficients are equally likely to be positive or negative. This may, of course, be due to noise in the measures; but it also may be due to decoupling effects produced by temporal or spatial distances and specialization in the rule-making processes.

The Effects of Organizational Agenda Attention

We examined the effects of the distribution of organizational attention in the academic area, as measured by the agendas for meetings of rule-making authorities (Academic Council before 1968 and the Faculty Senate after 1968). We caution that our measures of organizational attention are indirect and imprecise, and our findings are by no means conclusive. Nevertheless, the evidence seems to suggest two main findings: first, organizational attention allocation has similar effects on the processes of rule birth and rule revisions. The rates of rule birth and rule revision are positively affected by the presence of rule-related agendas in the respective student and faculty areas. This finding is consistent with the results on rule ecologies discussed earlier. That is, attention in a particular area increases the rate of both rule birth and rule revision in that domain.

Second, there are important variations in the flow of attention and their effects across different areas. We speculated that rule-unrelated agendas might distract organizational attention and thus reduce the rate. The findings show that rule-unrelated agendas have no significant effect on the overall rate; although most of the parameters of unrelated agenda tended to be negative. We also find that rule-related agenda in the faculty area increases the rate of births in the student area, but not vice versa. In our analysis, attention to the faculty area, especially attention to faculty rules, appears to be the main driving force in the rate of rule births in both the faculty and the student areas. This finding indicates that the contagion of organizational attention, in this case, is unidirectional, perhaps reflecting the centrality of the faculty in a university organization.

EIGHT

Toward an Understanding of Rules

The regularities summarized in Chapter 7 provide a start to an understanding of the dynamics of rules. That understanding can be organized around a vision of written organizational rules as responding to internal and external pressures through processes of learning and problem solving, accumulating the residues of those processes into a collection of rules. Within such a vision, we have tried to identify some important factors that influence rule birth and rule change and to provide suggestions for some small parts of a theory. It remains, however, to revisit theories of rules to see whether these results provide any hints with respect to central theoretical issues in the study of rules.

Revisiting Theories of Rules

The results summarized in Chapter 7 and our interpretations of them allow us to comment briefly on three sets of theoretical issues that have been central to earlier discussions of the role of rules in organizations. The first set of issues concerns the place of rules as carriers of organizational knowledge, in particular as depositories of political contracts and technical solutions. The second set of issues concerns the place of rules as elements of organizational structure, stability, and change. The third set of issues concerns the efficiency of the historical processes that generate rules and rule changes. The three issues are far from independent, but taken together they define a possible framework for considering what the present study can contribute to theories of rules and rule changes.

RULES AS CARRIERS OF KNOWLEDGE

One of the main notions underlying organizational learning theories and the conception of rules explored in this study is a conception of rules as carriers of organizational knowledge. The basic idea is that organizations confront internal and external problems, draw inferences from their experiences in those confrontations, and encode the inferences in rules. Lessons encoded in rules represent knowledge about solutions to problems found in the past. Rules retain knowledge and allow reuse of solutions to problems.

Rules record solutions to two major kinds of problems that organizations face. The first consists in what might be called *political* problems; the second consists in what might be called *technical* problems. The distinction can easily be overdrawn. Most problems are mixes of the two, and allocating a particular problem to one category or the other is itself an exercise in politics. Nevertheless, the distinction may provide a useful approximation. We distinguish problems of negotiating a reasonable agreement among interests that are explicitly in conflict from problems of finding solutions where conflict of interest is less salient than discovering effective routes to mutually desired outcomes.

Rules as Knowledge Relevant to Political Problems

Organizations are coalitions of diverse interests. For example, Stanford is a collection of coalitions of students (and their parents), faculties, governments, private donors, mass media, suppliers, research and professional associations, and other similar institutions. The interests that form these coalitions make demands on the university (and thereby on each other), demands that require negotiation of the terms of participation in the coalition. These negotiations involve various forms of politics, advertising, wheedling, lying, attention management, and bluffing, as well as discourse about possible compromises or creative partnerships.

Rules are outcomes of those negotiations among diverse interests. They are social contracts. When the consistency of organizational action to the desires of coalition members is in doubt, or when those desires are in conflict, rules are created or revised through political negotiation. The demands of the social system, as found in government regulators, competitors, outside sources of revenue or resources, and other groups and institutions of importance to the organization are rarely univocal and sometimes more attentive to the symbols of action than to its substantive effects; but they invite organizational response. A standard response that serves both symbolic and substantive purposes is the adoption of rules.

Rules are contractual substitutes for tacit understandings or extended negotiations when dealing with situations involving both conflict of interest and a substantial need for interpersonal predictability. As a result, rules are a major instrument for sustaining a social system of negotiated agreements among participants who do not share interests. A tendency to substitute rules for tacit understandings, and vice versa, has been used to explain the relative density of rules in large, heterogeneous countries or organizations compared with smaller, more homogeneous ones (Ouchi 1981). The American propensity for regulating social life through rules, laws, and courts, rather than more informal understandings, is legendary; but even in the United States, there are substantial differences between a small, stable community and a large, multicultural city in the dependence on formal rules, rather than tacit understandings, to order social relations.

The way in which rules are, in effect, substitutes for shared, informal understandings in what could be called political relations suggests an explanation for one of the more surprising results of the present study. Although government funding has positive effects on the rates of rule birth and revisions in the academic area in some of our analyses, the data also indicate that the creation and revision of rules is negatively (rather than positively) affected by government funding in the administrative area. Increases in funding are likely to result in decreases in rule making. The result is initially surprising, but it is consistent with casual observations on financial support, whether extended by governments to agencies, business firms to research laboratories, foundations to scholars, or parents to children. In general, there is often a negative relation between the amount of support provided and the amount of regulation associated with it. We believe this stems from the simultaneous effect of trust on funding and rule making. The higher the trust, the greater the funding and the less the insistence on detailed rules. This would suggest that regulatory cost as a proportion of financial support would increase very rapidly as the amount of support declines, a result of obvious (but not unique) significance for understanding fluctuations in administrative staff in modern universities.

This funding effect has to be contrasted with the somewhat more transparent effect of legislation. Increases in legislation lead to increased birthrates of both administrative and academic rules and increases in the revision rates of administrative rules (but not or much less in the revision rates of academic rules). Laws generate rules. Although any legal system relies on trust as well as rules, the natural organizational response to legislation is to adopt rules, partly because such a response is often mandated but also partly because it is conventional and safe. Rules provide procedural defenses in domains in which substantive defenses are difficult to establish and trust is problematic.

Rules, once established, affect political processes. Rules of the political game guide and constrain actions of individual actors, establish differential rights and responsibilities for participants, enhance the consistency of simultaneous and possibly dispersed behavior, and provide opportunities and obstacles for strategic action (March and Olsen 1989). The outcome is a process shaped by the collective political knowledge derived from past political experiences and encoded in the rules of the game. In some instances this can have a deep impact on the subsequent political dynamics of the organization, for example, when new rules establish new rule-making bodies and thereby give rise to new rule regimes which then suspend old rules and produce new and different rules. In other cases it can facilitate a vesting of interests of groups of actors which then inhibit or accelerate changes of specific rules, for example, when rules of the university facilitate or impede political action of students, or when rule-user competencies inhibit rule changes.

The feedback between the knowledge encoded in rules and political problems is more complex, though. Many political solutions are never encoded in rules (e.g., when the dominant coalition does not want to be bound by general rules), and many rules are inconsequential for subsequent political experience (e.g., when problems are purely exogenous). It is likely that the feedback is tighter in closed political systems with a small number of different interests, and less tight in open systems with many cross-cutting cleavages (Lipset 1960) and with unpredictable, complex interdependencies. Frequently, the feedback between rules and political problems is complicated by interactions among different learning processes. Collective learning processes that generate new rules and change old ones affect local learning processes of local political actors seeking to gain advantage within the contractual frame set by the rules. And the latter, when successful, can result in impulses to change or preserve established rules and thereby affect collective learning processes.

Rules as Knowledge Relevant to Technical Problems

An organization can be seen as a coalition of diverse interests requiring negotiated political agreements, but it can also be seen as a team with shared problems requiring technical solutions (Marschak and Radner 1972). Thus the second kind of problem that organizations face consists in what might be called *technical* problems. The distinction between technical and political problems is a notoriously hazy one, since even the purest technical issue involves questions that are ultimately political, and vice versa. Nevertheless, it is a distinction that conforms to ordinary experience. Organizations solve problems in which conflicts of interest are less significant elements than are gaps of technical knowledge.

As attention moves from relatively political systems involving conflict and goal ambiguity (as perhaps in the academic parts of universities) to relatively bureaucratic systems involving relatively shared and relatively clear goals (as perhaps in the administrative parts of universities), rules become less a record of politically negotiated contracts and more a record of solutions to technical problems. Rules are repositories of technical knowledge, substitutes for uninformed action or prolonged calculation especially when dealing with relatively complex, analyzable situations under some time pressure.

Just as political knowledge develops as part of a struggle to maintain a system of politically viable coalitions, technical knowledge develops as part of a struggle to assure technical efficiency in a system. Both struggles are fueled by external factors, and both are channeled by learning. When the consistency between organizational action and the political or technical demands of a problem environment is in doubt, rules are created or revised. Solutions to difficult recurring problems are coded into formal rules, thereby converting problematic calculations into routine operations with reliable, consistent outcomes.

If the desires of constituents or the demands of technical conditions are stable, either because the world is unchanging or because attention is focused elsewhere, organizational rules are gradually made consistent with them. The fit of rules to the political and technical environment improves over time as rules are shaped to deal with the claims on organizations, and organizations learn to operate within or around the rules. In such situations, rule regimes mature and individual rules stabilize, thereby reducing the rates of creating new rules and revising old ones. As a result, rules tend to be created at a decreasing rate as the density of rules increases and rates of rule revisions decline with regime age and rule age.

Each new rule or revision moves the system closer to being in balance with the pressures on it, but this movement is faster and more consistent in meeting pressures from the technical environment than it is in meeting political pressures. Problems in the technical realm are more likely to be responsive to analysis and less likely to deal with balancing inconsistent conflicting demands than are problems in the political realm. This gives written rules a greater comparative advantage over tacit rules, as well as greater cumulative efficiency as repositories of lessons learned, in the technical realm. Thus the decline of the rule birthrate as a function of density is steeper in administrative rules than in academic rules. Among administrative rules, it is steeper in accounting rules than in personnel rules. Similarly, the revision rate declines as a function of rule age at the time of last revision, and that decline is steeper in administrative rules than in academic rules.

This pattern of gradual accommodation to the political and technical requirements of an environment (and within an ecology of knowledge encoded into rules) is a major part of the story. It is a part that emphasizes the adaptation of organizational rules to external pressures through a combination of explicit change and internal flexibility. There are two reasons why it is not the whole story, however. First, the environment is not stable, either in its demands or in the energy it devotes to imposing them. So, the adaptation of rules is adaptation to a pulsating and moving target; and traces of earlier histories condition adjustments to the present. Second, there are two kinds of organizational learning involved and they interact. Type 1 learning is the adjustment to external pressures through changes in the rules. Type 2 learning is the adaptation of internal procedures and practices to the rules and internal pressures. Each Type 1 revision disturbs the adaptation of the organization to the rules (Type 2 learning), thereby slows the effectiveness of the rules, and thereby increases the likelihood of subsequent revisions, as we observe in the data. Con-

versely, Type 2 learning involves the accumulation of competencies with existing rules, increasing capabilities for maintaining them and thereby impeding
rule changes (Type 1 learning). In effect, the development of competence with
existing rules reduces experimentation with alternative rules, a classical competency trap (Levitt and March 1988).

The Ecological Structure of Knowledge

In a broad sense, studies of rules abound in the social science literature. These
include studies of the development of legal rules of liability, of administrative
rules for equal treatment of gender and ethnic minority groups, of judicial
rules of due processes, and of practical procedures for quality control. They
also include studies of informal rules of trust, reciprocity, and reputation. Conventional approaches typically involve focusing on a single rule or one set of
rules and treating individual rules in isolation. Such approaches have clear limitations. Knowledge does not exist as isolated kernels; rather, it is embedded in
an interconnected network that provides an ecological context for changes in
knowledge. As our findings suggest, births and revisions of rules seldom occur
in isolation. They are affected by both spatial and temporal distances to other
rules in the system.

We have speculated about several processes that regulate the ecology of organizational rules. First, problem-generating processes may produce collections
of problems, rather than isolated ones, hence force existing rules to respond to
them as a group. Second, the organization of attention in the rule-making processes may generate clustered attention to problem areas, rather than to specific
rules, leading to simultaneous changes in the rule system. Third, the knowledge represented by rules is organized in a way that highlights their interconnections. Rules create links by making reference to each other, by residing in
the same area, and by attachment to the same rule-making bodies. As a result,
attention to one rule in a particular area significantly increases the probability
of rule births and rule revisions in the same area. Moreover, as we have shown,
the likelihood of rule birth may also depend on the space "occupied" by existing rules or "freed" by the suspension of other rules already in that area. The
knowledge stored in rules is stored in a network of interrelations.

Ecological effects are important, but they are constrained by buffers among
rules in a system. The effects of changes in one part of a rule system on
changes in another depend on temporal and spatial distances among rules.

There are boundaries that limit the connections among rules. Some of those boundaries are found in specialization that divides the domains of different rule-making bodies. Some are found in the ways in which rules are seen as belonging to relatively distinct categories (e.g., procurement, personnel). Some are found in the substantive organization of knowledge that treats changes in some areas as irrelevant to changes in some others. Some are found in the time subscripts associated with rule changes. These temporal and spatial distances absorb impulses of change. As a result, an ecological treatment of rule change requires some ideas about the dimensions and metrics of distances among rules, about the ways in which networks of connections create isolated pockets of rules, and about the forms of autonomy and mutual interdependence typically prevailing among organizational rules.

RULES AND BUREAUCRACY

Rules are a fundamental element of bureaucracy. As such they are sources of concern to social philosophers of modern bureaucratic institutions. On the one hand, there is concern about rule proliferation. Bureaucracies seem increasingly crowded with rules. No one likes rules, yet everyone insists on them. At the same time, there is concern about the contribution of rules to stability. For the most part, this is concern about the possibility that rules may be excessively stable, that they may build rigidities into the responses of human institutions to a changing world. To a lesser extent, there is concern about the possibility that rules may be excessively plastic, that they fail to preserve responses that have been shown to be good ones.

Rules as Proliferating Viruses

Modern life appears to become more and more bureaucratized with time, regulated by increasingly intrusive and comprehensive rules, many of them enforced by increasingly remote and automated instruments of control. In organizational life, concern about the proliferation of rules often takes the form of speculations that rules grow without limit in organizations, perhaps at an exponential rate as each birth leads to subsequent progeny in a cascade of generations. The vision is one of sensible intentions defeated by virulent and explosively reproductive rules.

Our studies of the creation and transformation of organizational rules suggest a less explosive process than do most speculations about rule proliferation. Rule births exceed rule suspensions in the Stanford history. Rules accumulate. The proliferation of rules, however, appears to be connected to the solution of political and technical problems imposed on, or at least recognized by, the organization. Rules encode a history of reacting to such problems. They proliferate in much the way a good library proliferates, adding new regulations when new problems are encountered while retaining solutions to old problems. These solutions accumulate in inventories of rules.

Because they record problem solutions, rules increase in number as the organization copes with new problems. However, they do not proliferate at an increasing rate. If new rules were created by a birth process in which old rules gave birth to new rules, the population of rules would grow exponentially. That is not what we observe. Rather rules proliferate at a decreasing rate. Our interpretation is that rules are recipes for dealing with problems that have been encountered by an organization. As organizations learn how to deal with their problems, they add rules to standard operating procedures and, in effect, subtract items from the list of potential problems. As long as the supply of potential problems is fixed, each rule reduces the problem space available for subsequent rules and thus slows the rate of rule birth until something happens to replenish the problem supply. In this respect, the proliferation of rules is more like a decelerating process of learning than an accelerating process of reproduction.

Such an interpretation may provide an overly optimistic characterization of rule proliferation. To picture rule accumulation as equivalent to knowledge accumulation is probably too generous. Nevertheless, such an understanding may serve to temper descriptions of bureaucratization as necessarily pathological. If rules are seen as accumulating in much the same way knowledge does, then we can expect them to exhibit many of the same benefits and many of the same costs. The costs are well known. They include the ways in which rules and knowledge habitually annoy ignorance by imposing restrictions that appear arbitrary or foolish because the reasons are obscure to those with less knowledge. They include the ways in which rules and knowledge encourage quick actions that cannot easily be explained by, or to, less knowledgeable individuals involved. They include the ways in which rules and knowledge grow richer with experience but become obsolete as the world changes. They include the ways in which rules and knowledge defend themselves not only against incursions from ignorance but also against incursions from improved knowledge.

Rules as Instruments of Stability and Change

Although social philosophers spend substantial energy articulating the need for both stability and change in social institutions, they provide rather little help in determining what mix of stability and change will serve us best. The collection of rules that we have observed at Stanford illustrates the difficulty. We cannot say whether the rate of rule change at Stanford matches any conception of optimality. Defining an optimal rate for rule change is hopelessly complicated by the fact that optimality is not only difficult to calculate but also dependent on very difficult estimations of the future. Even more profoundly, any optimum change rate can be defined only for a particular time and space perspective (March 1994, 222–31).

Stanford rules appear to be neither hyper-stable nor hyper-plastic. They endure. They also change. The population of rules changes through births and suspensions; individual rules change through revision. Rules and organizations adapt to each other over time. As an organization learns how to cope with a problem area, each rule birth represents an increment of learning. As a rule endures, the organization becomes more accustomed to it and more competent at dealing with it. Periods of rule stability allow this competence to accumulate. At the same time, the accumulation of competence stabilizes rules. As a result, both the aging of a rule and the aging of a rule regime lead to reductions in the rate of rule birth and change. Rules become more stable as their revisions are based on greater organizational experience. The older a rule is when it is revised, the more enduring is the revision. On the level of the population of rules, stabilization results from absorption of problems by prior rules and through a shift of the rule-making process from recurrent problems to rare problems.

On the other hand, changes in rules tend to destabilize rules, both rules that have been changed and other rules that are in their neighborhoods. Revisions reflect learning, but they tinker with practices and challenge parts of knowledge that have themselves become embedded in rules. Just as changes in the external world induce changes in rules, changes in rules induce changes in other rules. The changes do not explode into hyper-instability, however. Although a rule change upsets competence and stimulates new changes by other rules, the resulting ripple of change is severely restricted by two factors. First, responsibility barriers ("jurisdictions," in Weber's terminology) between domains assure that although changes in one domain are likely to increase the rate of changes in nearby rules, their effect dwindle over time and space barriers. Second, attention limitations restrict the explosive contagion of change. Rule changes require attention, time, and energy. Thus rule changes are contagious, but the contagion does not produce general epidemics. It is contained within relatively narrow domains and within relatively brief time periods.

INEFFICIENCIES IN RULE HISTORIES

Many macroperspectives on organizations, including institutional theory and contingency theory, tend to emphasize the importance of environments for organizations. An emphasis on the ways in which rules serve the survival requirements of organizations is a common feature of both treatments, as well as of discussions of organization design. Organizations are seen as shaped by mimetic, normative, and coercive pressures. In this vein, organizations are described as externally legitimized institutions or as structures matched to environmental demands. For the most part, these arguments suggest a simple, direct, and immediate relation between organizations and their environments. Variations in rules are attributed to variations in functional necessities for communication, coordination, and control, or to variations in the requirements for social legitimacy. At the limit, rules are pictured as optimal solutions to problems of organizing, the optimality being assured either by conscious rationality on the part of organizers or by survival of the fittest. In somewhat less extreme form, the assumption is that changes in rules result in incremental improvements of the match between the organization and its environment.

Our results suggest that the relation between organizations and their environments is more complex. Organizational learning processes mediate impulses from the environment in various ways. Impulses can be deflected and relayed to other parts of the system (via attention diffusion). They can be absorbed (by existing rules). They can be selected, filtered, or amplified by the structure of attention. They can be integrated with other elements adopted in the past (rule resilience). They encounter more susceptibility when rule regimes are young and less when regimes are mature. External environments are important, but our empirical findings show that the effects of external environments are complicated by the way organizational learning shapes the connection between technical problems and environmental demands, on the one hand, and organizational rule production and change, on the other.

The results have important implications for understanding organizational change. Throughout the analysis, we have contrasted two broad views of the ways rule histories develop: the first sees individual rules as necessary products of functional necessities as reflected in contemporaneous requirements for survival and effectiveness. In this view, history is efficient in matching rules to their current environments. The second sees individual rules as evolving through time in a way that is sensitive to a variety of local (in time and space) conditions and that accumulates features over history. In this view, history is inefficient and path dependent. We think the data are much more consistent with the second view than with the first. The ecological contexts and histories of rules make a difference. There is no simple direct relation between current technical and environmental demands and current rules.

The relation between an organization and its environment is structured by rule residues from different historical contexts. The knowledge that rules embody reflects knowledge derived from a history of problem solving. Both because rules tend to resolve the problems and because problem instigators are distracted by other concerns and other targets for their attention, the problems that produce rules tend to be more transitory than the rules. Rules endure as traces of a history of problems, as warnings of potential future problems, and as records of practical arrangements that worked. Thus, without a history-dependent perspective, the processes that generate the observed organizational changes are likely to be misspecified. In particular, there is a tendency to give undue credit to contemporaneous actions and pressures. The patterns of rule births and changes that we observe, and consequently the collections of rules at any point, reflect not only a contemporaneous context but also a history of contexts whose effects have cumulated in the rule system.

Even the concept of "organization" appears as a convenient fiction that conceals an intensely path-dependent process in which old rules impose a specific organizational course of action and thereby lead to a specific stream of experiences and problems which are then resolved by adding new traces of experience that connect the current context to a history of earlier contexts. A key to understanding this path-dependent dynamic lies in understanding the organizational learning processes that determine how experiences are made, processed, and codified in organizational rules and how these rules in turn affect subsequent learning processes.

For example, the analyses reported here cast doubts on a view that treats organizational rules primarily as rational attempts to coordinate and manage organizational complexity. Such a view has been common since bureaucratic phenomena were first discussed in social science, but we find little empirical evidence in our study that changes in organizational size and complexity are primary factors in rule development. We cannot dismiss the role of size and complexity entirely, but we can question their power in explaining rule evolution. Several pieces of evidence, as noted above, point to different processes. Those processes include the self-regulation and learning associated with internal rule dynamics, the problem-generation and recognition processes, the structure of attention, and the ecological relationships among rules. All of these factors limit the capacity of rational agents to manipulate rules at will and raise questions about explaining rule phenomena simply as a product of rational design, functional elaboration, or pressures for conformity with external institutions.

Inefficient histories also have implications for organizational diversity. If rule evolution in organizations is path dependent, then different organizations facing the same environments are likely to carry different rule sets at a given time. Thus, even in the presence of homogenizing institutional pressures, organizations can develop individuality. Heterogeneous past adaptations to internal or external challenges affect subsequent adaptation to new demands, thus producing a tendency toward divergence through cascades of amplifying differences. This tendency to produce diversity is constrained, however, by the spread of rules from one organization to another. As organizations become more effectively connected to each other, rule heterogeneity is likely to be tempered by inclinations toward standardization.

A Learning Interpretation of Rules

Alfred North Whitehead (cited in Auden and Kronenberger 1962, 345) saw formal rules and routines as the foundation of civilization. He wrote, "It is a profoundly erroneous truism, repeated by all copy books and by eminent people when they are making speeches, that we should cultivate the habit of thinking what we are doing. The precise opposite is the case. Civilization advances by extending the number of important operations which we can perform without thinking about them."

The Whitehead argument depends on some assumptions about the relation between rules and intelligent behavior (March and Simon 1993, 10–13). If rules and routines encode the correct lessons to be gained from analysis and history and if the lessons of analysis and history are relevant to contemporary situations, then rules are, indeed, a major basis of civilization; for they facilitate not only the utilization of knowledge but also its transfer across time and space. On the other hand, if the histories and analyses underlying rules are incorrect or relevant only to a previous historical world that no longer exists, civilization probably advances more by ignoring rules than by following them.

The empirical results reported in the present book cannot validate the more heroic implications of the Whitehead perspective, but they are consistent with a conception of rules that sees them as summarizing the lessons gained from experience and thus as repositories of learning and carriers of knowledge. For example, earlier speculations in the "liability of newness" tradition associated rule age with increasing embeddedness of a rule and thus with increased durability. Using a learning framework, the present study decomposes rule age into two components. The first is the time between the birth of a rule and its last previous revision. This component measures the knowledge component of the rule and is associated negatively with rule change. The second component is the time that has passed since the last previous revision. This component measures the obsolescence of the knowledge in the rule and is associated positively with rule change.

We think the dominant story emerging from these studies is one of organizational rules and routines as vital parts of organizational learning. Rules are codings of inferences from an organization's own experience and the experiences of others. They are an organization's cumulative repository of learning. As such, formal rules play an especially important role as repositories of knowledge. In contrast to informal rules, formal rules capture historical imprints more accurately and extensively. This is not only because they provide more reliable and durable records of history but also because formal rules encourage rule responsibility more than tacit rules do. Once a set of formal rules is in place, they are seen as responsible for problems, and subsequent responses are likely to involve either changes of the formal rules or establishment of more formal rules.

The rules in our study are consistent with such a view. On the one hand, rules play an important role in organizational learning processes because they retain organizational lessons learned in the past. As such, they are necessary for intelligent adaptation of organizations to environmental demands. On the other hand, the processes that produce, change, and suspend the rules of this study display characteristics which make it unlikely that organizational rules are perfect tools of intelligent adaptation. As has been noted frequently in recent explorations of organizational adaptation, learning is an indispensable tool for organizational intelligence, but it is also an unreliable tool (March 1999). Learning is hampered by errors in interpreting history (March 1994a), by its own myopia (Levinthal and March 1993), by its tendency to eliminate the variation that it requires (March 1991; Schulz 1998b; Axelrod and Cohen 2000), and by the intricate relations among different levels of a nested and conflictual learning system (March 1994a; March and Olsen 1995). Rules, as instruments of learning, encapsulate all of these features. They record and reinforce erroneous interpretations of experience. They adapt locally in time and space to the detriment of the more distant. And they accumulate competence in ways that reduce experimentation. Furthermore, they develop with local autonomy sufficient to assure inconsistencies and conflict.

In that spirit, many of our results suggest that organizational rules track environmental changes and pressures, but the tracking is imprecise. For example, we find that change impulses emanating from political pressures, resource dependence, and technical problems are mediated by a number of organizational learning processes which involve problem absorption, problem diffusion, rule resilience (rules with broad experience change less), attention contagion, and maturation of regimes (and their rule-making routines). The most direct statistical evidence is that external change impulses often lose predictive power when intraorganizational learning processes are controlled: the legislation effect is significantly weakened in administrative models of rule births when suspension and density variables are included. Legislation has no statistically significant effect in multivariate models of revision of academic rules. The same is true for government funding effects in models for academic rules. There is strong indication that rules that are close to one another change together, but rule changes that are distant in time or space tend to be uncoupled.

More generally, the major results of the present study are amenable to learning interpretations. Rule births are affected particularly by internal and external problems and record solutions to them. As a result, the birthrate of rules is associated less with the number of problems previously solved than with the number of problems still remaining, a pattern characteristic of learning processes. Rule changes are particularly sensitive to rule histories. The longer a rule regime endures and the more experience it gains with rules, the less likely it is that rules will be changed. The later a rule has been revised, thus the greater the experience on which a revision draws, the less likely it is to be revised. And the more frequently a rule has been changed in the past, thus upsetting the gaining of experience with it, the more likely it is to be changed in the future. Each of these results is net of the others in a multiple regression sense, and each contributes to reinforcing a learning perspective.

Limitations and Hope

This book has explored written rules in formal organizations. Clearly, ours has been an incomplete exploration. Although we have tried to be attentive to other kinds of studies and to a history of speculation about rules, we have relied heavily on a small set of quantitative studies of rule births and changes in a single organization. We believe the results reveal important phenomena that might prove to be robust across organizations and might suggest a few fundamentals for understanding the dynamics of rules; however, the limitation of the empirical data to a single organization invites the usual caution in interpreting the generality of the results.

Similarly, the focus on quantitative event histories of rule births and changes is limiting. It directs attention away from the detailed content of a rule and the orchestration of its changes to the rudiments of its life history. Such a shift removes important information from consideration. It is quite possible, for example, that a rule change that almost anyone would view as major could appear here as merely one change in one rule. On the whole, however, we believe that the risks in the opposite direction are actually greater. The elaborate stories that can be told about the adoption or change of specific rules seem to us likely to miss the more subtle effects we have examined. The contextual detail of specific historic events in the history of rules is essential to a complete understanding, but so is an appreciation of the statistical structure of change.

Any quantitative study of rules in a single organization is an invitation for others to do similar kinds of studies in other organizations and to do different kinds of studies. Having profited considerably from other kinds of studies in thinking about our own, we can only applaud new efforts in new directions. We can also applaud efforts to make similar quantitative studies in other places. Many organizations do not have histories as well documented as we found at Stanford, but we are confident that some do and that similar studies are possible elsewhere. We hope that our studies may be helpful to others, and we invite our colleagues to solve the many conspicuous problems that we have left undisturbed.

In particular, we should note two substantial areas that require attention: the first is the problem of making reliable causal inferences. Our longitudinal research design and the observation of entire rule histories offer powerful vantage points for examining the processes that generate rule dynamics. However, as we have cautioned before, the statistical associations we have identified in this study are not necessarily causal. To complicate interpretations, the processes underlying those associations tend to move in concert. As an organization evolves over time, organizational size and complexity increase; so do regime age, rule density, and perhaps the (unobservable) interconnections among rules, and between rules and agents. It is unlikely that we will ever be able to untangle the effects of these processes completely. Nor are these processes necessarily separable in the real world. Thus we have offered moderate interpretations, rather than definite conclusions.

Event history analyses, in particular, face the well-known interpretive problems associated with unmeasured heterogeneity. Most discussions in the literature tend to treat rules as homogeneous, or seldom make an effort to differentiate different kinds of rules (for exceptions, see Edgerton 1985; Gouldner 1954; Kennedy 1976). Our findings show important variations between rule births and rule changes, among different areas of rules, and among different historical periods. As a result, they both provide caution about generic speculations about rules and provide some modest protection against the complications in interpretation introduced by unmeasured heterogeneity in rules. The protection is incomplete, however, and future efforts should emphasize identifying and measuring heterogeneity in rules.

The second problem is the problem of coevolution, of understanding the interactive ecology of rules. We have explored some aspects of the ecology of learning in rules, the way learning in one part of a rule set affects (or does not affect) learning in another part. Similarly, we have explored some aspects of the way changes in the environment affect the learning process surrounding rules. As we have tried to show, these interactions make a difference. We have, however, hardly touched the ecological intricacy of rule development. Rules are embedded in a host of other learning phenomena that are simultaneously affected by and affect rule development.

For example, one important but underexplored element in our story of rule dynamics is the implementation of rules and how it feeds back to rule dynamics. As rules are implemented, those who use the rules learn how to adjust to and use them. These adjustments affect subsequent rule development. Another neglected aspect of the context of rules is their symbolic role. Rules and rule changes are symbols that acquire meaning through social interpretation. The transformation of those interpretations is affected by experience with rules and, in turn, affects the development of rule histories.

It is a tradition of scholarly discourse to pray that one's successors will honor one's efforts while correcting one's inadequacies. We are happy to join the tradition. We believe that understanding the dynamics of rules is critical to understanding much human behavior, particularly in organizations. We have tried to use a set of studies of rules at Stanford University as a basis for theoretical speculations about rules and how they change. We hope that these results and speculations will be replicated, elaborated, refuted, and superseded in future reams of scholarship by hordes of future scholars. It is, of course, an optimistic fantasy; but having discovered beauty in the mundane realities of written rules, we claim the right to a certain amount of unjustified euphoria in contemplating the future possibilities for research.

Reference Matter

Notes

CHAPTER FOUR

1. The data on legislation were taken from: National Center for Educational Statistics, *Digest of Educational Statistics* (Washington, D.C.: National Center for Educational Statistics, 1980–1987). These data are also available through the internet at www.ed.gov/pubs/Edsearch94/. The data on funding came from the same source and from U.S. Bureau of the Census, *Historical Statistics of the United States* (Washington, D.C.: Government Printing Office, 1975).

CHAPTER FIVE

1. Some of the data used in this chapter have been previously reported in different form in Schulz (1992, 1998b) and Zhou (1993). They are used here with the permission of the *Administrative Science Quarterly* and the *American Journal of Sociology*.

2. This procedure suffers somewhat from the assumption that the effects of the covariates, conditional on the control of the historical period effects, are invariant over time. Since this study covers a nearly one-hundred-year history, the assumption may be questionable. We will relax this assumption in our analysis of period-specific rule-birth processes below.

3. Overdispersion is adjusted by a procedure that uses "the deviance divided by degrees of freedom" as an estimate of the scale parameter (see "SAS/STAT Software," in *SAS/STAT Software: Changes and Enhancements through Release 6.11* [Cary, N.C.: SAS Institute Inc., 1996], 263).

4. Organizational growth in terms of number of faculty was not included in the analyses of this section, mainly because growth in faculty showed no significant effects in the models set forth earlier in this chapter.

5. As suggested by Hannan and Freeman (1989, 210), the dummies are 1 in the years greater or equal to the beginning of the presidential tenure period, and 0

205

before that. The first period (the tenure of president 1) starts at 1891, the second (the tenure of president 2) at 1913, the third at 1943, the fourth at 1949, the fifth at 1968, the sixth at 1970, and the seventh at 1980. The first period is used as the reference category.

6. The main reason for not using lagged suspension variables is that the suspension effects are thought to occur more or less instantaneously. Problems, once part of rules, are generally acknowledged as issues worthy of some regulation. A second reason is methodological. A fair amount of recycling of problems occurs during "overhauls" of groups of rules (i.e., when a group of related rules is suspended and replaced with a new group of rules dealing with most of the issues of the suspended group). It is possible that births which occur during these overhauls are different from regular births; in particular, they are probably not independent of each other (thus violating assumptions of the Poisson model). Inclusion of contemporary suspensions captures the bulk of these "overhauls" and thereby reduces potential misspecifications of the models.

7. Overdispersion, when count data show a variance substantially larger than the mean, can result in biased results with Poisson models (e.g., Gourieroux, Monfort, and Trognon 1984; Lomi 1995). Overdispersion is particularly likely to occur in cases involving unobserved heterogeneity (Hannan and Carroll 1992, 239). The usual approach for dealing with overdispersion is to use the negative binomial model, as we have done earlier. The negative binomial model involves mixing the Poisson model with a gamma distribution (see, e.g., Mood, Graybill, and Boes 1974, 123). Because the negative binomial model requires an arbitrary specification of the relationship between the variance and the mean (e.g., Hannan and Carroll [1992] explored several specifications), alternative specifications seek to use the data to estimate the shape of the mixing distribution (e.g., Brannas and Rosenqvist 1994; Lomi 1995). We do this by allowing intercepts (as well as slopes) to vary among subpopulations.

8. This was accomplished by using two different kinds of local densities and suspensions. Joint local density is the pooled vector of local densities. Separate local density is the vector of local density for a given subpopulation (appended with 0 for all other subpopulations). Because of the existence of an intermediate level in academic rules, density and suspension measures were also defined on an intermediate level. In an analogous fashion, joint and separate variables are defined for suspensions.

9. Because models that replace single slopes for the local density and suspension effects with multiple slopes are not nested, likelihood ratio test of improvement of fit statistics cannot be used. For those models, the rho-squared statistic (Ben-Akiva and Lerman 1985) was used. It measures the degree of consistency of a model with the data (see also Lomi 1995, 128). It is defined as

$$\rho^2 = 1 - \frac{L_m - n_m}{L_0}$$

where L_m is the log-likelihood of the current model, L_0 is the log-likelihood of the restricted model containing only the intercept, and n_m is the number of parameters of the current model. All parameter estimates of these Poisson models of rule birthrates were estimated with Limdep.

10. These results are taken from Schulz (1998b).

11. The likelihood ratio statistic is 100.07 with two degrees of freedom, which is highly significant (p<0.01). The rho-squared statistics is 0.332 for this model, which is larger than the rho-squared statistics of the preceding models in Table 5.6.

12. Although the data have been disaggregated into subpopulations and many covariates have been included in the models, overdispersion is still a possibility. To test this possibility a negative binomial version of Model 2 was estimated. Its parameters are presented in Model 3 of Table 5.7. The estimated dispersion parameter is not significant. Nor is the likelihood ratio improvement of fit statistics (it is 2.7 with 1 d.f.). Thus overdispersion does not seem to play a role.

13. We again test for overdispersion. Model 5 in Table 5.9 is a negative binomial version of Model 4. The estimated dispersion parameter is not significant. Nor is the likelihood ratio improvement of fit statistics.

CHAPTER SIX

1. Some of the data used in this chapter have been previously reported in somewhat different form in Schulz (1993, 1998a) and Zhou (1993). They are used here with the permission of the *Administrative Science Quarterly* and the *American Journal of Sociology*.

2. Figure 6.1 uses a Kaplan-Meier life table estimation procedure. Figure 6.2 uses an Aalen-Nelson estimation procedure. For samples of this size, the two procedures yield essentially equivalent results.

3. We used split-spell technology as outlined in Blossfeld, Hamerle, and Mayer (1989) to estimate the effects of dynamic covariates.

4. We experimented with alternative model specifications in which we estimated the effects of rule suspensions and rule revisions separately, but the effects were not significantly different. We also explored the effects of number of births on the rate of rule change, but we found no significant effects.

5. We did not include information on rule changes in the administrative area because the time span for the academic rules was the period between 1891 and 1987 whereas that for administrative rules covers only the 1961–1987 period. In our preliminary analyses, we also explored the effects of the number of rule births in the previous year, but we found no significant effect.

References

A NOTE ON STANFORD REFERENCES

The research reported here draws from a number of reference books and publications associated with Stanford University. These are identified by name in the text and include the *Campus Report*, *Courses and Degrees* (the Stanford University catalog), the *Stanford Daily*, the *Stanford Directory*, the *Stanford Faculty Handbook*, the *Stanford Observer*, the *Stanford University Bulletin*, and the *Stanford University Register*. These items are archived in the Stanford University Archive. In addition, the text refers to several other official Stanford documents. These include the Academic Council minutes (archived in the Academic Secretary's office), the *Administrative Guide* (archived by the *Administrative Guide* editor), the Faculty Senate minutes (archived by the Academic Secretary's office), the Policy on Campus Disruptions (archived in the Academic Council's minutes), and the Procedures for Appointment, Reappointment, and Promotion (archived in the university archive).

Abdel-Khalik, R. 1988. Hierarchies and size: A problem of identification. *Organization Studies* 9: 237–51.

Abzug, R., and S. J. Mezias. 1993. The fragmented state and due process protections in organizations: The case of comparable worth. *Organizational Science* 4: 433–53.

Allison, G. T. 1971. *Essence of decision.* Boston: Little, Brown.

Allison, P. D. 1984. *Event history analysis.* Beverly Hills, Calif.: Sage.

Altbach, P. G., and R. O. Berdahl. 1981. *Higher education in American society.* Buffalo, N.Y.: Prometheus Books.

Amburgey, T. L., D. Kelly, and W. P. Barnett. 1993. Resetting the clock: The dynamics of organizational change and failure. *Administrative Science Quarterly* 38: 51–73.

Andersen, C. J. 1981. *Fact book for academic administrators (1981–82).* Washington, D.C.: American Council on Education.

Anderson, J. R. 1983. *The architecture of cognition.* Cambridge: Harvard University Press.

Arthur, W. B. 1989. Competing technologies, increasing returns, and lock-in by historical events. *Economic Journal* 99: 116–31.

Astley, W. G. 1985. The two ecologies: Population and community perspectives on organizational evolution. *Administrative Science Quarterly* 30: 224–41.

Astley, W. G., and C. J. Fombrun. 1987. Organizational communities: An ecological perspective. *Research in the Sociology of Organizations* 5: 163–85.

Auden, W. H., and L. Kronenberger, eds. 1962. *The Viking book of aphorisms: A personal selection.* New York: Viking Press.

Axelrod, R. 1984. *The evolution of cooperation.* New York: Basic Books.

Axelrod, R., and M. D. Cohen. 2000. *Harnessing complexity.* New York: Free Press.

Bacchetti, R. 1988. Interview with Xueguang Zhou at Stanford University.

Baier, V. E., J. G. March, and H. Sætren. 1986. Implementation and ambiguity. *Scandinavian Journal of Management Studies* 2: 197–212.

Barnett, W. P., and M. T. Hansen. 1996. The red queen in organizational evolution. *Strategic Management Journal* 17: 139–57.

Beck, N., and A. Kieser. 1997. *Standard operating procedures and organizational learning.* Unpublished manuscript. Department of Economics, University of Mannheim.

Ben-Akiva, M. E., and S. R. Lerman. 1985. *Discrete choice analysis: Theory and application to predict travel demand.* Cambridge: MIT Press.

Bendor, J., and T. H. Hammond. 1992. Rethinking Allison's models. *American Political Science Review* 86: 301–22.

Berger, P. L., and T. Luckmann. 1967. *The social construction of reality: A treatise in the sociology of knowledge.* Garden City, N.Y.: Anchor Press.

Blau, P. M. 1955. *The dynamics of bureaucracy.* New York: Random House.

———. 1970. A formal theory of differentiation in organizations. *American Sociological Review* 35: 201–18.

Blau, P. M., and R. A. Schoenherr. 1971. *The structure of organizations.* New York: Basic Books.

Blossfeld, H., A. Hamerle, and K. U. Mayer. 1989. *Event history analysis: Statistical theory and application in the social sciences.* Hillsdale, N.J.: L. Erlbaum Associates.

Boeker, W. 1989. Strategic change: The effects of founding and history. *Academy of Management Journal* 32: 489–515.

Brannas, K., and G. Rosenqvist. 1994. Semiparametric estimation of heterogeneous count data models. *European Journal of Operational Research* 76: 247–58.

Braybrooke, D., ed. 1996. *Social rules: Origin, character, logic, change.* Boulder: Westview Press.

Brennan, G., and J. M. Buchanan. 1985. *The reason of rules.* Cambridge: Cambridge University Press.

Bromiley, P., and A. Marcus. 1987. Deadlines, routines, and change. *Policy Sciences* 20: 85–103.

Brunsson, N. 1989. *The organization of hypocrisy: Talk, decisions and action in organizations.* New York: John Wiley and Sons.

Brunsson, N., and B. Jacobsson, eds. 1998. *Standardisering.* Stockholm, Sweden: Nerenius and Santérus.

Burns, T. R., and H. Flam. 1987. *The shaping of social organization.* London: Sage.

Cameron, A. C., and P. K. Trivedi. 1986. Econometric models based on count data: Comparison and application of some estimators and tests. *Journal of Applied Econometrics* 1: 29–54.

Carroll, G. R., and M. T. Hannan. 1989. Density dependence in the evolution of populations of newspaper organizations. *American Sociological Review* 54: 524–41.

Child, J., and A. Kieser. 1981. Development of organizations over time. In *Handbook of organizational design*, edited by P. C. Nystrom and W. H. Starbuck. Oxford: Oxford University Press.

Cohen, M. D., J. G. March, and J. P. Olsen. 1972. A garbage can model of organizational choice. *Administrative Science Quarterly* 17: 1–25.

Cohen, W. M., and D. A. Levinthal. 1989. Innovation and learning: The two faces of R&D. *The Economic Journal* 99: 569–96.

Coleman, J. S. 1990. *Foundations of social theory.* Cambridge: Belknap Press of Harvard University Press.

Comfort, L. K. 1985. Action research: A model for organizational learning. *Journal of Policy Analysis and Management* 5: 100–18.

Covington, C. R. 1985. Development of organizational memory in presidential agencies. *Administration and Society* 17: 171–96.

Cox, D. R., and D. Oakes. 1984. *Analysis of survival data.* London: Chapman and Hall.

Crozier, M. 1964. *The bureaucratic phenomenon.* Chicago: University of Chicago Press.

Cyert, R. M., and J. G. March. 1963. *A behavioral theory of the firm.* Englewood Cliffs, N.J.: Prentice-Hall.

Czarniawska, B., and B. Joerges. 1995. Winds of organizational change: How ideas translate into objects and actions. *Research in the Sociology of Organizations* 13: 171–209.

Dasgupta, P. 1988. Trust as a commodity. In *Trust: Making and breaking cooperative relations*, edited by D. Gambetta, 49–72. Oxford: Basil Blackwell.

Delacroix, J., A. Swaminathan, and M. E. Solt. 1989. Density dependence versus population dynamics: An ecological study of failings in the California wine industry. *American Sociological Review* 54: 245–62.

DiMaggio, P. J., and W. W. Powell. 1983. The iron cage revisited: Institutional isomorphism and collective rationality in organizational fields. *American Sociological Review* 48: 147–60.

Donaldson, L. 1996. *For positivist organization theory: Proving the hard core.* Thousand Oaks, Calif.: Sage.

Douglas, M. 1986. *How institutions think.* Syracuse, N.Y.: Syracuse University Press.

Douglas, M., ed. 1973. *Rules and meaning.* Harmondsworth, England: Penguin.

Downs, A. 1972. Up and down with ecology: The issue attention cycle. *Public Interest* 28: 38–50.

Durkheim, E. 1933 [1893]. *The division of labor in society.* Reprint, New York: Free Press.

Dworkin, R. M. 1967. The model of rules. *University of Chicago Law Review* 35: 14–46.

Edelman, L. B. 1990. Legal environments and organizational governance: The expansion of due process in the American workplace. *American Journal of Sociology* 95: 1401–40.

Edgerton, R. B. 1985. *Rules, exceptions, and social order.* Berkeley and Los Angeles: University of California Press.

Egeberg, M. 1998. The policy-administration dichotomy revisited: The case of transport infrastructure planning in Norway. In *Organizing organizations,* edited by N. Brunsson and J. P. Olsen, 133–46. Bergen, Norway: Fagbokforlaget.

Eisenstadt, S., and S. Rokkan, eds. 1973. *Building states and nations,* vols. I, II. Beverly Hills, Calif.: Sage.

Elsbach, K. D., and R. I. Sutton. 1992. Acquiring organizational legitimacy through illegitimate actions: A marriage of institutional and impression management theories. *Academy of Management Journal* 35: 699–738.

Elster, J. 1989. *The cement of society.* Cambridge: Cambridge University Press.

Fombrun, C. J. 1986. Structural dynamics within and between organizations. *Administrative Science Quarterly* 31: 403–21.

Freeman, J., G. R. Carroll, and M. T. Hannan. 1983. The liability of newness: Age dependence in organizational death rates. *American Sociological Review* 48: 692–710.

Fuller, L. L. 1969. *The morality of law.* Rev. ed. New Haven: Yale University Press.

Geertz, C. 1973. *The interpretation of cultures.* New York: Basic Books.

Goffman, E. 1967. *Interaction ritual.* New York: Pantheon Books.

Goldburg, C. B. 1994. The accuracy of game theory predictions for political behavior: Cumulative voting in Illinois revisited. *Journal of Politics* 56: 885–900.

Goode, W. J. 1973. *Explorations in social theory.* New York: Oxford University Press.

Gouldner, A. W. 1954. *Patterns of industrial bureaucracy.* Glencoe, Ill.: Free Press.

Gourieroux, C., A. Monfort, and A. Trognon. 1984. Specification pre-test estimator. *Journal of Econometrics* 25: 15–27.

Granovetter, M. 1985. Economic action and social structure: The problem of embeddedness. *American Journal of Sociology* 91: 481–510.

Grossman, S., and O. Hart. 1982. Corporate financial structure and managerial incentive. In *The Economics of Information*, edited by J. J. McCall, 107–40. Chicago: University of Chicago Press.

———. 1986. The costs and benefits of ownership: A theory of vertical and lateral integration. *Journal of Political Economy* 94: 691–719.

Hall, R. H., J. E. Haas, and N. J. Johnson. 1967. Organizational size, complexity and formalization. *American Sociological Review* 32: 903–12.

Hannan, M. T., and J. Freeman. 1984. Structural inertia and organizational change. *American Sociological Review* 49: 149–64.

———. 1989. *Organizational ecology*. Cambridge: Harvard University Press.

Hannan, M. T., and G. R. Carroll. 1992. *Dynamics of organizational populations*. New York: Oxford University Press.

Hart, H. L. A. 1961. *The concept of law*. London: Oxford University Press.

Hart, O., and B. Holmström. 1987. The theory of contracts. In *Advances in economic theory*, edited by T. Bewley. Cambridge: Cambridge University Press.

Hausman, J., B. Hall, and Z. Griliches. 1984. Econometric models for count data with an application to the patents-R&D relationship. *Econometrica* 52: 909–38.

Hayek, F. A. 1967. The results of human action but not of human design. In *Studies in philosophy, politics, and economics*, edited by F. A. Hayek, 96–105. London: Routledge and Kegan Paul.

Heiner, R. 1983. The origin of predictable behavior. *American Economic Review* 73: 560–95.

Herriott, S. R., D. Levinthal, and J. G. March. 1985. Learning from experience in organizations. *American Economic Review* 75: 298–302.

Hey, J. D. 1981. Are optimal search rules reasonable? And vice versa? (And does it matter anyway?) *Journal of Economic Behavior and Organization* 2: 47–70.

———. 1982. Search for rules for search. *Journal of Economic Behavior and Organization* 3: 65–81.

Hilgartner, S., and C. L. Bosk. 1988. The rise and fall of social problems: A public areas model. *American Journal of Sociology* 94: 53–78.

Hodgson, G. M. 1994. The return of institutional economics. In *The handbook of economic sociology*, edited by N. J. Smelser and R. Swedberg, 58–76. Princeton: Princeton University Press.

Holmström, B. 1979. Moral hazard and observability. *Bell Journal of Economics* 10: 74–91.

Isaac, L. W., and L. J. Griffin. 1989. Ahistoricism in time-series analyses of historical process: Critique, redirection, and illustrations from U.S. labor history. *American Sociological Review* 54: 873–90.

Jensen, M. C., and W. H. Meckling. 1976. Theory of the firm: Managerial behavior, agency costs, and ownership structure. *Journal of Financial Economics* 3: 305–60.

Kennedy, D. 1976. Form and substance in private law adjudication. *Harvard Law Review* 89: 1685–778.

Kingdon, J. W. 1984. *Agendas, alternatives, and public policies*. Boston: Little, Brown.

Kolak, N. 1988. Interview by Xueguang Zhou at Stanford University, October 21.

Kratochwil, F. V. 1989. *Rules, norms and decisions: On the conditions of practical and legal reasoning in international relations and domestic affairs*. Cambridge: Cambridge University Press.

Kreps, D. M. 1990. Corporate culture and economic theory. In *Perspectives on Positive Political Economy*, edited by J. E. Alt and K. A. Shepsle, 90–143. Cambridge: Cambridge University Press.

Kreps, D. M., P. Milgrom, J. Roberts, and R. Wilson. 1982. Rational cooperation in the finitely repeated prisoners' dilemma. *Journal of Economic Theory* 27: 245–52.

Langlois, R. N. 1986. *Economics as a process*. Cambridge: Cambridge University Press.

Langton, J. 1984. The ecological theory of bureaucracy: The case of Josiah Wedgewood and the British pottery industry. *Administrative Science Quarterly* 29: 330–54.

Lave, C. A., and J. G. March. 1975. *An introduction to models in the social sciences*. New York: Harper and Row.

Laver, M. 1997. *Private desires, political action: An invitation to the politics of rational choice*. London: Sage.

Leblebici, H., and G. R. Salancik. 1989. The rules of organizing and the managerial role. *Organization Studies* 10: 301–25.

Levinthal, D. A., and J. G. March. 1981. A model of adaptive organizational search. *Journal of Economic Behavior and Organization* 2: 307–33.

———. 1993. The myopia of learning. *Strategic Management Journal* 14: 95–112.

Levitt, B., and J. G. March. 1988. Organizational learning. *Annual Review of Sociology* 14: 319–40.

Levitt, B., and C. Nass. 1989. The lid on the garbage can: Institutional constraints on decision making in the technical core of college-text publishers. *Administrative Science Quarterly* 34: 190–207.

Levy, J. S., 1986. Organizational routines and the causes of war. *International Studies Quarterly* 30: 193–222.

Lipset, S. M. 1960. *Political man*. Garden City, N.Y.: Doubleday.

Lomi, A. 1995. The population ecology of organizational founding: Location dependence and unobserved heterogeneity. *Administrative Science Quarterly* 40: 111–44.

March, J. C., and J. G. March. 1978. Performance sampling in social matches. *Administrative Science Quarterly* 23: 434–53.

March, J. G. 1981. Footnotes to organizational change. *Administrative Science Quarterly* 26: 563–77.

———. 1988. *Decisions and organizations*. Oxford, England: Blackwell.

————. 1991. Exploration and exploitation in organizational learning. *Organization Science* 2: 71–87.

————. 1994a. *A primer on decision making: How decisions happen.* New York: Free Press.

————. 1994b. *Three lectures on efficiency and adaptiveness in organizations.* Helsinki, Finland: Swedish School of Economics.

————. 1999. *The pursuit of organizational intelligence.* Oxford, England: Blackwell.

March, J. G., and J. P. Olsen. 1984. The new institutionalism: Organizational factors in political life. *American Political Science Review* 78: 734–49.

————. 1989. *Rediscovering institutions: Organizational basis of politics.* New York: Free Press.

————. 1995. *Democratic governance.* New York: Free Press.

March, J. G., and H. A. Simon. 1958. *Organizations.* New York: John Wiley and Sons.

————. 1993. *Organizations.* 2d ed. Oxford, England: Blackwell.

Marschak, J., and R. Radner. 1972. *Economic theory of teams.* New Haven: Yale University Press.

Marshall, G. J., 1995. The survival of colleges in America: A census of four-year colleges in the United States, 1636–1973. Ph.D. thesis, School of Education, Stanford University.

Mayhew, L. B. 1979. *Surviving the eighties.* San Francisco: Jossey-Bass.

Mayntz, R., and F. Scharpf. 1975. *Policy-making in the German federal bureaucracy.* Amsterdam, Netherlands: Elsevier.

McCubbins, M. D., R. G. Noll, and B. R. Weingast. 1987. Administrative procedures as instruments of political control. *Journal of Law, Economics, and Organization* 3: 243–77.

Merton, R. K. 1957. Bureaucratic structure and personality. In *Social theory and social structure*, by R. K. Merton, Chap. 8. New York: Free Press.

Merton, R. K., A. P. Gray, B. Hocky, and H. P. Selvin. 1952. *Reader in bureaucracy.* Glencoe, Ill.: Free Press.

Meyer, J. W., J. Boli, and G. M. Thomas. 1987. Ontology and rationalization in the Western cultural account. In *Institutional structure: Constituting state, society, and the individual,* edited by G. M. Thomas, J. W. Meyer, F. O. Ramirez, and J. Boli, 12–37. Newbury Park, Calif.: Sage.

Meyer, J. W., and B. Rowan. 1977. Institutionalized organizations: Formal structure as myth and ceremony. *American Journal of Sociology* 83: 340–63.

Meyer, J. W., and W. R. Scott, with the assistance of B. Rowan and T. E. Deal. 1983. *Organizational environments: Ritual and rationality.* Beverly Hills, Calif.: Sage.

Meyer, J. W., W. R. Scott, D. Strang, and A. Creighton. 1985. Bureaucratization without centralization: Changes in the organizational system of American public education, 1940–1980. In *Institutional patterns and organizations,* edited by L. G. Zucker. Boston: Pitman.

Meyer, M. W. 1985. *Limits to bureaucratic growth.* Berlin, Germany: W. de Gruyter.

Mezias, S. J., 1990. An institutional model of organizational practice: Financial reporting at the Fortune 200. *Administrative Science Quarterly* 35: 431–57.

Mezias, S. J., and M. Scarselletta. 1994. Resolving financial reporting problems: An institutional analysis of the process. *Administrative Science Quarterly* 30: 654–78.

Miller, R. I. 1987. *Evaluating faculty for promotion and tenure.* San Francisco: Jossey-Bass.

Mills, A. J., and S. J. Murgatroyd. 1991. *Organizational rules: A framework for understanding organizational action.* Philadelphia: Open University Press.

Mintzberg, H. 1979. *The structure of organizations.* Englewood Cliffs, N.J.: Prentice-Hall.

Mirrielees, E. R. 1959. *Stanford, the story of a university.* New York: Putnam.

Mitchell, J. P. 1958. *Stanford University: 1916–1941.* Stanford, Calif.: Stanford University Press.

Moe, T. 1990. The politics of structural choice: Toward a theory of public bureaucracy. In *Organization theory,* edited by O. E. Williamson, 116–53. New York: Oxford University Press.

Mood, A. M., F. A. Graybill, and D. C. Boes. 1974. *Introduction to the theory of statistics.* 3d ed. New York: McGraw-Hill.

Nelson, R., and S. Winter. 1982. *An evolutionary theory of economic change.* Cambridge: Harvard University Press.

Nisbett, R., and L. Ross. 1980. *Human inference: Strategies and shortcomings of social judgment.* Englewood Cliffs, N.J.: Prentice-Hall.

North, D. C. 1990. *Institutions, institutional change and economic performance.* Cambridge: Harvard University Press.

Oliver, C. 1991. Strategic responses to institutional processes. *Academy of Management Review* 16: 145–79.

Ouchi, W. 1981. *Theory Z: How American business can meet the Japanese challenge.* New York: Avon Books.

Parsons, T. 1968 [1937]. *The structure of social action,* vols. 1, 2. Reprint, New York: Free Press.

———. 1982. *On institutions and social evolution: Selected writings,* edited by L. H. Mayhew. Chicago: University of Chicago Press.

Pentland, B. T., and H. H. Rueter. 1994. Organizational routines as grammars of action. *Administrative Science Quarterly* 39: 484–510.

Perrow, C. 1986. *Complex organizations: A critical essay.* 3d ed. Glenview, Ill.: Scott Foresman.

Pfeffer, J., and G. R. Salancik. 1978. *The external control of organizations.* New York: Harper and Row.

Posner, M. I., ed. 1989. *Foundations of cognitive science.* Cambridge: MIT Press.

Provan, K. G. 1987. Environmental and organizational predictors of adoption of cost containment policies in hospitals. *Academy of Management Journal* 30: 219–39.

Pugh, D. S. 1993. The measurement of organizational structures. Does context determine form? *Organizational Dynamics* 1: 19–34.

Pugh, D. S., D. J. Hickson, C. R. Hinings, and C. Turner. 1969. The context of organization structures. *Administrative Science Quarterly* 14: 91–114.

Radner, R., and M. Rothschild. 1975. On the allocation of effort. *Journal of Economic Theory* 10: 358–76.

Rose, R. 1984. *Understanding big government.* London: Sage.

Sagan, S. D. 1993. *The limits of safety.* Princeton: Princeton University Press.

Sandelands, L. E., and R. Stablein. 1987. The concept of organization mind. *Research in the Sociology of Organizations* 5: 135–61.

Schotter, A. 1981. *The economic theory of social institutions.* Cambridge: Cambridge University Press.

Schulz, M. 1992. A depletion of assets model of organizational learning. *Journal of Mathematical Sociology* 17: 145–73.

———. 1993. Learning, institutionalization, and obsolescence in organizational rule histories. Ph.D. thesis, Department of Sociology, Stanford University.

———. 1998a. A model of obsolescence of organizational rules. *Computational and Mathematical Organization Theory* 4: 241–66.

———. 1998b. Limits to bureaucratic growth: The density dependence of organizational rule births. *Administrative Science Quarterly* 43: 845–76.

Scott, W. R. 1975. Organizational structure. *Annual Review of Sociology* 1: 1–20.

———. 1981. *Organizations: Rational, natural and open systems.* 1st ed. Englewood Cliffs, N.J.: Prentice-Hall.

———. 1995. *Institutions and organizations.* Thousand Oaks, Calif.: Sage.

Searing, D. D. 1991. Roles, rules and rationality in the new institutionalism. *American Political Science Review* 85: 1239–60.

Selznick, P. 1957. *Leadership in administration.* New York: Harper and Row.

Shapira, Z. B. 1997. *Organizational decision making.* Cambridge: Cambridge University Press.

Shils, E. 1975. *Center and periphery: Essays in macrosociology.* Chicago: University of Chicago Press.

Silcock, H. 1954. The phenomenon of labour turnover. *Journal of the Royal Statistical Society* Series A, 117: 429–40.

Simon, H. A. 1951. A formal theory of the employment relationship. *Econometrica* 19: 293–305.

———. 1957. *Models of man.* New York: John Wiley and Sons.

Singh, J. V., D. J. Tucker, and R. J. House. 1986. Organizational legitimacy and the liability of newness. *Administrative Science Quarterly* 31: 171–93.

Spilerman, S. 1970. The causes of racial disturbances: A comparison of alternative explanations. *American Sociological Review* 35: 627–49.

———. 1971. The causes of racial disturbances: Test of an explanation. *American Sociological Review* 35: 427–42.

———. 1976. Structural characteristics of cities and the severity of racial disorders. *American Sociological Review* 41: 771–93.

Stinchcombe, A. L. 1965. Social structure and organizations. In *Handbook of organizations*, edited by J. G. March, 142–93. Chicago: Rand McNally.

Strang, D., and P. M. Y. Chang. 1991. World polity sources of the welfare state: An institutional analysis. Paper presented at the American Sociological Association Conference.

Strang, D., and S. A. Soule. 1998. Diffusion in organizations and social movements: From hybrid corn to poison pills. *Annual Review of Sociology* 24: 265–90.

Sugden, R. 1989. Spontaneous order. *Journal of Economic Perspectives* 3: 85–97.

Sutton, J. R., F. R. Dobbin, J. W. Meyer, and R. W. Scott. 1994. The legalization of the workplace. *American Journal of Sociology* 99: 944–71.

Taylor, F. W. 1947. *Scientific management.* New York: Harper and Brothers.

Thomas, G. M., and J. Meyer. 1984. The expansion of the state. *Annual Review of Sociology* 10: 461–82.

Tolbert, P. S., and L. G. Zucker. 1983. Institutional sources of change in the formal structure of organizations: The diffusion of civil service reform, 1880–1935. *Administrative Science Quarterly* 28: 22–39.

Tucker, D. J., J. V. Singh, and A. G. Meinhard. 1990. Founding characteristics, imprinting, and organizational change. In *Organizational evolution*, edited by J. V. Singh, 182–200. London: Sage.

Tuma, N. B., and M. T. Hannan. 1984. *Social dynamics: Models and methods.* Orlando, Fla.: Academic Press.

Tushman, M. L., and E. Romanelli. 1986. Convergence and upheaval: Managing the unsteady pace of organizational evolution. *California Management Review* 29: 1–16.

Van Maanen, J., and E. Schein. 1979. Toward a theory of organizational socialization. *Research in Organizational Behavior* 1: 209–64.

Veysey, L. R. 1965. *The emergence of the American university.* Chicago: University of Chicago Press.

Walker, G. de Q. 1988. *The rule of law: Foundations of constitutional democracy.* Melbourne, Australia: Melbourne University Press.

Wallerstein, I. M., and P. Starr. 1971. *The university crisis reader.* New York: Vintage Books.

Warglien, M. 1995. Innovation and evolution in a population of R&D projects: Early results from an empirical study. Unpublished manuscript, Department of Business Economics, University of Venice.

Weber, M. 1946. *From Max Weber: Essays in sociology*, edited by H. H. Gerth and C. W. Mills. New York: Oxford University Press.

———. 1978. *Economy and society*, edited by G. Roth and C. Wittich. Berkeley and Los Angeles: University of California Press.

———. 1988. *The Protestant ethic and the spirit of capitalism*. Gloucester, Mass.: Peter Smith.

Weick, K. E. 1979. *The social psychology of organizing*. 2d ed. Reading, Mass.: Addison-Wesley.

———. 1982. Management of organizational change among loosely coupled elements. In *Changes in organizations*, edited by P. S. Goodman and Associates, 375–408. San Francisco: Jossey-Bass.

Williamson, O. E. 1975. *Markets and hierarchies: Analysis and antitrust implications*. New York: Free Press.

———. 1985. *The economic institutions of capitalism*. New York: Free Press.

———. 1996. *The mechanisms of governance*. New York: Oxford University Press.

Winter, S. G. 1971. Satisficing, selection, and the innovating remnant. *Quarterly Journal of Economics* 85: 237–61.

Witt, U. 1985. Economic behavior and biological evolution: Some remarks on the sociobiology debate. *Journal of Institutional and Theoretical Economics* 141: 365–89.

Zhou, X. 1991. The dynamics of organizational rules. Ph.D. thesis, Department of Sociology, Stanford University.

———. 1993. The dynamics of organizational rules. *American Journal of Sociology* 98: 1134–66.

———. 1997. Organizational decision making as rule following. In *Organizational decision making*, edited by Z. Shapira, 257–81. New York: Cambridge University Press.

Zucker, L. G. 1977. The role of institutionalization in cultural persistence. *American Sociological Review* 42: 726–43.

———. 1983. Organizations as institutions. In *Research in the sociology of organizations*, edited by S. B. Bacharach, vol. 2, 1–47. Greenwich, Conn.: JAI Press.

———. 1987. Institutional theories of organizations. *Annual Review of Sociology* 13: 443–64.

Zucker, L. G., ed. 1988. *Institutional patterns and organizations: Culture and environment*. Cambridge, Mass.: Ballinger.

Zytkow, J. M., and H. A. Simon. 1988. Normative systems of discovery and logic of search. *Synthese* 74: 65–90.

Index

Aalen-Nelson estimation procedure, 207n2
Academic Council, 39–40, 86–87, 91,
92, 150; attention allocation of, 152;
historical significance of, 164, 166;
local effects of rules made by, 136;
resolutions, 46; rule births under, 113,
116 table 5.3, 128; rule changes under,
155–56; rule populations under, 171
Academic rules, 35, 38–40; births, 87,
94, 100–103 tables 4.4–4.5, 106–7,
113–18, 120–24, 134–39, 166;
changes, 87, 88–89, 104–5 table 4.6,
115, 134, 142, 143 fig. 6.2, 148–60,
173–74, 183; density, 94, 140, 180–81;
effects of presidents on, 134; federal
government and, 134, 167; independence from administrative rules, 132,
136; problem areas, 126; regimes, 92,
113, 115–18, 123, 124, 136, 140, 164;
relationships among, 151; spells, 84;
at Stanford, 86–89, 113–18, 165–66;
suspensions, 87, 115, 140; variables
of, 94; variations among rule areas,
136
Accounting, 35, 41–42
Action: environment for, 15; rule-based,
6–8, 10, 193, 196; theories of individual, 6–7 translations of rules into, 22,
23
Adaptation, 24–27, 58, 175–76, 190; of
rules, 2, 25–27, 190; of rule users to
rules, 73, 169. *See also* Changes; Learning; Revisions; Selection process
Administrative conduct, 41

Administrative Guide, 36–37, 42, 85, 91,
111, 164
Administrative rules, 35–38; births, 86,
87–88, 94, 95–97 tables 4.1–4.2,
106–7, 109–13, 129–34; changes,
87–88, 98–99 table 4.3, 112, 142,
145–48, 173–74; density, 94, 129, 132,
140, 180–81; federal government and,
167; independence from academic rules,
132, 136; problem areas, 126; regimes,
109–11, 131–32, 147, 148, 164; relationships among, 148; spells, 84; at
Stanford, 85–88, 109–13; suspensions,
86, 87–88, 112, 129, 132, 140; variables of, 94; variations among rule areas,
129, 131
Affirmative action programs, 34
Age, regime, 77–78, 91–92, 123, 124,
131–32, 136, 140, 147, 148, 159,
170–72, 190
Age, rule, 77–79; academic rules, 148,
150; administrative rules, 145, 147;
changes and, 142–43, 148, 150, 156–
59, 173–76, 178–79; effect on rule
population, 170–72, 190; measurement
of, 175–76; rule histories and, 93–94,
145–47, 172–73; stability and, 72–74
Agenda items: Academic Council, 119,
152, 153; attention allocated to, 121,
123, 153, 158, 183–84; Faculty Senate,
119, 152, 153, 183; rule births and,
119
Appropriateness, 6, 18–19; logic of, 6, 7,
10, 22

221

Competence: accumulation, 4, 57, 72–82, 191, 194; differential strengthening of, 77; external influences and, 74; in problem solving, 182; regime age and, 171; rule changes and, 53–54, 73–75, 80, 173–74. *See also* Knowledge; Learning

Competition, 15–16, 24; attention allocation and, 65, 68–70, 182–83; ethics of, 43–44; rule changes and, 148, 151, 159

Complexity, organizational, 31–32, 61; measurement of, 92–93; rule births and, 111, 113; rule changes and, 147, 150–51, 158, 169–70. *See also* Organizational structure

Compliance, 19, 60

Conflict, 12–13, 48–51

Consequences, 6–7, 10

Construction: of organizational reality, 14–16; of rules, 6. *See also* Social construction of problems

Contagion: of attention allocation, 67, 71, 121, 182–84; of problem generation, 57, 67–72; of rule changes, 148, 151, 155–56, 159, 194–95; technology and, 67–71

Contemporaneous changes, 148, 151

Content, 181–82

Contracts, 12, 13

Controller's office, 35, 36

Cooperation, 20

Coordination, 12, 41

Courses and Degrees, 86–87

Covariates, 84, 89–90, 94–105; of rule births, 107–8, 120–21; in study of rule change, 143–44

Crises, 51–53

CUBA Manual, 42

Darwinian models, 25

Deaths. *See* Suspensions

Debate, 21–22

Decentralization, 34, 41

Decision-making: processes, 50; theories of organizational, 68. *See also* Action

Delegation of authority, 39

Demands: rules as responses to, 50

Demonstrations, 32–33, 46, 59, 91; student, 43–44, 88, 120

Density, 64–66, 80–82; academic rules, 94, 140, 180–81; administrative rules, 94, 129, 132, 140, 180–81; environment and, 66, 94; global, 128–29, 131, 134, 136; local, 128–29, 131–32, 136, 139–40, 206–7n9, 206n8; organizational structure and, 64, 187; regime age and, 172; rule births and, 64–65, 80–82, 125–29, 132, 139–40, 179–82; rule regimes and, 131–32, 136; variations in, 132, 137. *See also* Problem space

Development, rule. *See* Evolution, rule

Diffusion, 27, 48, 71. *See also* Contagion

Discipline, 47, 49

Dismissals, 45–46

Dissolutions. *See* Suspensions

Distances, 71–72, 179, 199

Diversity in rule development, 197

Domains: contagiousness of revisions among, 72, 183; responsibility barriers of, 195; rule changes within, 155. *See also* Faculty rules; Student rules; Subpopulations

Durability. *See* Stability

Duration. *See* Age, rule; Rules, endurance of

Dynamic covariates, 144

Ecology, 57, 64, 196; attention allocation and, 67, 70; need for future study of, 201–2; problem recognition and, 70–71; regulation of, 191; of rule births, 112, 115, 169; of rule changes, 147–48, 151, 169, 179–84. *See also* Environment; External influences; Internal influences

Ecological structure of knowledge, 191–92. *See also* Knowledge

Economic change, theories of, 11

Economic institutions, 12, 24, 25, 26

Efficiency of history, 16, 195–97

Embeddedness, 42, 48, 58, 78, 163, 191, 198

Employment. *See* Organizations

Enforcement, 19, 60

Environment, 4; organizational structure and, 10, 15, 60–62, 195; rule age and,

Personnel administration, 35, 36, 131
Poisson models, 84, 108–9, 120–21, 128,
206n7, 206n7, 206–7n9
Policies, 12, 86; on campus disturbances,
44–45, 47, 50; changes in, 37–38;
creation of, 40; research, 8; tenure,
45–49
Political problems, 186–90, 193
Political processes, 26, 188
Politics: in higher education, 32–33;
within organizations, 12, 15–16
Population, rule, 168–69
Predictability, 12, 187
Predictions. See Patterns
Presidents, 38, 126, 129, 134
Problem absorption, 64–66, 76, 81–82,
126, 129, 159–60. See also Problem
solving
Problems: exogenous flows of, 63; influ-
ence of existing rules on, 165; political,
186–89, 193; recognition of, 63–64,
67–72; recycling of, 126, 129, 168,
206n6; sources of, 58–66; technical,
186, 189–91, 193
Problem instigators, 65, 66, 165, 172, 196
Problem recognition, theory of, 63, 67
Problem solving, 8; rule births and,
49–51, 56–57, 75, 125, 140; rule
changes and, 26, 63; rules as records of,
162, 193, 196; stability of rules and, 53.
See also Problem absorption
Problem space, 168–69, 181–82. See also
Density
Problem supply, 131, 136
Procedural interdependence, 71–72, 155,
182
Procedures, 72, 86
Procedures for Appointment, Reappoint-
ment, and Promotion, 46
Proliferation, 13–14, 192–94. See also
Births
Protestant Ethic, The (Weber), 14
Protests. See demonstrations

Quantitative analysis, 54–55, 200–201

Racial incidents, 43, 49, 50
Rationality, 7, 9–11, 13–14; logic of con-

sequences, 6, 10, 22; theories of calculated, 10. See also Limited rationality
Records. See Archives
Recycling of problems. See Problems, recycling of
Regimes: academic rules and, 92, 113,
115–18, 123, 124, 136, 140, 164;
administrative rules and, 109–11,
131–32, 147, 148, 164; age, 77–78,
91–92, 123, 124, 131–32, 136, 140,
147, 148, 159, 170–72, 190; effect
on rule system, 170–72, 190; environment and, 165; histories of, 147, 150,
166–67; maturation of rule regimes,
68–69, 77, 170–72; rule births and,
109–11, 113, 115–18, 123, 124, 140;
rule changes and, 77–78, 147, 148,
151–52, 159, 164; rule density and,
131–32, 136; at Stanford, 91–92,
163–65. See also Academic Council;
Faculty Senate
Repeated events, 144–45
Research malpractice, 47
Residues of prior adaptation, 4, 168–69,
185, 196
Responsibility barriers, 195
Retention of experience, 21, 25, 28, 139,
169. See also Experience; Knowledge;
Learning; Rules
Revisions, 2–4, 40–41; academic rules,
87–88, 115, 121, 134, 148–50; administrative rules, 85–86, 145–47; attention allocation and, 184; effect on stability, 79–80, 176–78, 194; government
role in, 187–88; learning process and,
76; obsolescence and, 176; patterns of,
87–89; previous, 145, 148–50, 159,
176–78; problem absorption and, 76;
rate of, 142, 175–79; rule age and, 79,
157–59, 173–74; in rule histories,
83–84, 93, 145, 147, 172–73; at
Stanford, 37, 85–89; time distances
between, 179, 180, 182–83. See also
Changes; Plasticity; Suspensions
Right-censoring, 144
Ross, Edward A., 45
Rule-based action, 6–8, 10, 193, 196
Rules: areas of, 35, 49, 60, 127; as

Library of Congress Cataloging-in-Publication Data

March, James G.
  The dynamics of rules : change in written organizational codes / James G. March,
Martin Schulz, Xueguang Zhou.
      p.   cm.
  Includes bibliographical references (p.) and index.
  ISBN 0-8047-2744-4 (cloth : alk. paper) — ISBN 0-8047-3996-X (pbk. : alk. paper.)
  1. Stanford University—By-laws.   2. Stanford University—Administration.
3. Organizational change—United States—Case Studies.   4. By-laws—United
States—Case studies.   I. Schulz, Martin.   II. Chou, Hsüeh-kuang.   III. Title
LD3000.5 .M27   2000
302.3'5—dc21   99-042233

∞   This book is printed on acid-free, archival-quality paper.

Original printing 2000
Last figure below indicates year of this printing
09   08   07   06   05   04   03   02   01   00

Designed by Janet Wood
Typeset by James P. Brommer in 10.5/14 Garamond
and Franklin Gothic Display